# The Campus and the State

# The
# Campus
# and
# the
# State

MALCOLM MOOS

FRANCIS E. ROURKE

with the assistance of Glenn Brooks and Leo Redfern

The Johns Hopkins Press, BALTIMORE

# Foreword

THIS IS a study of challenge and response in the day-to-day relationships between our public institutions of higher education and American state governments.

The central concern of this volume is, in fact, with the impact of state administrative controls upon the management of state colleges and universities. Do state controls tend to have a suffocating effect upon educational policy under certain conditions? What evidence is there that the actions of a state budget officer in reversing the priority of expenditures proposed by educational institutions seriously impair the vitality of an educational program? Are centralized administrative controls simply added annoyances that we must learn to live with side by side with burgeoning bureaucracies and budgets, or are they fundamentally disruptive—do they threaten, however remotely, the essential conditions for freedom on the campus? Finally, quite apart from the influence of state administrative controls, how do the politics of the legislature and the governor's office affect the operating climate of the campus? It is principally to such queries that this study is addressed.

The paternity of this inquiry is the responsibility of several leading educational associations: the Association of Governing Boards of State Universities and Allied Institutions; the National Association of State Universities; and the American Association of Land-Grant Colleges and State Universities. For many years a growing concern with the issues arising from state controls over higher education has prompted several resolutions urging that a special study be undertaken that would review the status of state-supported colleges and universities within the larger context of state government. This volume represents such an attempt.

It was prepared under the guidance of the Committee on Government and Higher Education and financed by a grant from the Fund for the Advancement of Education of the Ford Foundation. On the initiative of the Fund for the Advancement of Education, the Committee on Government and Higher Education was organized to conduct this study under the chairmanship of Dr. Milton S. Eisenhower, President of The Johns Hopkins University. This committee, appointed in January, 1957, brought together a distinguished group representing education, business, and the professions. It included:

> Milton S. Eisenhower, chairman
> A. Boyd Campbell
> Rev. John J. Cavanaugh, C.S.C.
> Margaret Clapp
> Charles W. Cole
> James B. Conant
> Arthur S. Flemming

Clinton S. Golden
Virgil M. Hancher
J. L. Morrill
Herbert R. O'Conor
R. Sargent Shriver, Jr.
Edgar W. Smith
J. Russell Wiggins
Alfred H. Williams

To aid the Committee in its work, a small staff was organized to gather information and prepare preliminary reports. This book is the report of the Staff, which accepts full responsibility for all facts and judgments presented here.

The Committee itself has prepared a shorter document based on the Staff findings and published as a companion to this volume. It summarizes the problems in state-campus relations and makes specific recommendations for improvement. These recommendations are directed both to state governments and to colleges and universities.

In a sense, the real authors of this background staff report are the hundreds of college and state officials who patiently related their experiences and described the problems they encountered in state-campus relations for Staff interviewers.

Another important group of state officials and educators submitted valuable written statements to the Committee in response to letters or questionnaires. Several university presidents gave most welcome assistance by their efforts to analyze the unique features of higher education as distinguished from conventional state activities. Their thoughts are freely incorporated in the final chapter.

Throughout the book the reader will find a few quotations without footnotes. These quotations are taken from letters or statements addressed in confidence to the Committee.

A number of outstanding educators and state officials appeared before full meetings of the Committee to offer direct testimony on the relations between state government and higher education. To this group the Staff is heavily indebted. Among the consultants were: Frank Bane, former Executive Director, Council of State Governments; M. M. Chambers, Visiting Lecturer, University of Michigan; Carl Devine, Business School, University of Florida; John Lederle, Director, Institute of Public Administration, University of Michigan; John Millett, President, Miami University; Lloyd Morey, President Emeritus, University of Illinois; Arthur Naftalin, Commissioner of Administration, State of Minnesota; Richard Plock, Secretary-Treasurer, Association of Governing Boards of State Universities and Allied Institutions; A. Alan Post, Legislative Analyst, State of California; Floyd Reeves, Consultant to the President, Michigan State University; John Dale Russell, Executive Vice-President, New York University; Irvin Stewart, former President, West Virginia University; Russell Thackrey, Executive Secretary, American Association of Land-Grant Colleges and State Universities.

A total of 344 educational institutions are covered by this study—all state-supported colleges and universities offering the bachelor's degree or advanced degrees. Of this number, by far the largest group is made up of state colleges and teachers colleges (264), while 57 institutions are state universities, and another 23 are technical colleges offering the bachelor's degree or above. Junior colleges and schools under local jurisdiction are not covered in this study.

For their help and encouragement at many points the Staff would also like to thanks James Doi; Ted Driscoll and other members of the staff at the Council of State Governments; Ernest Hollis and his colleagues at the U.S. Office of Education; Charles McCurdy, John Walton, and William Young.

We would like to acknowledge the assistance of several

Staff members whose contributions to this project were many and varied: Barbara Johnson, who served as secretary of the Committee until December 1957; Audra Carter; Richard Cortner; Keith Johnson; Nan Ulle; Fred Weaver; Margaret Wiberg; and our secretary during the final year of this project, Joan Murrell.

Opinion as well as fact is presented, although in this study a careful effort has been made to separate and identify the two. Opinion is a very important matter in state-campus relations. Legally and technically a university may be free from state controls, but the militant views of state officials may have a harassing effect upon educational activity. A state office may work strenuously to get along with the colleges, but extremely hostile opinions among educators can quickly dampen any enthusiasm for improved relations. Conversely, a climate of opinion that is amicable can overcome many of the technical obstacles that lie between the statehouse and the campus. Therefore, whenever the report cites the views of college or state officials, it is seeking to describe a broader climate of opinion that invigorates—or enfeebles—the formal arrangements that tie the campus to the State.

Throughout the two years and two months devoted to the preparation of this report, the Staff has been favored with steady co-operation and helpful understanding from the Committee and its chairman, Dr. Eisenhower. His availability and advice in drawing this study into focus were invaluable. The Staff also wishes to add an admiring word for the work of his Administrative Assistant, Mr. Keith Spalding, who cheerfully ran interference for the Staff in its own administrative relationships and pulled a strong oar in drafting the report of the Committee. Finally, the Staff desires to acknowledge with thanks the generous assistance of the Fund for the Advancement of Education, and its Vice-President, Dr. Alvin Eurich, who encouraged a complete independence for the course of this project from its inception.

Almost every part of the report is the composite product of our several labors—carried on with complete freedom, but with encouragement and many helpful suggestions from the Committee itself.

April 22, 1959
Baltimore

*The Staff of the Committee on Government and Higher Education*

Malcolm Moos, DIRECTOR
Francis E. Rourke, ASSISTANT DIRECTOR
Glenn Brooks, RESEARCH ASSOCIATE
Leo Redfern, RESEARCH ASSOCIATE

# Contents

# CHAPTER I

# The pattern of conflict

FOR THE greater part of the century, the relations between public institutions of higher education and state government have been marked by increasing anxiety. This tension has been more visibly and deeply felt by educators than by state officials.

The point of departure for this development cannot, of course, be precisely fixed. But, generally speaking, it may be said to commence with the movement—beginning around 1917—to regroup state administrative units into a more centralized orbit and bring them under tighter executive control. During recent years this movement has gathered great momentum. Its acceleration has been sparked in good part by the steady rise in spending for all state activities, an increase to which higher education has contributed, even though its share of the state's dollar today is no larger than it was forty years ago.[1] Whatever its antecedents, the trend

1 See, in this connection, Figure 2, p. 72.

1

toward administrative centralization has been a major factor in introducing greater stress into relations between public colleges and universities and state government.

Quite a number of non-educational offices and agencies of state government stand out conspicuously as sources of conflict with colleges and universities. It may surprise some observers that so many of them are administrative rather than legislative in character. Of this group, the state budget office, beyond question, is now in a position to wield more actual or potential influence over higher education than any other state administrative agency. With the development of the executive budget in state after state, the budget office has moved forward to the point where its recommendations can have a decisive effect on the judgments reached by both the governor and the legislature on appropriations for higher education.

Other central control agencies that have brought closer supervision over the operations of state colleges and universities are state auditors, comptrollers, purchasing departments, personnel offices, and central building agencies. And the more traditional agencies of state control have begun to affect the operations of colleges and universities in a number of new ways. By means of riders to appropriation acts, legislatures can now exert close control over certain phases of university policy even where universities enjoy constitutional autonomy. More recently (largely since World War II) the appearance of new legislative fiscal agencies has brought the colleges under an additional budgetary analysis and review of their operations. These formal methods of legislative control are buttressed by a variety of informal contacts and pressures.

On another front, colleges and universities have also experienced some supervisory difficulties with personnel in the state chief executive's office. In some states, for example, the governor's office must now approve all out-of-state travel requests for faculty attendance at professional meetings. Still a different source of conflict in the story of the state and higher education is the central educational co-ordinating board which is beginning to dot the academic landscape in various parts of the United States. Although the eventual impact of these new master boards is unpredictable, they have nonetheless emerged as formidable elements of control over higher education—so much so in North Carolina as to provoke open conflict.[2]

## The Hazards of State Control

Potentially at least, the entrance of these new controls represents a grave threat to the tradition of the free college or university in America. For in their zeal to apply controls over higher education in the name of economy and tidy administration, some state officials have forgotten the compelling reasons that led to the grant of legal autonomy to institutions of higher education.

The basic function of a state university is essentially the same as the task of a private university—the conservation, dissemination, and advancement of the collective knowledge of society. Every test of experience has shown that this responsibility can only be discharged in an atmosphere of freedom. To be sure, even under an educational system run from afar by the state, the appearance of higher education can be preserved, but this is a far cry from the quality of performance to which all states aspire. Indeed, the importance of high-level education for American society can hardly be overstressed, for without a steady flow of graduates from schools

[2] For a discussion of the North Carolina situation, see Chapter IX, pp. 221-223. This conflict now appears to have been resolved.

of higher learning, the scientific and humane achievements of this civilization would perish in a generation.

With uncommon foresight the authors of early state constitutions and charters establishing state colleges and universities recognized that higher education, whether public or private, must be insulated from the momentary whims of statehouse politics. They knew this insulation should apply to all phases of academic life, not simply to the professor in the classroom. They feared lest political control over one phase of higher education might gradually encroach upon the vital center of academic freedom.

With the steady advance of state controls, the legal independence of higher education in many of the states now stands in serious danger of erosion. Traditionally, the law has assigned explicit responsibility for the management of higher education to independent lay governing boards. As the courts have repeatedly affirmed, this means that these boards are accountable to the state for the success or failure of higher education.

Now all this may be changed even without any official revision of the law. As one state agency acquires authority to allocate building funds as it sees fit, another to set the salaries of professors, and still another to approve the purchase of experimental apparatus, the responsibility vested in the governing board may become, in the long run, a legal fiction. And if extensive power over colleges and universities continues to be delegated to non-educational officials, the public may soon have difficulty identifying the seat of actual responsibility for the development of higher education in any state.

Moreover, some educators suggest that the steady deterioration of the independence of state colleges and universities may have adverse implications for the autonomy of private institutions.

The president of a leading state university made this point with great force:

> I think that private colleges and universities in this country have viewed with considerable equanimity the trials of their brethren in the publicly supported universities and have been sustained in that feeling by the conviction that they were safe and secure. However, most private universities would be out of business very shortly if their tax-exempt status were eliminated, or if the legislature used its various legislative powers to hamstring and restrict their activities. The periodic threats in the Massachusetts legislature are an indication of what can happen to institutions as venerable as Harvard if an aroused electorate acquires a dislike for the institution. The powers of the Attorney General in the investigation of the use of endowed funds and gifts and grants would be quite adequate to harass if not completely frustrate the administration of a university.
>
> It seems to me that this is a situation in which we all hang together or we shall all hang separately and that there is no argument for freedom in a privately controlled university which is not equally applicable to the publicly controlled university. Certainly the administration of tax revenues is not more sacred than the administration of trusts, nor is the educational process so different in the two types of institutions that one requires freedom for the performance of its functions and the other does not.

Responsible college officials have not made a unilateral denouncement of all centralized controls. They do not question the fact, for example, that the budget office serves an invaluable function in state government. They recognize that it provides a means by which demands for financial support from each state agency can be objectively appraised and balanced against the fiscal needs of other government activities. And they agree that a good budget office can be of great assistance, particularly to a small college, in the preparation of a budget. Moreover, college officials are aware that demonstrable benefits to non-educational agencies of state government have resulted from the application of such devices as centralized purchasing and civil service procedures.

But college administrators do question several matters. Foremost is the assumption that state agencies of central control can treat education in much the same manner as they deal with other departments of state government. This educators deny, and many state officials share their view. It is their conviction that education is a unique activity—so different in its essential nature that it withers in an atmosphere of control to which most state activities can accustom themselves. Education, college administrators stoutly insist, is not a function akin to highway, public welfare, or penal administration. They are convinced that strict adherence by institutions of higher learning to a bewildering array of centralized bureaucratic controls will ultimately endanger the academic as well as the administrative freedom of the college.

The educator understands the rationale behind the steady increase in executive as well as legislative agencies of central oversight. He recognizes that these centralized controls have been prompted by the obviously sound purposes of economy and efficiency and that they have come about in response to urgent public demand and need.

He despairs, however, of what he believes is the tendency of state officials to look at university life solely from the vantage point of fiscal procedures. Education is intricate in design and ancient in lineage, and it cannot be viewed merely in terms of unit costs, rigid personnel requirements, and audit exceptions. Moreover, the tendency of all topside controls is to squeeze the sovereignty of the college in the conduct of its vital responsibilities of teaching, research, and the selection of distinguished personnel as well as the procurement of intricate laboratory equipment. The educator pleads that central controls should not be imposed over any college in such a way as to jeopardize the performance of its essential functions.

In addition to doubting the applicability of uniform central controls to the special environment of higher education, college officials take exception to these controls on other grounds. They question the wisdom of supervisory techniques that consume an inordinate amount of time and money. Of course, some students of administration will dismiss irritations that arise out of uniform procedures by noting that these burdens are a small price to pay for the economies achieved under the new system. But to this reasoning there is a ready rejoinder. Petty controls exact a toll in time and energy that can never be shown on the ledgers of a state comptroller. Yet they can become immensely important in the race to learn the thermonuclear facts of life or in the relentless pursuit of new truths in science and the humanities.

Actually, the resistance of many college and university administrators to the intrusion of state officials into the day-to-day operations of educational institutions springs from the conviction that these controls do not actually realize the objective of good management they set out to achieve. It needs to be remarked that in so far as a heavily freighted system of controls overburdens the skill and capacity of a comparatively few officials at the summit of government, it is entirely out of harmony with the prevailing trend toward decentralization by both private management and the federal government. The establishment of some of these controls is pushing state government in directions different from those taken in modern management practice elsewhere.

In short, educators agree that the legislature and the governor acting through the budget office have clear authority to decide the initial question of what portion of a state's

economic resources should be committed to higher education. This decision is immovably a political one and under a
democratic system it must be made by elected representatives
in response to the public will. But the second phase of fiscal
control—the expenditure and internal allocation of state
funds once they have been appropriated—is another matter.
Here educators are convinced that, once the legislature has
spoken, fiscal control thereafter should be the responsibility
of the college or university itself. If this principle of fiscal
responsibility is accepted, then college officials believe that
the schools will not be impaled on controls that not only
frustrate day-to-day operation, but on occasion threaten a
decline in standards and quality at the institution itself.

*Encroachments: a Summary View*

By way of illuminating the more obvious areas where central control agencies have intervened on the campus, it may
serve a useful purpose to cite a few examples before beginning analysis on a larger canvas. In West Virginia the state
auditor took it upon himself to deny a state college the right
to pay the salary of a professor on sabbatical leave—on the
ground that a sabbatical only benefits the individual and not
the educational institution. In another state, trouble occurred
when a state purchasing office upset a carefully planned experiment in animal nutrition by substituting an inferior
grade of cattle feed for the one specified by the school of agriculture.

Shifting to a different area of control, college officials
strongly reject the idea that it is sensible, or in fact at all
feasible, that the status and future of academic personnel at
a university should depend upon decisions made in the state
personnel office. Reference here is to a unique situation, yet

it did exist and produce some harrowing results in Massachusetts until the state university fought its way free of state controls over the hiring of faculty members. In other states the inability of state personnel offices to adapt to the special needs of educational institutions has interfered with the recruitment of secretaries and laboratory technicians.

Legislative committees, particularly interim committees, seem more disposed to monitor university activities and internal affairs of the campus than was formerly the case. The multiplication of statutes affecting curriculum is another legislative source of discomfort for the college, for if it is carried too far this practice can lead to an imbalanced educational program. An extreme illustration here is a bill introduced in one state that would require each state college to give a course in embalming—a requirement that seems altogether out of line, even in the presence of an extraordinary death rate.

Legislatively launched research programs can present any university with unexpected problems. Louisiana yields a painful example. Here the sum of $130,000 turned up unexpectedly in a recent university appropriation, for the purpose of improving research and teaching in poultry. Apparently an enterprising legislator was able to convince his colleagues that the poultry problem in his district cried out for a fat appropriation. But, in the ensuing legislative session no support for poultry research could be found. And so, after being launched on a research journey upon which it did not wish to embark, the university was committed to operate a program and staff with no funds for continuing support.

Sometimes a college may be subject to more subtle control through the whisper of discontent in the legislature. In Minnesota the university press published a study by an anthropologist on Nova Scotia Indians. Subsequently in legislative hearings on the university budget before an appropriations committee, university officials were called to task. "Why should Minnesota taxpayers subsidize publication of a study of Indians living in a remote part of Canada?" The clear implication from this line of questioning was that this kind of research should never again be published by the university press. Without challenging the right of legislators to inquire into the expenditure of state funds, Minnesota's educators were disturbed that legislators might think that the quest for knowledge should stop at the state border. The progress of any society depends on the search for ideas in all areas of human activity, and to put geographical blinders on a university would greatly restrict its ability to be of service even to the people of a state.

Yet occasionally the "whispers" of discontent over research get louder. At one mid-western university an economist prepared a monograph on the leasing of farm lands, carrying the suggestion that a formula might well be used for determining land valuation that had been developed by the United States Department of the Interior for leasing lands on Indian reservations. This publication was roundly denounced by some legislators who forthwith urged some of the regents to have it withdrawn.

*The Argument for Control*

While the college administrator objects to this seemingly endless corridor of controls, the state official is simultaneously constrained to argue persuasively for the application of most of the rules he is compelled to uphold. And today his position is a strong one. For the plain truth of the matter is that the rationale for administrative centralization has great appeal for both the business and political community. From

FIGURE 1

# The pressure for control

An important factor contributing to the increase in administrative controls over institutions of higher education is the increasing amount appropriated by the states for these institutions. In 1932 state expenditures for higher education amounted to $234,000,000; in 1957, such expenditures had risen to $1,958,000,000, an increase of over 800% in 25 years. This increase in state expenditures for higher education is graphically presented in the chart below.

STATE EXPENDITURES FOR PUBLIC HIGHER
EDUCATION IN CURRENT AND
CONSTANT (1947–49) DOLLARS: 1932–1957

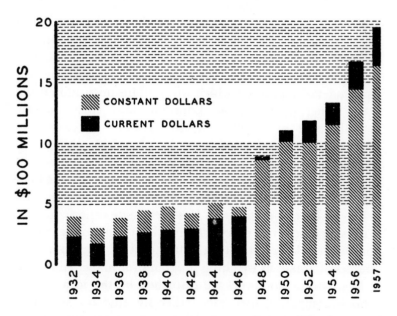

*Source:* U. S. Bureau of the Census, *Compendium of State Government Finances,* for the years shown (Washington: U. S. Government Printing Office). Constant dollars computed from U. S. Department of Labor, *The Purchasing Power of the Consumer Dollar in the United States* (mimeo.).

the view point of business and taxpayer groups, fiscal and management controls promise savings in public expenditures that can be quickly translated into reduced spending. The expanding costs of all public services including higher education also give any device that offers the hope of saving money a promising future with the legislature. Moreover, a great many executive leaders, especially governors, are already on record as favoring some system of central supervision. Only by such action do they believe it possible to pull together the discordant strands of state administration into one cohesive pattern of improved public service.

Many state officials are convinced that certain practices in higher education cry for remedy. A particular grievance here is the lack of co-ordination in higher education—a weakness which can breed duplication of curriculum and a waste of the state's resources. Of course, the college official has long had well-grounded apprehension over the course that attempts at co-ordination may take. He fears that co-ordination will bring a levelling process which will pull his institution downward rather than upward. Educators also worry that the establishment of so-called "master boards" to co-ordinate higher education may bring on jurisdictional conflict with the traditional governing boards.

At the capitol, legislators are concerned that if the schools will not themselves co-ordinate higher education, then the state will have to do so itself. Not every state college can have a nursing school nor every state university an atomic reactor, for the legislator cannot be unmindful of the limited resources of a state in weighing programs for higher education.

Legislators, moreover, are disturbed by the idea of state schools competing with each other for students as well as programs. While by no means a universal problem, an occasional recruitment device in this field has left legislators staring in disbelief. One example cited by state officials as particularly offensive was a birthday greeting from one state college sent to high-school students on their eighteenth birthday. Clearly, argue state officials, such practices are hardly befitting an institution of higher learning and degrade the very idea of a college education.

On another front, campus reporting to the legislature and to the executive agencies of government often leaves much to be desired. Here perhaps it is fair to say that nothing strains relations between capitol and college more than the uneasy feeling that university authorities are not making full disclosure of the facts, and that certain fiscal practices on the campus will not bear close scrutiny.

## The Campus and the Capitol

From the perspective of the educator, the widespread anxiety over state controls in higher education rests upon three essential considerations.

First, it is indubitably clear that government controls have penetrated institutions of higher education in some states at a number of critical points and in a remarkable variety of ways. Certainly the impact of such encroachments is well-documented in the following chapters by the experiences of Massachusetts, West Virginia, Kansas, and New York, and educators are deeply disturbed by recent developments in these states.

Second, cases of particularly bad controls—state officials sometimes refer to them with disdain as atrocity stories— are disquieting to college administrators in states more fortunately situated, because of their fear that these stringent controls may be exportable.

Third, this fear is sometimes intensified by the pale beginnings of new controls over higher education that are

cropping up in states that have so far been relatively free
from centralized supervision.

Despite reassurance that unwarranted controls will not
penetrate his own institution, the college official casts uneasy
glances at experiences elsewhere, and wonders anxiously
whether similar practices will overtake his own institution.
He is not unmindful of the human equation in this matter
of state interference. Some state personnel directors have the
authority to apply certain rigid procedures to college and
university nonacademic recruitment, but they do not as yet
do so. But the college administrator always wonders what a
change in staff in any state agency might bring. Quite understandably, therefore, he resists the extension of further
controls by statutory authority, while simultaneously working to remove restrictions that have already harried the operations of his institution or threatened its essential freedom
in a deeper and more disturbing domain.

While an inquiry of this nature necessarily concentrates
upon grievances, it should be remembered that a remarkable
amount of good will exists among educators, legislators, and
state officials in all parts of the country. On balance, the
problems of readjustment in the persistent partnership of
the state and higher education are not as difficult as they are
sometimes painted to be. Any picture of the campus and
capitol set off against each other as two hostile camps would
be highly inaccurate. The truth of the matter is that on
some very fundamental issues they are not so much divided
as they are united in the search for solutions to common
problems.

Nor can it be said that partisan conflict in state politics
has played havoc with higher education. Actually there has
been an extraordinarily unpartisan approach to educational
policy in many states, an approach which began long before
the term "bipartisan foreign policy" slipped into the legis-

lative vocabulary of national politics. There is, moreover, every reason to believe this will continue. For the seven thousand state legislators across the nation, along with executive officials, take great pride in their colleges and universities and in the advancement of these schools. And most of them want these institutions to grow upward to higher levels of achievement and distinction.

The abiding concern of state official and educator for faithfully fulfilling their obligations in a time of unparalleled growth and unsettlement is understandably great. For the legislator and executive fiscal officer, mounting appropriations inevitably impose sterner demands for more stringent controls over colleges and universities. From the educator's viewpoint, students, salaries, and satellites, also inspire moments of apprehension. Enrollments may soon soar beyond belief, and in the matter of salaries campus competition for academic talent has never been keener.

In the face of these conditions it should come as no surprise that in some areas of conflict the task of moderating differences between college administrators and state officials is beset with difficulty. Here we are reminded that in striving for improved relations, the colleges and the state cannot always concentrate on easy solutions but must sometimes direct their efforts toward the avoidance of costly errors. For in its totality a university is an organism whose sensory apparatus can be damaged very easily.

It needs always to be remembered that a damaged college or university leaves scar tissue upon each succeeding generation. For academic institutions reach the summits by painstaking effort. Highway departments in an inert condition can be elevated into vigorous organizations in a relatively short period, but not so the university. No massive transfusion of the energies of main street will swiftly revive the school that has slumped in decline. It is for this very reason that any practices that blunt or make more difficult the mission of the university must be carefully weighed in the balance. Education is far too precious a matter to be threatened, however remotely, by misunderstanding, misinformation, or genuine grievances between the capitol and the campus.

CHAPTER II

# Higher learning and the law*

LEGAL PROVISIONS governing the relationship between the
state and public colleges and universities in this country
bear eloquent witness to the fact that the states are as capable
of diversity in the field of higher education as they are in
any other area of social and economic life.[1] There is a great

* In preparing this chapter, a questionnaire was sent to each of the state
attorneys-general in the United States. Detailed replies were received from
forty states, and we would like to express our gratitude for the help extended
us by each of these state officers.

[1] While comparatively little has been written on the political and administrative contacts between state government and higher education, the legal
side of this relationship has been subjected to intensive analysis. See, for
example, Alexander Brody, *The American State and Higher Education*
(Washington: American Council on Education, 1935); Edward C. Elliott and
M. M. Chambers, *The Colleges and the Courts* (New York: Carnegie Foundation for the Advancement of Teaching, 1936), pp. 115-64; and M. M.
Chambers, *The Colleges and the Courts, 1941–1945* (New York: Carnegie
Foundation for the Advancement of Teaching, 1946), pp. 37–43. Upon the
request of this committee, M. M. Chambers also prepared for its use a memorandum entitled "State Government and Higher Education in the United

17

variety in the constitutional and statutory provisions relating to higher education among the several states, and even where there appears to be similarity in statute or fundamental law, there is wide diversity in the way in which judges interpret the law. Nor is judicial interpretation itself a sure guarantee of uniformity, for the play of diverse personalities and varying traditions tends to pull the states far apart in the actual administration of their separate systems of higher education.

But even in the face of this inherent and intended diversity of a federal system, the body of law dealing with the relationship between state government and higher education does tend to divide itself rather naturally into the familiar categories of constitutional and statutory law. The part of the law of higher education originating directly in state constitutions is relatively small in most areas, but it is, nevertheless, of considerable significance even where it has only very limited practical effect. For the continued attention given higher education in state constitutions does serve to suggest the concern that has historically existed in the public mind over this topic. And those states which have given the university constitutional recognition as virtually a fourth branch of government have honored higher education with a status that has lifted it high above the common run of state activities.

But by far the greater part of the law defining the status

---

States: Some Opinions of the Higher Courts." During the past decade M. M. Chambers and T. E. Blackwell have both published widely on this topic in educational journals. See especially the recent articles by T. E. Blackwell in *College and University Business,* e.g., "Legislative Control of Tax Supported Universities," XXVI (September, 1956), pp. 34–35; "Power of the Legislative Auditor to Control Disbursement of Colleges," X (February, 1951), p. 31; "Legality of Revenue Bonds Issued for Building Dormitories," XI (September, 1951), pp. 49–50; "Deposit of University Funds with State Treasurers," VIII (March, 1950), pp. 48–49.

of higher education is legislative rather than constitutional in its immediate origins. Teachers' colleges, for example—institutions that are today winning increasing recognition as state colleges—number about one-half of all public institutions of higher education in the United States, and these schools are ord arily subject to continuing control by the legislature. Most state universities are also creatures of the legislature rather than the constitution, or at least subject to such controls as the legislature may choose to impose over their operations. None of these schools can appeal to any system of higher law in justification of their right to enjoy a degree of independence within the framework of state government. They must make their case for the freedom of higher education in the legislature or in the forum of public debate, unprotected by any shield of legal autonomy. The independence of these schools thus stands in constant need of being nourished and replenished by the support of the community.

It needs, moreover, to be borne in mind that however much the law may separate higher education from the other branches of state government or distinguish it from the rest of state activities, it also serves to hold state colleges and universities within the web of government. For public higher education is by law a function of the state, even where it may not be subject to state control. And institutions of higher education derive substantial benefit from their position as governmental agencies, since this status affords them advantages that are of considerable assistance in their day-to-day operations. Consequently the law of higher education also serves to affirm the kinship of public colleges and universities with the family of government activities.

In so far as the law may provide state colleges and universities with protection from unwarranted interference by government agencies and officials, it is no small factor in shoring up their independence. And yet, even at best, the law is only one of the factors upon which the freedom of institutions of higher education depends. For a state university may, like any private institution, be legally free and yet subject to a pervasive and penetrating array of controls, ranging from the pressures which can be brought to bear by dominant groups in the outside community to inhibitions which have internal origins in an institution's own need for financial support. Important as the law may be, a state university can never buy freedom for itself with legal currency alone.

## Higher Learning and Higher Law

Provisions relating to higher education are to be found in the constitutions of over half the states.[2] In some cases, however, the higher law deals mainly with such matters as the place where the university is to be located. Wisconsin is a state in this category, the constitution of Wisconsin requiring that the university be established at or near the seat of state government. But in other states, constitutional provisions go to the heart of organization and administration in the area of higher education. The size and method of selection of members of governing boards are spelled out in the fundamental law of several states, including Texas, Virginia, Nebraska, Alabama, and Louisiana.

In still other areas the constitution places control over

2 For detailed analyses of constitutional provisions affecting state colleges and universities, see Elliott and Chambers, *op. cit.*, pp. 505-12; Brody, *op. cit.*, pp. 215-25; Council of State Governments, *Higher Education in the Forty-Eight States* (Chicago: Council of State Governments, 1952), pp. 131-32; and "Provisions of State Constitutions for Higher Education," a study prepared for the Council for the Study of Higher Education in Florida (mimeographed).

the affairs of a university in the hands of its governing board, subject only to the restriction that this power be exercised in accord with laws passed by the legislature. Typical here is the Constitution of South Dakota, which states that: "The general control and supervision of the State University and the various other state educational institutions shall be vested in a state board of education, whose powers and duties shall be prescribed by law." [3] In a situation of this kind, the university is legally entitled to as much autonomy as the legislature allows it to enjoy, or the courts decide it must have. Ordinarily, however, the constitutional origins of a governing board's authority give it a claim to independence that other departments of government cannot lightly dismiss.

Over the years the support of higher law has served to create a very formidable barrier against governmental interference with the independence of state universities. And the importance that law has come to play in this regard stems only in part from the remedies it affords in court against infringements upon the university's freedom. For the law creates as well as sustains a community's traditions, and in some states the tradition of freedom which constitutional law has helped to shape discourages visible attempts at interference with the university. In this environment, the university's purely legal independence comes in time to be buttressed by the force of public opinion, and strong political liabilities are attached to assaults upon the university. In the end a sphere of independence may emerge that is broader by far than that which the law itself necessarily requires.

---

[3] South Dakota, *Constitution*, Art. 14, sec. 2. A similar provision is contained in Art. 8, sec. 10 of the Nebraska constitution: "The general government of the University of Nebraska shall, under the direction of the legislature, be vested in a board of six regents. . . . Their duties and powers shall be prescribed by law. . . ."

*The Constitutional Corporation*

The attempt to root higher education in fundamental law has reached its greatest achievement in American society with the establishment in six states of institutions of higher education that have been granted constitutional status as virtually a fourth branch of government.[4] In these states the public university holds co-ordinate legal status with the legislature, the executive, and the judiciary. It is subject to legal control by these other branches of government only in so far as it seeks their assistance in attempting to attain its own objectives, as when it requests financial aid in the way of appropriations from the legislature.

The establishment of these so-called constitutional corporations has had effects that reach far beyond the borders of the states in which they have been located. The very existence of institutions of this kind, legally insulated from the pressures of state politics, has furnished a model for higher education in all parts of the country, throwing into bold relief the image of a state university as a unique institution within the web of government. The force of the

---

[4] In a recent survey, William P. Wooden lists seven universities as enjoying this degree of constitutional independence: Oklahoma State University; Michigan State University; the University of California; the University of Colorado; the University of Idaho; the University of Michigan; and the University of Minnesota. See "Recent Decisions," *Michigan Law Review*, LV (1957), p. 728. This listing follows that presented earlier in Elliott and Chambers, *op. cit.*, pp. 134–54 and Brody, *op. cit.*, pp. 165–214. However, in the 1956 Utah decision referred to *infra*, note 20, the University of Georgia is also included in the category of constitutional corporations, and Chambers in his more recent book states that a constitutional amendment adopted in 1943 clearly establishes the constitutional independence of the University System of Georgia; Chambers, *op. cit.*, pp. 37–38. In all, twenty-seven states make explicit reference to higher education in their constitutions, but most do not guarantee genuine constitutional autonomy for their colleges and universities.

attraction thus exerted by the constitutionally independent university has been greatly reinforced by the fact that several of these schools have acquired distinguished reputations as centers of learning. Not that legal status alone can confer the touch of greatness upon any public university, for the place of the university in the history and tradition of the state and the availability of economic resources for the support of higher learning are of vital importance in shaping the destinies of all state colleges and universities. And even without constitutional autonomy, schools such as the University of Wisconsin were quick to reach a position of eminence in the academic world.

But the role of the university as a constitutional corporation deserves attention for another reason besides the role that this type of institution has played in setting a national tone for higher education. The fact of the matter is that recent developments with respect to the relations between these constitutionally independent universities and the offices and agencies of state government bring into sharp focus the pressures toward governmental control which are today converging upon state institutions of higher education. For if a university that enjoys constitutional immunity from government control cannot hold itself aloof from these pressures, it is clear that other colleges and universities will feel their impact even more keenly.

PLANTING THE SEED

It was in Michigan that a constitutionally autonomous state university was first established. The special status granted the University of Michigan under the terms of the state constitution of 1850 was a direct result of dissatisfaction with the shifting fortunes of the university as it had previously been operated under state control. Prior to 1850, the legislature had taken it upon itself to intervene directly in the internal affairs of the university, through capricious use of its law-making power and through a constant reshuffling of the membership of the university's board of trustees. The depressing effect of this system of state control upon the quality of university operations was graphically summarized by a legislative committee appointed to look into the affairs of the university:

> When legislatures have legislated directly for colleges, their measures have been as fluctuating as the changing material of which the legislatures were composed. . . .
> Again, legislatures . . . have not been willing to appoint trustees for a length of time sufficient for them to become acquainted with their duties. . . . A new board of trustees, like a legislature of new members not knowing well what to do, generally begins by undoing and disorganizing all that has been done before. At first they dig up the seed a few times to see that it is going to come up and after it appears above the surface they must pull it up again to see if there is sufficient root to support so vigorous branches; then lop off branches for fear they will exhaust the roots, and then pull it up again to see why it is so sickly and puny and finally to see if they can discover what made it die. And, as these several operations are performed by successive hands, no one can be charged with the guilt of destroying the valuable tree.[5]

As indicated by this metaphor, so well-directed toward an agricultural community,[6] the primary reason for the estab-

---

[5] Michigan, House of Representatives, *Report of the Select Committee to Inquire into the Conditions of the University*, House of Representatives Documents, 1840, p. 470.

[6] State college and university officials have often demonstrated great skill in the use of metaphors which will bring the needs of higher education home to agricultural communities. Witness, for example, this celebrated defense of academic freedom by the regents of the University of Wisconsin:

. . . In all lines of academic investigation it is of the utmost impor-

lishment of the University of Michigan in a position of constitutional independence was a desire to promote its efficiency. For it was pointed out that comparable private institutions operating within the state had far outstripped the University of Michigan in educational achievement.

Over the years the constitutional provisions guaranteeing the university's independence have blocked a variety of attempts designed to bring the school under closer state control.[7] Early in Michigan history the efforts of the legislature to force the university to introduce the study of homeopathic medicine into its medical school curriculum brought about a lively series of court tests.[8] None of these efforts was suc-

---

tance that the investigator should be absolutely free to follow the indications of truth wherever they may lead. Whatever may be the limitations which trammel inquiry elsewhere we believe the great State University of Wisconsin should ever encourage that continual and fearless sifting and winnowing by which alone the truth can be found.

Richard Hofstadter and Walter P. Metzger, *The Development of Academic Freedom in the United States* (New York: Columbia University Press, 1957), p. 427.

And in Texas, one educator protested that efforts to force the university to spend money from its reserve fund would deprive the school of its "seed-corn."

7 Michigan, *Constitution* (1850), Art. 13, secs. 6, 7, and 8. The key phrases appear in section 8: "The board of regents shall have the general supervision of the University, and the direction and control of all expenditures from the university interest-fund." When the constitution was amended in 1909 (Art. 11, sec. 5), the word "interest" was removed from this clause and the word "fund" was changed to "funds" so as to give the board of regents control over all university income from whatever source derived.

8 See *People* v. *Regents of University*, 4 Michigan 98 (1856), where the legislature by statute sought to establish a chair in homeopathy at the university; *People* v. *Auditor General*, 17 Michigan 161 (1868), wherein the university's use of a legislative appropriation was made contingent upon the establishment of a chair in homeopathy; *People* v. *Regents of University*, 18 Michigan 469 (1869) and *People ex. rel. Attorney General* v. *Regents of the University*, 30 Michigan 473 (1874), two cases where the attorney general of the state sought a writ of mandamus to compel the university to obey a law requiring it to appoint a homeopathic professor. In *Weinberg* v. *Regents of*

cessful, the court holding in every case that the university was entitled to ignore the legislative directive in question. In many of these early decisions the exact degree of independence the university enjoyed under the constitution was left in doubt. But finally, in a decision that has come to be looked upon as a landmark in the history of the university, the court spelled out the school's independence in clear and unmistakable terms: "The board of regents and the legislature derive their power from the same supreme authority, namely, the constitution. . . . They are separate and distinct constitutional bodies, with the power of the regents defined. By no rule of construction can it be held that either can encroach upon or exercise the powers conferred upon the other." [9]

## FREEDOM FROM ADMINISTRATIVE CONTROL

General satisfaction with this experiment of granting autonomy to the University of Michigan was evident at the constitutional convention of 1908. For at that time the constitution was amended so as to grant constitutional autonomy to the land-grant college of the state, the school that now bears the name of Michigan State University.[10] And as far as both Michigan and Michigan State are concerned, the courts have upheld their independence not only from direct and immediate control by the legislature, but also from

---

the University of Michigan, 97 Michigan 246, 56 N. W. 605 (1893), the courts also held that the university was not within the scope of a building statute enacted by the legislature.

[9] Sterling v. Regents of University, 110 Michigan 369, 68 N. W. 253 (1896). This case grew out of a legislative act directing the university to establish a homeopathic medical college as a part of the university at Detroit.

[10] Michigan, Constitution, Art. 11, sec. 8. See especially the clause, "The board shall have the general supervision of the college, and the direction and control of all agricultural college funds. . . ."

attempts at intervention by administrative officials, acting pursuant to what they consider to be legislative authority. On one occasion, the auditor-general of the state refused to approve traveling expenses incurred by various employees of the university, including President Angell, on the grounds that these expenses were not, as required by law, for a "reasonable purpose." The court, however, reversed this decision, holding that the auditor's duties with regard to university expenditures were purely ministerial and did not allow him to substitute his own judgment for that of college administrators on the propriety or good sense of university expenditures. The Board of Regents, the court said, "is made the highest form of juristic person known to the law, a constitutional corporation of independent authority, which, within the scope of its functions is coordinate with and equal to that of the Legislature." [11]

In the other states in which schools have been granted a constitutional status of complete independence, the courts have similarly ruled that this "elevation of the university to the place and dignity of a constitutional department of the body politic" [12] provides protection from administrative as well as legislative attempts at control. Judicial rulings to this effect are, of course, of critical importance to the schools concerned, for with the current trend toward administrative centralization in state government, it is executive rather than legislative officials who are today regarded as represent-

11 *Regents* v. *Auditor General,* 167 Michigan 444, 132 N. W. 1037 (1911). However, as noted in the Chase decision, cited *infra,* note 12, the state itself is actually the "highest form of juristic person known to law."

12 *Williams* v. *Wheeler,* 23 Cal. App. 619, 138 Pac. 937 (1913), a case in which the court upheld the right of the University of California to refuse admission to a student who had not been vaccinated, even though a state law on this subject allowed him to claim the privilege of conscientious objection to such innoculation.

ing the chief threat to the independence of institutions of higher education.

This growth of topside power has been in good measure designed to insure closer control over expenditures by the line agencies of state government. As might be expected, the conflict between college official and state administrator has largely centered on the university's use of its appropriated funds. And in every case, the issue presented for judicial decision has been essentially the same as that which came before the courts in Michigan. Is it the university or a state office of fiscal control which has the primary legal right to determine how university funds are to be spent to promote the goals of higher education?

Perhaps the most famous of all decisions upholding the independence of the university from administrative control was handed down in Minnesota. Here, although the university's autonomy can be traced back to the state constitution adopted in 1851, its status of constitutional independence was not clearly confirmed until 1928. In that year the state auditor refused to approve payments for expenses incurred by the university in connection with a survey it made of group insurance plans for members of the faculty. The auditor's refusal was based on the fact that the Commission on Administration and Finance disapproved of the university's insurance plan, a power the commission claimed to exercise under a statute enacted by the legislature in 1925.

In granting the university's application for a writ of mandamus to compel the auditor to honor the voucher in dispute, the court clearly spelled out the factors which had impelled the framers of the constitution to place the university beyond the reach of control by the other branches of government:

> The purpose of the Constitution remains clear. It was
> to put the management of the greatest state educational

institution beyond the dangers of vacillating policy, ill-informed or careless meddling and partisan ambition that would be possible in the case of management by either Legislature or executive, chosen at frequent intervals and for functions and because of qualities and activities vastly different from those which qualify for the management of an institution of higher learning.[13]

This decision nullified any possibility that the Minnesota legislature might authorize an executive agency to impose controls that it was itself constitutionally prohibited from exercising.

The issue of administrative control over a constitutionally independent university has also been joined in Idaho and Oklahoma. In Idaho the court upheld the university in its refusal to clear all expenditures with the State Board of Examiners, an agency of fiscal control.[14] And in Oklahoma the judiciary set aside an attempt by the State Board of Public Affairs to pass on all university vouchers.[15] In each case the court held that control over money was central over policy and that a state fiscal agency could not intervene in one without controlling the other.

[13] *State* v. *Chase*, 175 Minn. 259, 220 N. W. 951 (1928). More recent decisions affirming the constitutional autonomy of the University of Minnesota include *Fanning* v. *Regents*, 183 Minn. 222, 236 N. W. 217 (1931), where it was decided that the university does not need legislative approval to construct a dormitory; *State ex rel. Peterson* v. *Quinlivan*, 198 Minn. 65, 268 N. W. 858 (1936), the method of appointing regents is beyond change by legislative or executive act; *State ex rel. Sholes* v. *University of Minnesota*, 54 N. W. 2d 122 (1952), the courts cannot compel the regents to enact a regulation prohibiting religious activity on the campus. In this last case the independence of the university from judicial as well as legislative and executive control was proclaimed.

[14] *State* v. *State Board of Education*, 33 Idaho 415, 196 Pac. 201 (1921).

[15] *Trapp, State Auditor* v. *Cooke Construction Co.*, 24 Okla. 850, 105 Pac. 667 (1909).

## BREAKING THE CONSTITUTIONAL BARRIER

In spite of the array of judicial decisions handed down in their behalf, universities that enjoy the status of constitutional corporations by no means feel that their independence is entirely free from jeopardy today. The source of their anxiety stems from the fact that the fiscal power of government is making itself increasingly felt as a somewhat subtle and publicly unrecognized mechanism of control over constitutionally independent institutions. This trend is in good part a product of the expanding costs of higher education. Mounting legislative appropriations bring in their wake increased pressure toward more stringent control over expenditures by colleges and universities. And it is their own growing need for financial support that has placed the constitutionally autonomous universities in the position of having to yield some of their traditional freedom of action.

Striking examples of the manner in which the fiscal power of the legislature can penetrate the constitutional barrier have occurred in Michigan, the state in which the precedent of the constitutional university was first established. In recent years, the legislature has passed capital outlay appropriation acts which specify that no money can be spent on a construction project until approval had been secured from the Buildings Division of the state Department of Administration.[16] While this power has not to this point been abused, it confronts the university with clear evidence that its independence in an important area of its operations has been whittled away. And there are some misgivings that

16 Michigan, *Public Acts of 1957*, No. 306, sec. 6: "Expenditures under the provisions of this act for buildings and construction shall be authorized when the release of the appropriations for buildings and construction items is approved by the state administrative board. . . . No agency included within the provisions of this act shall make any commitments for any project until after the release of the appropriation."

this shift in control to an executive agency will some day lead to political interference with the university.

The institutions of higher education in Michigan have also been made subject to the requirement that all self-liquidating projects receive legislative approval prior to construction.[17] The enactment of this provision sprang originally from a practice that had greatly incensed the Michigan legislature, the policy followed in some cases of charging off utility costs on self-liquidating projects to state appropriations and then claiming in public pronouncements that the buildings involved no cost to the taxpayer. Although the legislature no longer allows schools to charge off such costs to the state, it still requires that all plans for self-liquidating projects receive legislative approval in advance. Up to the present time, however, the approval has been little more than a formality.

The legal standing of this roundabout method of legislative control is not altogether clear. Two decisions handed down by the Michigan courts point up the ambiguity in this area of the law. In one case, decided in 1911, the courts ruled that the legislature has the power to attach conditions to appropriation acts, and if the university accepts the appropriation, it must comply with the conditions.[18] Some years later, however, the legislature sought to have Michigan State

17 Michigan, *Public Acts of 1957*, No. 307, sec. 12: "In view of the fact that state appropriations have been used for certain expenses in connection with self-liquidating projects, no contract shall be let for construction as to any self-liquidating project at any of the state supported institutions of higher education without prior approval therefor by the legislature."

18 *Board of Regents of the University of Michigan* v. *Auditor General*, 167 Michigan 444, 132 N. W. 1037 (1911). This principle may also be found stated in a dissenting opinion in *Weinberg* v. *The Regents of the University of Michigan*, 97 Michigan 236, 56 N. W. 605 (1893): "In making appropriations for its support, the legislature may attach any conditions it may deem expedient and wise, and the regents cannot receive the appropriation without complying with the conditions."

College clear all its expenditures through a state administrative board, by means of a rider attached to an appropriations act. This time the court held that the rider in question violated the constitution since it put a state administrative agency rather than the Board of Regents in the position of governing the university.[19] The net effect of these two decisions has been to limit the power of the legislature to attach conditions to appropriations acts to those restrictions which do not invade the constitutional authority of the regents. This leaves it to the courts to decide in cases where a test arises whether legislative restrictions actually impinge upon the governing board's legal authority.

It is, however, of critical importance to note that a constitutional university does not always have complete freedom of action in deciding whether or not to challenge what it may regard as an unconstitutional rider coupled to an appropriations act. For a state university has a heavy dependence upon public and legislative good will for financial and other support, and even in the case of a successful court challenge, it risks a Pyrrhic victory in which its legal autonomy would be upheld at considerable cost to its relations with the community. It is considerations of this kind which militate against a court challenge of legislative riders in states in which the university enjoys constitutional autonomy. The plain fact of the matter is that a state university cannot always afford to cast itself in the role of standing on its legal rights when this may be interpreted within the state as a willful defiance of public opinion.

However, in thus accepting without protest legislative riders that are in fact infringements upon the university's con-

[19] *State Board of Agriculture* v. *State Administrative Board,* 226 Michigan 417, 197 N. W. 160 (1924). There is an excellent discussion of these cases in Wilfred B. Shaw (ed.), *The University of Michigan: An Encyclopedic Survey* (Ann Arbor: University of Michigan, 1942), I, pp. 116–36.

stitutional autonomy, a state university may well give such provisions a legality they would not otherwise have. This is the apparent meaning of a decision recently handed down in Utah, where the state university found that its acceptance of controls over a long period of time was itself held by the courts as contributing to the legal validity of this pattern of supervision.[20] The university's efforts to secure a declaratory judgment upholding its constitutional immunity from legislative control over the school's internal operations thus met with rebuff.[21] And as partial proof of its contention that the university was legally subject to legislative jurisdiction, the court pointed out that "for over 50 years the University has never raised the point of independent control . . . and has acquiesced in and complied with the legislative enactments relating to its purposes and government."

As is obvious from the success of the attempts currently being made to circumvent the legal safeguards by which schools of this kind have been protected in the past, the independence of constitutional universities must ultimately rest upon the support of public opinion as well as upon the provisions of fundamental law. For even constitutional law is not beyond the possibility of amendment,[22] and legislative and other governmental bodies can always harass an institu-

20 *University of Utah* v. *Board of Examiners of State of Utah*, 4 Utah 2d 408, 295 Pac. 2d 348 (1956).

21 The relevant portion of the Utah constitution (Art. 10, sec. 4) reads as follows: "The location and establishment by existing laws of the University of Utah, and the Agricultural College are hereby confirmed, and all the rights, immunities, franchises, and endowments heretofore granted or conferred, are hereby perpetuated unto said University and Agricultural College respectively." The court ruled that the university had not, by this or any other provision of the constitution, been rendered independent of legislative control.

22 See Chapter VII, p. 178 for a discussion of an effort in California to pass a constitutional amendment depriving the University of California of full control over nonacademic personnel.

tion of this kind through investigations and burdensome reporting requirements even where they cannot bring it under direct control. Thus, a constitutionally independent university, like all state institutions of higher education, faces a continuous job of maintaining public understanding of its role in the community, explaining, justifying, and defending the administrative as well as the academic freedom that the university has traditionally enjoyed.

## Legislation on Higher Education

In the great majority of states, colleges and universities do not enjoy this constitutional recognition as separate branches of government. On the contrary, the general right of the legislature to exercise control over their organization and operations is rooted in the fundamental law of the state and has frequently been affirmed by the courts. In Nebraska, for example, where the university's governing board can trace its origins to the constitution, it has been declared that "the Board of Regents is but a mere governmental agency expressly subjected by the Constitution to the will of the Legislature to work out its projects for higher education." [23] And in Montana the court denied that the governing board is an autonomous agency of state government, pointing out that the board "is a part of the executive department, and is but an agency of the state government." The legislature was thus upheld in its right to "prescribe the extent of the powers and duties to be exercised by the board in the general control and supervision of the University of Montana." [24]

[23] *State ex rel. Bushee* v. *Whitmore*, 85 Neb. 566, 123 N. W. 1051 (1909), a decision which ordered the university to obey a legislative directive to establish agricultural experiment stations in the western part of the state.

[24] *State ex rel. Public Service Commission* v. *Brannon*, 86 Mont. 200, 283 Pac. 202 (1929), a decision in which the court held that the legislature could

Similar statements upholding the plenary power of the legislature over higher education can be found in court decisions in many other states. Except where it is blocked by some constitutional provision, this power can legally penetrate into the most intimate details of university operations, and the freedom that most state colleges and universities enjoy is thus dependent in large measure upon legislative self-restraint. This legislative power to control higher education can also be delegated to administrative agencies if the legislature chooses to do so, and this is a practice commonly followed.

However, the authority of administrative officials over higher education is limited to the terms fixed in either constitution or statute. Recent decisions in both Arizona and West Virginia [25] have pointed out that a state auditor has no lawful right to pass on the propriety as well as the legality of university expenditures. An auditor's power is restricted to determining whether or not university expenditures are within the law. He is acting *ultra vires* when he goes beyond that to inquire into their wisdom. Similarly, a recent attorney general's opinion in New Mexico held that the chief of the state Budget Division was exceeding his prescribed authority in requiring that salary increases for all administrative per-

---

require the chairman of the chemistry department at the University of Montana to serve as state chemist.

[25] The Arizona decision was *Board of Regents of University and State College* v. *Frohmiller*, 69 Ariz. 50, 208 Pac. 2d 833 (1949), where the court held that expenses incurred in connection with the inauguration of a new president were legitimate items of university expenditure, thus striking down an auditor's decision to the contrary. In West Virginia the auditor sought to deny the right of a state college to pay a professor while the faculty member was on sabbatical leave, but was overruled in *State ex rel. West Virginia Board of Education* v. *Sims*, 81 S. E. 2d 665 (1954). Of course in the nature of things a state auditor who has the authority to disallow expenditures that are not for public purpose has a substantial amount of discretionary power vested in him under the law.

sonnel making more than $600 a month be cleared through his office. The attorney general pointed out that "nowhere in the Act creating the Budget Division is the power to pass upon or to approve or disapprove salaries of State employees to be found. It does not exist in terms. It cannot be implied from the language used." [26]

While some college administrators often feel themselves cramped and confined by their governmental status, the truth of the matter is that the schools derive great advantages from their legal position as agencies of the state. A look at legal precedents in virtually any state will show the great variety of circumstances in which an institution of higher education may find it highly useful to have its status as a governmental institution confirmed. In Colorado, for example, the schools have sought and obtained several attorneys general's opinions upholding their governmental status that have been of great benefit to them in their own operations. An opinion handed down on October 13, 1933, held that Adams State Teachers College was a governmental agency within the meaning of the law and was entitled to avail itself of the benefits of a statute enacted by the Colorado legislature authorizing governmental agencies of the state to accept loans and grants from the federal government. This opinion cleared the way for the school to make application to the Federal Emergency Administration of Public Works for a loan to be used for the construction of residence halls on the campus.

On March 10, 1941, a ruling by the Colorado attorney general extended the state Workmen's Compensation Act to employees of the University of Colorado. This opinion held that the university, even though constitutionally autonomous, was an instrumentality of the State and that members of its

---

[26] Opinion of Attorney General Fred M. Standley, August 15, 1957, No. 57–205 (mimeographed), p. 2.

staff were entitled to all the privileges of state employees. A more recent opinion delivered on April 18, 1952, pointed out that Fort Lewis A & M College could not, as a state agency, be sued for the torts of its employees in the absence of legislative consent, and that the university thus enjoyed the same immunity from tort liability as any other governmental agency. Elsewhere similar legal precedents have been of great benefit to colleges and universities.

## FREEDOM UNDER LAW

In legal theory at least, legislative bodies have a right to impose extensive statutory control over all aspects of college and university operations. Chapter XI reviews the manner in which legislatures have been involved in policy concerning research, admissions, courses, and tuition. But it remains true that legislative interference with the internal administration of institutions of higher education is the exception rather than the rule. It is the belief in most states that governing boards can only operate effectively where they are left by the legislature with a substantial degree of autonomous control over the affairs of the university. Whatever constitutions may allow, the common understanding seems to demand that higher education be granted administrative as well as academic freedom.

In some areas this freedom is not only supported by silent custom but is also articulated in law. The legal independence of a great many institutions of higher education is buttressed to some degree by the fact that these schools are chartered as public corporations of the state.[27] Not that too much importance should be assigned to a university's position as a corporate institution, for schools that enjoy corporate status are

[27] In former times state colleges in many areas were actually held to be private corporations. See Elliott and Chambers, *op. cit.,* pp. 116–21.

not by that fact alone protected from regulations imposed upon non-corporate institutions. But the fact that legislatures in a great many states have seen fit to bestow this special standing upon their institutions of higher learning does suggest the widely spread conviction that running a university demands a flexibility in internal management comparable to that of private business organizations.

And several court decisions broadly interpreting the authority of governing boards have placed particular stress upon the discretionary privileges that state universities derive from their corporate status. As an Illinois court once said of the university at Urbana:

> By creating the corporation and conferring upon it the powers delegated by the act of its creation, the State has committed to it the operation, administration and management of the University of Illinois. While the legislature has the power at any time to modify or change, or even take away entirely the powers thus conferred on the corporation, it can do so only by legislation. As long as the present statute is in force, the State has committed to the corporate entity the absolute power to do everything necessary in the management, operation and administration of the university.[28]

In Illinois corporate standing has in this way become a symbol of a school's right to internal self-government. Soon after this decision, in fact, legislation was passed conferring corporate status upon the other institutions of higher education in the state.

An equally striking indication of the legislative belief that

---

28 *People ex rel. Board of Trustees of the University of Illinois* v. *Barrett,* 382 Ill. 321, 46 N. E. 2d 951 (1943), a decision upholding the university's right to employ its own counsel. For a more recent Illinois decision to the same effect, see *Turkovich* v. *The Board of Trustees of the University of Illinois,* 11 Ill. 2d 460, 143 N. E. 2d 229 (1957), where the power of the university to operate a television station was confirmed.

an institution of higher education cannot be administered in the same way as other state agencies is provided by the common legislative practice of exempting the schools from controls imposed upon the rest of state administration. The fact that public colleges and universities are able to secure such privileged status reflects in part the political power that these institutions are able to muster in the legislatures of many states; this is a power that local political leaders often look upon with considerable respect. But it also reveals common acceptance of the notion that uniform procedures which are suitable for the general run of state activities encumber rather than assist effective management in the field of higher education.

An example of special legislation freeing the schools from topside control is provided by a statute enacted in Kentucky in 1952, which clearly excluded the university and the five state colleges from the terms of a state personnel act that had been passed two years earlier.[29] Prior to this legislative clarification, there had been considerable feeling among college administrators that the earlier law might give the state personnel agency jurisdiction over all college and university employees. And in the neighboring state of Tennessee, a revised purchasing act passed by the legislature in 1953 specifically exempted the state colleges and the university from its provisions.[30] In Tennessee as in other states, the schools are, however, required to carry on their purchasing in accordance with the standards of the uniform purchasing act.

The autonomy of the state colleges in Rhode Island was clearly established by a bill passed in 1939 by the state general assembly which had as its declared purpose "that the

[29] Kentucky, *Revised Statutes*, Ch. 11, secs. 164. 220, 164. 225, 164. 230, 164. 365.

[30] Tennessee, *Code Annotated* (1955), sec. 12–336 (*Public Acts of 1953*, Ch. 163, sec. 30).

control of the state colleges shall be removed from partisan political influence." [31] This bill granted corporate status to the trustees of the state college system and included several paragraphs designed to secure the fiscal independence of the university from overhead control by state administrative agencies. One such provision specified that the pre-audit conducted by the state controller "shall be purely ministerial, concerned only with the legality of the expenditures and the availability of the funds, and in no event shall the state controller interpose his judgment regarding the wisdom or expediency of any item or items of expenditure."

However, in 1955 two members of the legislature sought to pare away the autonomy of the schools by introducing a bill that would have greatly tightened statehouse controls over institutions of higher education. The most important section of the proposed legislation authorized the state director of administration to "establish and maintain a current system of financial controls and checks" over colleges within the state. For that purpose the director was authorized to "assign such subordinates or employees to the board of trustees of state colleges as he shall deem necessary, which subordinates or employees shall not be within the classified service." The possibility of patronage appointees moving into a position of close control over higher education aroused severe misgivings within the state. Newspapers carried the story under headlines referring to the "bill to hobble" the trustees and "an assault on the colleges." President Henry Wriston of Brown University, who had fathered the original autonomy act for Rhode Island's colleges, stated that enactment of this new piece of legislation would be a disaster. And although the bill was passed by the senate, it was defeated overwhelmingly when it came before the house.

[31] Rhode Island, *General Laws* (1956), Ch. 31, sec. 16–31–1 (Rhode Island, *Public Laws 1939*, Ch. 688).

In recent years a number of state schools have also been successful in persuading the legislature that certain controls previously imposed upon them should be removed. In 1952, for example, the University of Maryland was the beneficiary of legislation that gave the university freedom from central purchasing and personnel controls. This "Autonomy Act," as it is called, declared that "the Board of Regents shall exercise with reference to the University of Maryland . . . all the powers, rights, and privileges that go with the responsibility of management . . . and said board shall not be superseded in authority by any other State board, bureau, department or commission, in the management of the University's affairs. . . ." [32]

## Summary

Not all the legal precedents bearing on the relationships between government and higher education in the forty-eight states point the same way. In a very few areas, state constitutions have lifted institutions of higher learning almost out of the context of government altogether. Here the university has acquired a standing not wholly unlike the judiciary—a part of government and yet rigorously isolated from the pressures and inhibitions of politics. Ordinarily, however, the law places state colleges and universities in a favored though far less exalted position. Creatures of the legislature, they are subject to general legislative mandates on matters of both policy and administration.

But education is different. The law confirms even where it does not explain this fact. And state courts do not often probe deeply behind the letter of the law. In part at least, the difference springs from the fact that the university is an

[32] Maryland, *Annotated Code*, Art. 77, sec. 24 (e).

institution that carries on a complex and many-sided range of day-to-day activities, and it can only be operated effectively when those responsible for its management are left with enough flexibility and discretion to meet unexpected emergencies and to plan ahead. This is a practical case for the freedom of the university which rests essentially upon principles of business efficiency. Nor is this argument restricted in its application to higher education alone. Government enterprises in such other areas as resource development have traditionally been granted considerably more freedom than the conventional run of state activities.

However, the case for the freedom of the university goes deeper than this and rests upon a characteristic of higher education that it does not come close to sharing with any other state activity. This is the fact that in certain areas colleges and universities need freedom not merely as an administrative convenience to enhance their efficient co-operation but as a basic source of creative energy and an indispensable means to all their achievements. For without freedom, productive teaching and research in the Western tradition are impossible. To be sure, this freedom is not at all inconsistent with proper accountability to the community and to public officials in both the legislature and the executive branch on matters of general finance and university policy. And it cannot be invoked to escape such accountability. But it does stand in jeopardy when state officials responsive to political forces gain easy access to the corridors and decisions of the university in the area of either teaching or research. It has been to guard against this possibility that the law has given institutions of higher education their preferred status.

CHAPTER III

# The state story:
# administrative centralization

FINDING THE proper position for public institutions of higher education within the over-all scheme of state government is an old problem. Certainly the difficulty has not, as some modern observers have often believed, been born entirely of recent attempts to reshape the architecture of state government. The legitimacy of certain controls the state established over the campus first became an issue well back in the nineteenth century.[1] Early litigation before Michigan courts involved such pointedly contemporary issues as how far a legislature may legally attach conditions to funds appropriated for support of a state university. The same cases also discussed the propriety of attempts by a state fiscal officer to

[1] Chapter II, pp. 25-27.

43

control college expenditures from appropriations duly authorized by the legislature.

But the concern of college administrators with drawing a line between proper and improper controls by the state has become particularly acute in recent decades. Everywhere in state government there has been a gradual movement toward administrative centralization, and this move, coupled with the growth of state appropriations, has brought a burgeoning variety of controls over state colleges and universities. In some states it has opened up entirely novel avenues of supervision with the establishment of building authorities and central purchasing offices. In other instances it has meant the revival of previously dormant power in a comptroller's office to exercise a close pre-audit check upon the legality and economy of all state expenditures. Inspired as it is by the entirely praiseworthy goals of economy and efficiency, the new centralization has nevertheless seemed to many educators to pose a grave threat to the traditional freedom of state colleges and universities and to open up avenues of political pressure on the campus.

## The Growth of Concern

The fears of college officials have found their most visible expression at the meetings of educational associations. Back in 1922, the American Association of Land-Grant Colleges and State Universities established a committee to investigate "the administrative relationships of the land-grant colleges with their respective State governments with special reference to the increasingly frequent adoption of the system of centralized expenditure control, a system which is seriously encroaching upon the administrative officers of many land-grant institutions."[2] And in 1923 the association's Special Committee on Centralized Financial Control returned a report on its investigation to the association based upon replies it had received from forty-one states.[3]

This committee exhibited considerable restraint and detachment in reporting its findings to the association. It found "the replies revealed a much less difficult situation at present, taking the country as a whole, than might have been anticipated."[4] And its candor was evident also in the admission that "educational authorities are occasionally guilty of unbusinesslike methods and unwise or unnecessary expenditures. . . . Reporting and accounting systems are sometimes vague or difficult for either public officials or the public to understand. . . . Perhaps the surest means of escaping outside interference is for the executives of our institutions to administer them with scrupulous regard for the public interest, and with a view to inspiring public confidence in the efficient use of funds."[5]

Nonetheless, the committee reaffirmed its belief that state colleges should remain under the sole jurisdiction of those charged with official responsibility for administering their affairs. In an extremely forceful presentation of the college point of view it said:

> The tendency which has appeared in a few States to ruthlessly cut across established responsibilities by legislation giving sweeping authority to State fiscal or control

[2] Association of Land-Grant Colleges, *Proceedings of the Thirty-Sixth Annual Convention*, Washington, D. C., November 21–23, 1922 (Burlington, Vt.: Free Press Printing Co., 1923), p. 366. See also in this regard Edward D. Eddy, Jr., *Colleges for Our Land and Time* (New York: Harper & Brothers, 1956), pp. 153–54.

[3] Association of Land-Grant Colleges, *Proceedings of the Thirty-Seventh Annual Convention*, Chicago, Ill., November 13–15, 1923 (Burlington, Vt.: Free Press Printing Co., 1924), pp. 463–80.

[4] *Ibid.*, p. 463.

[5] *Ibid.*, p. 473.

bodies or officers, and almost without exception creating divided authority and responsibility, is a thoroughly disturbing trend. It almost inevitably results in uncertainty, loss of initiative on the part of institutional authorities where freedom of initiative is indispensable to good government, loss of time, and friction, or at least a measure of mutual distrust. . . . No general state board or fiscal officer, however honestly intentioned but from necessity removed from direct contact with the actual problems of the university, can approximate the wisdom of administration of the fiscal affairs of the colleges which the boards of trustees or regents are in a position to exercise. . . .

Perhaps the most serious of all is the fact that, since it is utterly impossible for such boards to control wisely and intelligently the affairs of all the State's varied departments and agencies in accordance with the intimate and particular needs of each branch, resort is usually had to a dead level of uniformity of procedure with little or no discrimination. . . . Those who see the dangers in dead uniformity of State administration should arise and protest with vigor. Under the present widespread tendency, agencies which are wholly unlike in every respect, and whose proper and efficient administration requires procedures adapted to their own needs, are subjected in some States to uniform administrative procedures which can result only in lessened accomplishment and ultimate retardation of progress.[6]

Succeeding meetings of the land-grant association kept the issue of state intervention in the internal affairs of colleges and universities burning. In 1925 the Special Committee on State Fiscal Policies of the Association of Land-Grant Colleges delivered a report sharply critical of the controls that budget offices were beginning to exercise over state institutions of higher education.[7] "Already," the group complained,

6 *Ibid.*, pp. 466–67.

7 Association of Land-Grant Colleges, *Proceedings of the Thirty-Ninth Annual Convention*, Chicago, Ill., November 17–19, 1925 (Burlington, Vt.: Free Press Printing Co., 1926), p. 377.

"the educational institutions in some states are being severely hampered by policies determined for them at the state capitol." And in the discussion that followed, it was pointed out "as an instance of the utterly unreasonable domination of statehouse bureaucracy . . . that two land-grant college presidents were unable to attend this convention except at their own expense." [8]

In 1928, with the co-operation of the land-grant association, the United States Office of Education undertook a survey of land-grant institutions, and the results of this survey were issued as a two-volume report in 1930.[9] Speaking on the emerging problem of state administrative controls over land-grant institutions, the committee concluded that "recent reorganizations of State governments, the creation of State budgets, and the extension of the power of State agencies over the finances and the internal affairs of the land-grant colleges have in many instances tended to supersede the authority of institutional governing boards and institutional administrative officers." [10]

Since 1930 this topic of fiscal controls has come up repeatedly at meetings of state educational officials. Among the more recent documentations of this continuing interest is the report outlining the scope of controls over land-grant

[8] *Ibid.*, p. 378.

[9] U. S., Office of Education, *Survey of Land-Grant Colleges and Universities,* Bulletin, 1930, No. 9 (2 vols.; Washington: U. S. Government Printing Office, 1930). Over the years the U. S. Office of Education has not lost its interest in the relationship between state government and higher education. Its studies in this area include the following by John H. McNeely: *Authority of State Executive Agencies Over Higher Education,* U. S. Office of Education Bulletin, 1936, No. 15 (Washington: U. S. Government Printing Office, 1936); *Higher Educational Institutions in the Scheme of State Government,* U. S. Office of Education Bulletin, 1939, No. 3 (Washington: U. S. Government Printing Office, 1939).

[10] U. S., Office of Education, *Survey of Land-Grant Colleges and Universities,* Bulletin, 1930, No. 9, p. 73.

institutions delivered by President A. L. Strand of Oregon State College at a meeting of the land-grant association in 1953.[11] Strand found a strong trend toward an increase in such supervision and identified control over publications as "the most dangerous and the most intolerable control that has been placed on any of the institutions." While Strand found that land-grant schools in a majority of the states he studied were "free, or relatively free, of controls," he also pointed out that even in some of these states "they feel sort of a condition of incipiency, they think they can see controls coming and that their freedom from controls is being compromised." [12]

Two years later Lloyd Morey of the University of Illinois presented a paper on this topic at the annual meeting of the National Association of State Universities.[13] And in both 1954 and 1955 fiscal control was a principal topic on the agenda of the Association of Governing Boards of State Universities and Allied Institutions at its annual meetings. Moreover, in the latter year, each of the major organizations representing state institutions of higher education established committees to deal with the question of fiscal control over higher education.[14] In increasing degree, then, the organized

[11] A. L. Strand, "Land-Grant Colleges and the State," *Proceedings of the Association of Land-Grant Colleges and Universities, Sixty-Seventh Annual Convention*, Columbus, Ohio, November 10–12, 1953, pp. 221–25.

[12] *Ibid.*, pp. 224–25.

[13] Lloyd Morey, "Governmental Control of Public Higher Education," *Transactions and Proceedings of the National Association of State Universities*, LIII (1955), p. 30. Morey goes on to comment on the drive for economy which motivates a number of these controls: "The much-worn phrase, *economy and efficiency*, under which many of these procedures parade, and which has a winning way with the legislatures and the public . . . overlooks the fact that institutional officers and boards are more interested in saving money for their institutions than anyone else possibly could be, since they will be the direct beneficiaries of such results." p. 39.

[14] The organizations concerned were the Association of Land-Grant Col-

associations of college officials have worked to quicken public interest in this subject and to stiffen resistance to state administrative control.

## Administrative Reorganization: the Wellspring of Control

College officials have been increasingly worried over the steady infiltration of state administrative power into the internal affairs of public institutions of higher education for almost forty years. At the same time, these have also been years in which there has been a growing effort in most of the states to redesign the administrative architecture of state government. Nor have these simultaneous developments been unrelated. For the trend toward administrative reorganization is widely believed to lie at the root of most of the controls attacked by college officials.

Historically, the movement to revamp state government had its origins in 1909, when the People's Power League of Oregon came up with proposals for centering executive power in the governor. It gathered much of its modern momentum in 1917, when Governor Frank Lowden won approval for a comprehensive plan of administrative reorganization in Illinois.[15] Since that time the Illinois experiment has served as something of a precedent as state after state has moved to streamline its executive machinery. As one author states it:

---

leges and Universities, the National Association of State Universities, and the State Universities Association.

[15] See in this regard A. E. Buck, *The Reorganization of State Governments in the United States* (New York: Columbia University Press, 1938), pp. 6–8.

The Progressive era was the period in which the doctrines of centralization began to be accepted as axiomatic, the period in which the formulae for reconciling "true democracy" and "true efficiency" became completely crystallized. Generally the case was accepted as proved in the following years, and the tenets of centralization were used as guiding principles in local, state, and national reorganization schemes.[16]

The zeal to reorganize has been particularly strong during the past decade, when "little Hoover Commissions" have been sprouting all over the landscape of state politics. No fewer than thirty-three states set up such agencies during the legislative biennium of 1950-51.[17]

The recommendations of reorganization groups are virtually uniform in all the states and parallel very closely the proposals usually set forth in the leading studies of national administration. Recent state reports have in fact been largely inspired by and modeled after the Hoover Commission studies of the organization of the executive branch of the government. Underlying all these surveys is the belief that administrative reorganization cheapens costs while improving the services offered by state government. The slogan of "economy and efficiency" with which it is associated has done more than anything else to promote the cause of reorganization with the general public.

### INTEGRATING STATE ADMINISTRATION

The most familiar aspect of the reorganization movement is the effort it has made to shift agencies around until they are located in a few recognizable departments and agencies

[16] Dwight Waldo, *The Administrative State* (New York: The Ronald Press, 1948), p. 136.
[17] Council of State Governments, *The Book of the States, 1952–53* (Chicago: Council of State Governments, 1952), p. 147.

within the executive branch of government. Traditionally every state activity has tended to move within its own private orbit. And this isolation has meant that policies followed in one area often duplicate or conflict with those pursued in closely related areas of administration. The consolidation of related activities in fields such as transportation, highways, and health, has been widely regarded as promising some savings as well as heightening the efficiency of executive operations.[18]

Yet studies calling for administrative consolidation ordinarily meet with stiff opposition in the rough and tumble of state politics. For any such proposal, however innocent on the surface, threatens some disturbance of vested interests within the state. Legislators and legislative committees have working arrangements with administrative agencies which a shift in their location may easily upset. The same fear of change grips interest groups that regard a more tightly knit administrative system as less accessible to their own influence. And as the third dimension of organized resistance to administrative integration, executive agencies themselves are less than enthusiastic about consolidation proposals that threaten to reduce their status or restrict their traditional freedom of operations.

In the face of stubborn opposition that proposals for administrative integration ordinarily generate, it is not surprising that a great many plans for consolidation in state

[18] Frequently the argument is also heard that consolidation will promote more democratic as well as more efficient government. For it is felt that the practice of scattering and dispersing authority among many government agencies necessarily makes it difficult for the public to fix definite responsibility anywhere for the conduct of governmental affairs. Woodrow Wilson made the classic statement of this point of view: "There is no danger in power, if only it be not irresponsible. If it be divided, dealt out in shares to many, it is obscured; if it be obscured, it is made irresponsible." "The Study of the Administration," *Political Science Quarterly*, II (1887), p. 213.

government never get off the ground. As one study reveals: "With very few exceptions, the numerous postwar movements for state reorganization appear to have resulted in only moderate or negligible legislative acceptance of the reorganization proposals." [19] In some instances, of course, the establishment of groups to suggest changes in executive organization represented merely an effort by a skillful governor to dramatize his own zeal for economy and efficiency. Once their reports are turned in, the political utility of a reorganization commission and the impulse to reform may both be exhausted.

The effort to weld state administration into a coherent unity through the reshuffling of agencies and functions has not in itself resulted in any substantial transfer of power from colleges and universities to other state agencies.[20] No state has proposed that governing boards be abolished and the colleges be absorbed by an ordinary state agency. In some states the lack of political vitality in consolidation plans serves to immunize institutions of higher education from the effects of these proposals, while in other areas the legal independence of the schools bars any drastic change in their status. What has actually happened is that in every state the system of higher education has been under growing pressure to "set its own house in order." Every year special state educational commissions are established to look into the way in which schools of higher learning are equipped to meet the challenge of present and future enrollment trends. And high on the agenda of these groups is the objective of developing some rational scheme for avoiding needless dupli-

[19] Karl A. Bosworth, "The Politics of Management Improvement in the States," *American Political Science Review,* XLVII (1953), p. 84.

[20] The quest for tighter administrative consolidation has, however, had some effect upon the organization and administration of higher education in the states. See in this regard, John H. McNeely, *Higher Educational Institutions in the Scheme of State Government,* U. S. Office of Education Bulletin, 1939, No. 3, pp. 22–45.

cation of facilities—the same goal that animates little Hoover Commissions in recommending administrative consolidation in state government.

## Centralized Fiscal Control

Nevertheless, the reorganization movement has had a very substantial impact upon day-to-day operations in higher education. By and large, this has come about as a result of the trend toward centralized fiscal control—a far more successful, though much less publicized, aspect of the reorganization movement in state government. Budgeting, auditing, and purchasing agencies have sprung up in state after state even while proposals for administrative consolidation were going down to defeat. What has been lost on one front has to some extent been retrieved on another.

For the creation of these instruments of central fiscal oversight has in fact represented something of a back-door approach to the objectives sought by administrative reorganization. Agencies that cannot be integrated through a formal process of consolidation can nevertheless be subject to a very close kind of co-ordination and control through supervision over the way in which they spend money. A most important development on this front has been the establishment of central budget offices in all parts of the country. For as one observer tells us:

> The reforms of organization were never completely successful. Political pressures, tradition, and inertia kept many states from achieving the symmetry of organization postulated by theory. The goal of unified co-ordination through organization was seldom reached with the satisfactory results predicted by theory.
> The executive budget system was a different story. Oper-

ational differences, tradition, and inertia—all were split as
if by a knife under the thrust of the executive budget.[21]
And nowhere has the cutting edge of this knife been felt
more keenly than in the area of higher education.

## THE POLITICS OF FISCAL CONTROL

Of course some of the same factors that impede proposals
for administrative consolidation block or blunt the development of centralized fiscal controls. State legislatures can
hardly be enthusiastic over establishment of fiscal agencies
that enhance the ability of a governor to direct and control
the entire range of activities under his jurisdiction. But legislatures are caught in a squeeze between mounting demands
for public services and the unrelenting pressure that exists
in all states to keep the costs of government down. Consequently, legislative support for the establishment of budgeting, purchasing, and other offices, has usually been
forthcoming. And it has come largely in response to the
belief that substantial economies will flow from the activities
of these state offices of central management and fiscal control.

Once it has established these new agencies, the legislature
ordinarily continues to support the growth of their power.
Nearly every legislative biennium brings new laws extending
centralized control over state administration. Characteristic
illustrations include a recent Florida statute requiring the
approval of the Budget Commission before hiring any state
employee at a salary in excess of $10,000, and a law passed
in Kentucky giving the Department of Finance virtually
complete control over the location, design, and construction
of all state buildings.

21 Leo F. Redfern, "State Budgets and State Universities in New England"
(unpublished Ph.D. dissertation, Harvard University, September, 1957), pp.
101–102.

Today, of course, legislatures are also stepping out with their own instruments of control such as interim committees and legislative auditors. These agencies have two principal advantages from the legislative standpoint. First, they can oversee administration on an around-the-clock basis, whereas the legislature itself is ordinarily in session only for a comparatively brief period every other year. Second, and most important, these interim agencies owe their loyalty entirely to the legislature. For while in some states the budget officer can maintain close relations with the legislature and enjoy its confidence, in other parts of the country he is regarded as primarily a servant of the governor rather than the legislature. This lack of confidence in executive fiscal officials has a particular tendency to develop in states in which the legislature and the governor's office are controlled by different political parties. And where this cleavage exists colleges and universities are often caught in the crossfire between rival political camps.

But however the winds of state politics may blow, the swing toward overhead control of state administration is deeply imbedded in current trends in state politics and government. In consequence, institutions like state colleges and universities which stand out against this development inevitably cast themselves in the role of the underdog. A few decades ago the burden of proof would have been placed upon budget and other fiscal officials to justify the utility of these new controls. Today, officials in higher education are faced with the necessity of explaining why they should not be subject to closer administrative supervision.

## THE SHAPE OF THINGS TO COME

There can be little doubt that the move toward fiscal control will accelerate rather than slacken in years to come.

Many states which already have the executive budget and other instruments of control are presently engaged in sharpening these tools. And where the trend toward centralization is still in its infancy, it may well move much farther in this direction. For there is a strong tendency for the states to imitate each other's innovations in the area of management practices—a tendency that receives strong reinforcement from organized associations of state officials. Through publications, annual meetings, and other means of communication, these organizations quickly spread the word from state to state about new devices and techniques of control.

Broadly stated, the emergence of agencies of central control has rarely occurred as the particular result, or discovery, of irregularities or abuses within the field of higher education itself. As a matter of fact, state officials will usually admit that these checks are less necessary in the case of colleges and universities than elsewhere in state government. For the prestige of higher education has generally been sufficient to attract men of great competence and integrity to its service. And this has meant that schools of higher learning have been less plagued by the fiscal irregularities and downright incompetence that have often prevailed in less fortunate areas of state administration.[22]

But this does not mean that the state officials are willing that colleges and universities be entirely removed from the scope of centralized administrative oversight. Their reluctance to see such decentralization occur stems in part from their desire to preserve uniformity in state administrative

[22] Of course even college administrators have been known to fall from grace. And even a rare instance of fraud or embezzlement may become a heavy club in the hands of those who wish to impose tighter fiscal control over colleges and universities. For a description of a flagrant case of embezzlement that occurred in Louisiana some years ago, see M. M. Chambers, *The Colleges and the Courts* (New York: Carnegie Foundation for the Advancement of Teaching, 1946), p. 32.

practice. For at the back of their minds is the fear that any exemption from central control granted to institutions of higher education will constitute a precedent. And this precedent, once established, will lead to demands from other state agencies that they be accorded a similar privilege. State officials in Massachusetts, for example, will privately admit that the personnel controls formerly imposed over the university defeated the very purposes of an efficient recruitment system. Nevertheless, they are quite fearful that the recent enactment of the Freedom Bill relieving the university from these controls, will soon lead other state agencies to demand equal and perhaps even greater independence for themselves. It is, in short, a common view among state officials that the whole edifice of central administration will collapse if but one block is removed.

Moreover, while state officials will ordinarily grant that college officials are less prone to the fiscal irregularities that sometimes overtake administration in other areas of state government, there is widespread skepticism in various parts of the country as to the competence of the educator to handle business matters. This skepticism is based in good part on the stereotype of the academic man as an impractical sort of fellow who needs all the help he can get in "meeting the payroll." Whether this stereotype of the academic man is justified or not, it is largely irrelevant today when so many college administrators come from a business rather than an academic background. Man for man, the administrative experience of officials at leading universities would compare favorably with that of administrators in any other area.

Some pressure for extension of uniform controls over all state administration comes from the lobbying activities of fiscal officers who are not at all averse to having their own power extended. But by far the most important element behind these controls is the mounting cost of state government.

The postwar years have driven expenditures for state government from 7 billion, in 1946, to more than 21 billion, in 1956. During this same period, expenditures for higher education have also climbed at a rapid pace. In 1946, expenditures for state institutions of higher learning stood at $397,000,000, but by 1956 they had expanded to $1,678,000,000.[23] In the face of this trend toward increased state expenditures, little difficulty is ordinarily encountered in winning broad public support for doubling the watch over state expenditures.[24]

*State Departments of Administration*

In states where the zeal for reorganization has waxed the strongest, an effort has usually been made to bring together all the instruments of control into a central department of finance or administration. This development has been described by the Council of State Governments as "one of the most spectacular trends in state administrative reorganization of the last decade." [25] In part, of course, establishment of an agency of this kind may be only a means of tying together

[23] However, it is interesting to note that although appropriations for higher education have risen dramatically in recent years, the percentage of state funds allocated to the support of state colleges and universities has actually declined since the early years of the century. In 1913 expenditures for higher education stood at 12.5 per cent of the total state budget, in 1922 at 10.2 per cent, in 1927 at 9.8 per cent, and in 1932 at 8.3 per cent. From that point the percentage of expenditures for higher education dropped sharply during the depression and war years, fluctuating between 5.1 per cent in 1934 and 7.4 per cent in 1944. By 1957, the percentage had climbed back to 8.1 per cent, which was still lower than the 8.3 per cent allocated to higher education in 1932.
Source: U.S., Bureau of the Census, *Compendium of State Government Finances,* for the years shown (Washington: U.S. Government Printing Office).
[24] See in this connection Appendix A.
[25] Council of State Governments, *Reorganizing State Government* (Chicago: Council of State Governments, 1950), p. 103.

activities that already exist. For if it makes sense to consolidate program agencies that provide related services to the public, it is also good administration to bring housekeeping tasks like budgeting, comptrolling, and purchasing into closer communion with each other.

Establishment of a department of finance or administration, however, may well represent more than a simple act of administrative consolidation. It may also generate pressure for the introduction of new techniques of fiscal or management supervision. In a study of state departments of administration the Council of State Governments lists nine separate functions or types of control which such an agency can be expected to exercise.[26] Certainly it is easy to conceive of this "ideal type" state department of administration's acting as something of a spur to the ambitions of administrators who are in charge of them. Where a top official lacks one of the functions identified as belonging to a solidly constructed department of administration, he may quite understandably feel a sense of deprivation unless and until the legislature has added this missing link to his chain of power.

The table below shows the trend toward the establishment of unified agencies of fiscal control.

As this chronology reveals, nine of the nineteen states having departments of administration have acted to establish these agencies since World War II.

The centralization of topside controls in a department of administration, of course, can have a very beneficial effect from the perspective of the line agencies over which these controls are exercised. It could, for example, bring an end to the duplicate reporting requirements that often prevail when each topside office is a law unto itself. The establishment of a department of administration could, therefore,

[26] Council of State Governments, *A State Department of Administration* (Chicago: Council of State Governments, 1957), pp. 5–6.

## State Departments of Finance or Administration *

| State | Year Established | Name of Department |
|---|---|---|
| Illinois | 1918 | Finance |
| California | 1921 | Finance |
| Ohio | 1921 | Finance |
| South Dakota | 1925 | Finance |
| Maine | 1931 (reorganized in 1951) | Finance and Administration |
| Kentucky | 1936 | Finance |
| Connecticut | 1937 | Finance and Control |
| Alabama | 1939 | Finance |
| Minnesota | 1939 | Administration |
| Utah | 1941 | Finance Commission |
| Louisiana | 1948 | Administration (Division in executive office) |
| Michigan | 1949 | Administration |
| New Hampshire | 1950 | Administration |
| Oregon | 1951 | Finance and Administration |
| Rhode Island | 1951 | Administration |
| Kansas | 1953 | Administration |
| West Virginia | 1957 | Finance and Administration |
| New Mexico | 1957 | Finance and Administration |
| North Carolina | 1957 | Administration |

Source: Data received from state governors.

* The following states have agencies which apparently possess most of the same powers as the departments of finance or administration in other states: Massachusetts, Commission on Administration and Finance (1922); Maryland, Department of Budget and Procurement (1939); Missouri, Director of Revenue (1945); New Jersey, Department of Treasury (1947); Montana, Controller (1951); Washington, Office of Director of Budget (1947); Wisconsin, Budgets and Accounts (1947); Pennsylvania, Office of Administration (1955).

lighten the load of overhead control that these line agencies ordinarily bear. And it is also true that the establishment of a more efficient topside organization can enhance the ability of staff agencies to deliver the services they are called upon to provide. These are certainly claims which supporters of this particular brand of overhead organization would advance.

But from the point of view of many institutions of higher education, these possibilities are purely speculative. The experience of Kansas seems to indicate that the establishment of a central department of administration may actually create more problems than it solves for state colleges and universities. Some years ago this state joined the "reform movement" in public administration by establishing a streamlined Department of Administration in the executive branch. According to a statement issued by a director of the department in 1956, "the primary duty of this division was to prepare and provide a systematic, efficient, and orderly transition from the state's antiquated financial administration to a modern system of doing business." [27] But today several college and university officials in Kansas say that the department has at times become a serious obstacle to effective administration in the field of higher education.

In the charts and diagrams of its organization, the Kansas Department of Administration appears extremely well equipped to provide assistance to operating state agencies as well as to serve the governor as an instrument of executive oversight. The statute establishing the department was drafted by experts from academic and professional life. It created four principal divisions within the department—Budget, Purchasing, Personnel, and Accounts—under the general direction of an executive director. While this executive director is himself an appointee of the incumbent governor, the division heads are professional classified employees who are at least legally isolated from the pressures of state politics.

Actually, the Department of Administration has done

[27] State of Kansas, *Report of Department of Administration* (January, 1956), p. 1.

much to weave together the loose strands of administrative authority within state government in Kansas. At the same time, however, there is a growing feeling that the department has failed to provide many of the services intended by the original statute. The Personnel Division, for example, is supposed to recruit, classify, and regulate all nonacademic personnel. But in point of fact the colleges have had to do much of their own recruiting and testing, since the division has not been able to turn up candidates for vacancies at state institutions of higher education. Here the colleges contend that the Department of Administration has added new paperwork and controls without providing them with any compensating assistance in handling the everyday burdens of personnel administration.

Friction has also occurred in the area of purchasing. By law the department's purchasing division is empowered to buy not only general supplies but also specialized research materials. A typical grievance here was the fact that cumbersome procedures in the purchasing division caused delays of up to ninety days in receiving equipment for a polio research project at the medical center of the university. And on several occasions the division has arbitrarily changed the specifications for equipment ordered by the schools. The music department of one Kansas institution ordered special library shelves for sheet music and received unsuitable bookshelves instead. And when the school asked for a balanced high-fidelity sound system, it received an assortment of component parts that did not match. These and other experiences have been a constant source of irritation in the relations between the Department of Administration and the state's institutions of higher education.

On occasion, the Department of Administration has added to the tension by releasing information to the press that is apparently intended to embarrass the colleges. Recently the

University of Kansas sent through a properly budgeted purchase order for a costly rare book. Persons in the Department of Administration, unable to block the order by any legal means, circulated the item to the press and to legislators in an effort to call public attention to the "wasteful" policies being followed at the state's institutions of higher education. And to compound concern, college business managers in Kansas must spend so much time handling matters generated by the Department of Administration—one official of a small college said it consumed 50 to 60 per cent of his time—that they are unable to devote sufficient attention to internal management. As a result of these and other experiences, college officials have come gradually to the belief that the department is more interested in control than in assistance, more anxious to regulate than to serve.

There is widespread agreement that the Department of Administration is staffed by alert and capable men. But uniform concern does exist over the extension of the department's authority into areas traditionally reserved for the Board of Regents and administrators of educational institutions. And nearly all parties concerned, including officials of the Department of Administration, would concur at this stage that the establishment of good relations between campus and the state is more than a matter of a tidy organization chart.

The problem of developing an attitude of service among rank-and-file employees of a department of administration is a particularly acute one, even where the director of such an agency may be firmly attached to the notion that it is his function to serve and not supplant the heads of operating agencies. A former controller speaks vividly of this problem out of first-hand experience:

> There is many a slip between the statement of policy by a state controller, expressing sympathy for vesting large

discretion in the educational institutions, and the actual
carrying out of this policy by the personnel of the central
controlling department. Time and again during my period
in Lansing, when conflicts between department personnel
and educational institutions were called to my attention, I
found it necessary to reverse over-zealous centralist activities by my staff. Some staff members were real martinets.
There are those who assert that there is a congenial tendency on the part of central purchasing, accounting and
budget people to get beyond their depth and to violate
the principles of service which they avow as their reason
for being. I believe there is much truth in this claim. External control personnel, particularly those in the lower
ranks, tend to "go by the book" and frequently show little
real judgment or discretion. Their frame of mind emphasizes negative values.[28]

Clearly, as this memo from the firing line implies, the task
of developing good relations between fiscal and operating
agencies is not one that can be solved by negotiations and
agreements between top-level administrators alone. Ultimately, the character of the relationship that develops will
turn very much on the behavior of rank and file employees
of these agencies in their day-to-day contacts with each other.
This is not, of course, to deny that the heads of such agencies
can do much to set the tone of relations by their own pronouncements and example.

## The Emerging Critique of Centralization

Within the world of public administration, the prevailing
trend in recent decades has been to stress the advantages of
concentrating authority at the summit of administrative
power. Administrative centralization has been used as a cure
for many of the difficulties that flow from a lack of co-ordina-

28 See, John W. Lederle, Appendix A.

tion of the varied patterns of government activity in the modern state. And the establishment of agencies of central management and fiscal control has certainly done much to encourage a more rational allocation of the state's limited resources among the unlimited demands now made upon the public treasury.

When this much has been said, however, it is equally true that "one good custom" can corrupt the world, and that carried too far, the pursuit of economy and efficiency through fiscal centralization quickly degenerates into little more than a fetish. Good government is more than a matter of tidy housekeeping. Budget and other fiscal officials can hardly be expected to know more about welfare, education, or highway administration than the officials in charge of those activities. And a system under which all significant administrative decisions must be channeled through an overhead fiscal office for approval, is perfectly designed to stifle initiative and responsibility and dampen enthusiasm among the operating agencies of government.

For precisely these reasons, more and more students of the administrative process are beginning to suggest that in the name of efficiency itself a halt must at some point be called to the trend toward administrative centralization. While it is only recently that this view has gained appreciable strength, its roots reach back into the very beginning of the reorganization movement. As early as 1922 Francis W. Coker denounced what he called "dogmas of administrative reform" by pointing out that "there is a vast amount of useful coordination that can be accomplished in our state administration without making too much of a fetish of the principle of one-man responsibility and control." [29]

Coker's criticism was prompted by an Ohio reorganization

[29] F. W. Coker, "Dogmas of Administrative Reform," *American Political Science Review*, XVI (1922), p. 411.

act which in his view revealed an unwarranted preference for concentration of executive power. For him, there were obvious advantages to a system of decentralized administration which proposals for reorganization, current at that time, failed to recognize. He noted that a decentralized administration secured "continuity of policy," helped establish "customs and traditions of non-interference by periodically changing political officers," elicited the participation of "disinterested citizens serving on unpaid boards," placed legal authority and responsibility in the officials "most likely to develop a sense of professional responsibility and pride" in their work, and did not extend the power of any official "beyond the limits" of his administrative competence.[30] Coker's last suggestion, that excessive centralization overloads administrative circuits at the top level, has surged to the fore in recent years.

Over the years, new dissents to prevailing theories of administrative centralization have sprung from several quarters. During the 'twenties and the 'thirties, W. H. Edwards published a number of articles critical of the tenets by which the reorganization movement was then nourished.[31] Later (1939) Charles Hyneman struck out at the assumptions underlying current reorganization plans in an article bearing the suggestive title, "Administrative Reorganization: An Adventure into Science and Theology." [32] And in a recent discussion of trends in state reorganization, John A. Perkins suggests that "taken function by function, the services of state government are more often than not carried on quite satisfactorily, in spite of their not being grouped or related properly to each

---

[30] *Ibid.*, pp. 410–11.

[31] See, for example, W. H. Edwards, "The Public Efficiency Experts," *Southwestern Political and Social Science Quarterly*, X (1929), pp. 301–12; "Has State Reorganization Succeeded?" *State Government*, XI (1938), pp. 183–84; Waldo, *op. cit.*, pp. 142-44, presents a thorough analysis of Edwards' views.

[32] *Journal of Politics*, I (1939), pp. 62–75.

other and to the chief executive. . . . Intimate acquaintance with state administrative activities can dull the enthusiasm for reorganization of even a doctrinaire political scientist." [33]

Curiously enough, the most challenging criticisms of administrative reorganization have recently come from central administrators themselves. Professional personnel administrators have been particularly vehement in their insistence upon the need to decentralize responsibility for recruitment and other personnel functions to the line agencies of government. The central personnel agency is beginning to lose much of the luster it once gained in delivering the public service from the evils of "spoils." For there is now impressive evidence that agencies such as TVA were much more successful in attracting superior personnel when they were freed from the cumbersome restrictions of central personnel controls. Here, as elsewhere, centralization has reached a point of diminishing returns, and the direction of change has begun to reverse itself.

## Summary

Up until recent times, state government was characterized by a high degree of dispersion of authority in its operations. Activities like welfare, education, highways, and public health were administered in virtual isolation from each other. Over the years the conviction developed that this system of fragmented administration made for expensive government. It did so because it allowed some state agencies to spend more extravagantly than others and did nothing to prevent duplication of facilities and even dishonesty in operations. And it was also felt that the development of instru-

[33] John A. Perkins, "Reflections on State Reorganizations," *American Political Science Review,* XLV (1951), pp. 509–10.

ments of central observation and control would provide a means by which demands for financial support from each state agency could be objectively appraised and balanced against the fiscal needs of other governmental activities.

On this set of beliefs the "efficiency and economy" movement strode into state politics. Its primary objective has been to establish agencies of management and fiscal control that will help plan and then police the operations of every state agency and prevent extravagance and irregularities in the management of the state's business. Throughout each succeeding decade of this century the strength of this movement has continued to grow. And there can be no doubt that the strong public support it has received has been fed in good part by the mounting costs of higher education along with all other state activities.

It is important to recognize that budget officers, auditors, purchasing agents, and other state officials do have a strong rationale and justification for their contemporary role in state government. It would be folly for anyone, least of all educational administrators, to overlook the inefficiencies and abuses in traditional areas of state administration that have brought these instruments of central inspection and control. Behind each lies a long history of scandal or mismanagement in such matters as the handling of contracts or the disposition of the state's resources. There is, then, good reason for keeping a close watch over the way in which the state's funds are handled. Sentiment for doing so is especially strong among taxpayer and business groups, which tend to line up behind every administrative device and development that offers the hope of saving money.

Elsewhere the efficiency and economy movement has won many friends in both the executive and legislative branches of government. Governors in particular have long found the scattering of authority in state administration a handicap in their efforts to carry out their own personal or party plat-forms. They have come to look upon the establishment of instruments of central direction and control as steps by which their leadership in state government can be rendered more effective. Consequently, chief executives have proposed and supported a study of state administration by a variety of so-called "little Hoover Commissions." Inevitably, each of these groups returns recommendations designed to integrate all state activities under a web of centralized control that will shore up and extend gubernatorial power.

On the horizon of state administration today, there is a dawning recognition that while sprawling decentralization has been the problem of the past, excessive centralization will be the problem of the future. Surely there is widespread appreciation of the gains that have been won through the establishment of instruments of central oversight. And there is considerable agreement that innovations like the executive budget are here to stay. But the burgeoning tendency of over-zealous central offices to run rather than serve all state activi-ties, prompts a growing concern lest the "architects of orderliness" sap the vitality and creative initiative of the very agencies that render the services which state government exists to perform.

CHAPTER IV

# The art of budgeting

FROM AN administrative standpoint, the agency at the pivot
of relations between campus and capitol is the state budget
office. Customarily this office receives the budget requests of
the individual institutions, analyzes all fiscal plans in terms of
their inherent worth and the over-all needs of the state, and
finally welds these requests into a unified state budget to be
submitted by the governor to the legislature. And in most
places the budget office also enjoys extensive additional
power to supervise and control expenditures after a legislative decision on appropriations has been made. Under these
circumstances, differences of opinion between the schools
and the budget office are not unusual, especially in states that
have vigorous and skilled personnel in both the budget office
and in higher education.

Of course, any generalization about budgeting must recognize that there are wide disparities among the states as to the

70

real power of the budget officer over colleges and universities. In states like North Carolina, New York, and Florida he is in a very strong official position, able to exert substantial influence over both the size and the direction of expenditures for higher education. In a state like Arkansas, on the other hand (the only state which still relies solely upon a legislative budget) the budget officer acts mainly in a clerical capacity, preparing the forms on which all agencies submit their fiscal requests to the legislative council. And up until 1957, budgeting in Colorado consisted, for all practical purposes, of one man and an adding machine. It is still little more than that in Delaware. Elsewhere (Minnesota and Michigan, for example) the constitutional immunity of the major universities protects them from any save the most general control over university expenditures.

But through the years the general growth in the stature of state budgeting has been an impressive one.[1] Since 1910, state after state has moved to strengthen its budgeting process, and the National Association of State Budget Officers now lists members in every state.[2] In forty-one states the budget officer serves as an instrument of gubernatorial control over the budget. In six other states a plural body of executive (and sometimes legislative) officials has responsibility for the presentation of a comprehensive budget, and the budget officer acts as staff adviser to this group. In either case the recommendations of the budget officer are of critical importance in determining not only the aggregate of appropriations to be made for higher education but also the way in which these

1 For recent discussions of the development of state budgeting, see Jesse Burkhead, *Government Budgeting* (New York: John Wiley & Sons, 1956), pp. 21–25, and Leo Redfern, "State Budgets and State Universities in New England," (unpublished Ph.D. thesis, Harvard University, 1957), pp. 96–132.

2 Arkansas has an executive officer who handles budgetary matters, even though his role, under a legislative budget system, is necessarily a restricted one.

FIGURE 2

# Higher education's share
# of the State budget: 1957

The chart below presents a comparison between expenditures for higher education and other major areas of state spending in 1957. The total budget of all state governments in 1957 was $24,234,000,000. Higher education's share, $1,958,000,000, represented 8.1%—an amount that was less than state expenditures for insurance trusts, public welfare, and other forms of education, and only one-third the amount spent for highways.

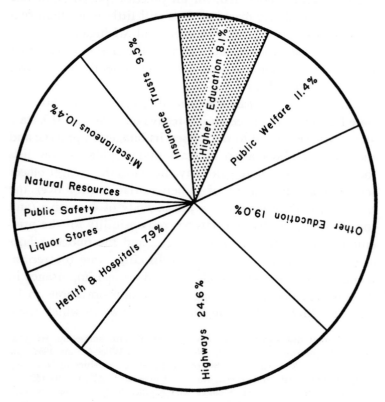

*Source:* U. S. Bureau of the Census, *Compendium of State Government Finances in 1957* (Washington: U. S. Government Printing Office, 1958).

appropriations are used in the day-to-day operations of colleges and universities.

## Frontiers in Dispute

One fact stands out with respect to each of the major roles that the budget office has assumed in state government. In the case of both the preparation of an executive budget and its administration, difficulties are greatest where state officials take upon themselves the task of substituting their own judgment for that of academic administrators on the details of college and university expenditures. For this practice introduces a note of acrimony in the relations between campus and capitol that is seldom found where the budget office simply confines itself to the task of balancing the over-all needs of higher education with those of such other state activities as highways, health, and conservation.

In providing means by which a balanced program of state expenditures can be determined, executive budgeting has proved a progressive development in state administration. Before the adoption of this practice of having a single executive agency co-ordinate all requests for financial support, appropriations were commonly parceled out among state agencies entirely in terms of the political support they could muster in the legislature through skillful lobbying. One observer has described the end-result of this process in the following terms:

> At the end of a legislative session a group of appropriation bills would have been passed which reflected the skill, determination, and luck of certain legislators rather than a considered, well-balanced program of expenditures to meet all the needs of the state in proportion to its resources. Some very important services would be almost

crippled because their needs were not championed by skill-ful advocates. Other services, much less important, would be granted far more than they really needed or deserved because some competent people had pressed their cause. And, more serious than this, appropriations would have been made without due regard for the resources of the state.[3]

It should be stressed that this highly political system of budg-eting was not one under which higher education always pros-pered. For at his best, a modern budget officer can help make a strong clear case for those activities like higher education which are vital to the welfare of the state but which may not have commensurate political strength in the legislature.

Of course, friction on budgetary matters is by no means peculiar to the relationship between the campus and the capi-tol. A budget office whose assigned task is that of whittling away at all unnecessary expenditures for program activities can hardly expect to become an object of affectionate esteem anywhere in state government. A certain measure of unpopu-larity is a built-in feature of the budgetary role. And the standing of the budget office with both the governor and the legislature may very well depend upon its ability to pinch pennies successfully. One governor is reported to have re-marked, when informed that his budget officer hadn't a friend in state government, that he'd fire him if he discovered he had. And in North Carolina, where the legislature was faced with a $10,000,000 deficit and the unpleasant possibility of having to raise taxes, the way out was found when one legislator declared: "We don't need to raise taxes at all. The budget officer will save $10,000,000 in this budget. He always has and he will do it again." In this instance the budget officer was quick to reply that if the legislature was actually

[3] Kirk H. Porter, *State Administration* (New York: F. S. Croft & Co., 1958), pp. 134-35.

convinced that there was $10,000,000 "fat" in the budget, it should be removed before and not after appropriations had been made.

Moreover, there is no disputing the fact that many a budget officer plies his trade of saving money in the face of formidable obstacles within the state. The common practice of earmarking the revenue obtained from some state taxes for the support of specific functions effectively isolates large portions of the budget from central control. And there are many agencies whose political support is so formidable that the budget office is able to perform little more than a perfunctory review of their requests for financial support. Budget office decisions to which these agencies object can be quickly reversed through political channels.

## Submitting the Budget

Few college officials will deny that requests for funds from all state agencies need to be channeled through a single administrative office under either legislative or gubernatorial jurisdiction.[4] For the task of appraising the complex variety

4 The rationale for budget analysis in higher education has been persuasively stated by Frank Landers, Budget Director of the State of Michigan, in a letter to the Committee on November 28, 1958: "The institutions of higher learning have got to accept the fact that if they want the large increases in annual appropriations which the enrollment figures all predict they will need, they will have to learn to live with the state governments. Certainly no governor nor legislature can blindly put out these kinds of annual sums without being able to say, 'Yes, we have looked into the matter and verified the needs.' It is *not* enough for the educational institution—no matter how great its reputation—to say to the state budget authorities, 'this is what we need; please give it to us without asking any questions.' There are simply too many pressures from other competing responsibilities of government and the dollars requested are getting so large that the day of just handing over money without any information as to why it is needed is probably gone forever. This does not mean that no one trusts the higher education authorities. It is just that . . .

of demands now made upon the resources of a state demands the attention of a skilled, experienced, and permanent staff. And budget offices in at least the more advanced parts of the country today attract the services of some of the most talented individuals on the roster of state civil service. In a state like California, for example, the level of ability manifest in the Department of Finance compares favorably with that to be found anywhere in either national or state government.

And it has now become standard practice for the schools to clear their budgets through a central executive office before submitting them to the legislature. Only 8 of the 284 institutions covered in a committee survey were altogether free of this requirement.[5] Of course in the case of 19 additional schools, the clearance obligation was of a purely formal nature, since the fiscal agency simply acted as an instrument of traffic control, sending the budget on to the legislature without revision or recommendations as to changes. But two-thirds of the schools (230) are compelled to submit their budgets for actual review by an executive agency. And in the case of 138 of these schools, only the revised budget is thereafter submitted to the legislature. (In the case of 48 institutions a permanent legislative agency also steps into the picture for the purpose of reviewing proposed expenditures.)

BUDGETS IN REVIEW

Inevitably a budget office which begins as a staff arm of the governor comes to exercise considerable power in its own

there has to be some explanation and some way of publicly demonstrating the reasonableness, comparatively speaking, of the requests."

[5] In the spring of 1958 the Committee on Government and Higher Education sent a questionnaire to all college business officers. Replies were received from 289 of the 345 officials to whom this "Checklist of State Controls over Public Higher Education" was sent. Unless otherwise noted, the figures given in this chapter on budgetary controls are based on the returns to this questionnaire.

right. Its expertness on matters of finance is translated in some eyes into wisdom on matters of policy, so deferential is the layman to anyone who can move with ease through the intricacies of government accounting. An indication of the respect often accorded the budget officer is provided by the practice followed in Florida, where it is customary for the legislature to rely upon the advice of the budget officer alone when the appropriations committee goes into executive session for its final consideration of budgets. Given the very limited resources with which most states operate, it is plausible to suggest that the power of the budget office derives in good part from the pressure upon state legislatures to view all problems primarily in terms of their fiscal dimensions.

Many college officials are now afraid that the most important decisions on higher education will come in time to be made without adequate opportunity for the views of college administrators themselves to be heard. Most disturbing in this regard is the fact that effective power over decisions on higher education is often lodged at very low echelons of authority within the budget office. The budget recommendations of the governor on higher education, which might normally be expected to mirror the advice of his budget director, may actually turn on the findings of a budget examiner buried deep within the hierarchy of a department of finance. Thus, co-ordination which in budget theory is carried on by top officials having a broad perspective, may actually reflect the views and opinions of a budget examiner with a relatively narrow perspective.

In New York, for example, the budget office is a hundred-man agency, and colleges and universities are obliged to submit minutely detailed requests to this office. Because of the complexity of New York's budget, initial budget hearings are held, not with the budget director or his deputy, but with an associate budget examiner, fourth in the chain of command within the budget office. This is followed by a formal hearing with the budget director and members of the legislative committee, but the fact is that most of the decisions as to budget recommendations in the state are made by the associate examiner or his immediate superior, the principal budget examiner. Only a few decisions are actually made by the budget director and virtually none by the governor. While such developments may be an inevitable consequence of bigness, they nevertheless serve to separate higher education from policy officials of the state.

Some of the tensions that develop are based on pure status considerations. College presidents are offended by the fact that they must go hat in hand and present their programs for approval by a minor budget official. One college president in New Jersey commented that having to refer matters involving higher education to the director of the budget was like walking into the hall outside his office and saying to the janitor, "This is my professional opinion and recommendation. I wonder if you will go along with me on that." Similar resentment against having to deal with subordinate officials crops up in many other states.

But these considerations of status aside, the important issue here is whether any budget official is competent to reverse the considered judgment of specialists in the field on how best to pursue the goal of higher learning. Does the expertness of budget examiners go so far as to surpass that of professionals who have spent their entire careers working in the field of higher education? This issue boils up frequently when college and university budget requests are being subjected to detailed and critical examination by the budget office. In Michigan it came to the fore when the budget office moved to reverse the university's judgment on the order of priority it intended to follow in its building construction program. The budget office acted, it said, to carry out the governor's policy (in the 1958–59 budget) of emphasizing projects connected with science. California was stirred up by a difference of opinion over the necessity of purchasing microscopes at a state college. And in Florida the issue arose when the university's plan to hire an additional staff member was questioned by the budget office.

There would be a good deal more of this sort of conflict were it not for the fact that the review process as carried on in many states is still a very rudimentary operation. Quite commonly it is restricted to areas where increased financial support is being asked for. In New Hampshire, for example, the university does not submit any completely itemized budget to either the governor or the legislature. Instead, it sends along a single page on which it explains in detail only the amount needed above the current level of mill-tax support. This kind of arrangement tends to confine the area of dispute by assuming that previous appropriations were justified. But it might not be an advantageous system for colleges and universities in a period when drastically increased expenditures for higher education were called for.

Perhaps the most peculiarly informal system of budget presentation is that practiced in Georgia. Contrary to the procedure followed in other states, Georgia agencies do not submit any formal budget requests prior to the passage of an appropriation act. Rather they present a general sketch of their needs to the governor. In the case of higher education, this request consists of a letter from the Board of Regents (which has jurisdiction over all public institutions of higher learning in Georgia) to the governor outlining the fiscal needs of the schools. Appropriations legislation is then based on the governor's broad estimate of the overall needs of the state. After and only after an appropriation act has been passed, do state agencies come forward with their detailed budget requests. Although the proposed expenditures of the schools are stated in rather precise terms, the board receives a lump-sum grant to be spent at its own discretion.

In North Carolina the Department of Administration has recently introduced a system under which the budgets for all state agencies are divided into two categories.[6] The first category, which is called the "A" budget, consists of requests for funds needed to support all existing programs at current levels of support. Separately, in a so-called "B" budget, each agency submits its requests for what it considers to be needed improvements, expansions, or additions. It is the firm expectation of the director of the state's fiscal department that this system "will permit a great deal more fiscal authority and responsibility to be placed in the administrators in charge of the state's programs." And it is worth noting that the director then went on to say that "we feel it is common sense to expect the head of an agency to know best how to supervise the expenditures of that agency's appropriations to accomplish certain directed results for which that agency is held responsible." [7]

Most conscientious fiscal officers feel that it makes no sense to pit the judgment of budget examiners against that of skilled professionals in each program area on detailed items of appropriations. All too often this process of budget review degenerates into futile disputes as to whether the university could get along with one less automobile or two fewer secretaries. A former state budget officer delivered a blistering indictment of the kind of "nit-picking" into which examination of detailed object-code budgets often degenerates:

> Just why an agency head should be expected to itemize and thus to justify his plans among other things to buy two

[6] For a description of this system, see Paul A. Johnston, "New Budget Procedures in North Carolina," *State Government* (June, 1958).

[7] *Ibid.*, p. 120.

new typewriters and a new automobile and to hire an additional clerk-typist at $247.80 is a mystery. His job, after all, and the task he is held accountable for, is that of getting results through an effective performance of his department. If he decides to spend more on his auto fleet and less on train travel, the presumption is that as a good administrator he knows what he is doing and is acting for the good of the service in making this decision. . . .

. . . To go much further than this, I submit, constitutes unwarranted interference with the internal affairs of the operating agencies. A list of individual positions and an itemization of new equipment purchases will intrigue the citizen and legislator but they will hamstring the responsible and competent administrator who needs a good deal of latitude if he is to allocate his over-all spending authority in the most efficient way possible. A rigid object and character itemization of spending authority constitutes an almost insurmountable obstacle to responsive and resourceful public management.[8]

This kind of criticism of the excessively detailed review process would meet with fervent agreement from many college officials.

Before leaving the topic of budget presentation, it should be noted that the technical side of this subject also provokes controversy, although nothing like the tension that builds up on matters involving conflict of judgment. Issues crop up here on such matters as the suitability of state forms for school budget requests, the timing of the budget submission, and other matters of procedure. Happily, in most of the surveyed states, a working compromise on the routine to be followed in budget submission has been reached between the schools and the budget officer. Often schools are the only institutions permitted to use their own forms. Moreover,

---

8 George W. Mitchell, "Recent Trends in State Budget Practices," Remarks at Annual Meeting, National Association of State Budget Officers, September 12, 1955, pp. 4–5.

because of the need for establishing actual enrollment figures, schools are frequently allowed to submit their budget requests at a later date than operating agencies. Complaints still occur that the forms used in preparing state budgets do not always fit the fiscal needs of the schools, but in most places the campus and the capitol have been able to arrive at a working agreement on budget forms sufficient to keep the peace.

NEW DIRECTIONS IN BUDGETING

In some areas attempts are being made to take some of the soreness out of the process of budget appraisal and review through innovations in the techniques by which budgets are constructed. One such development has been the introduction of program budgeting in state government. Program budgeting is a deliberate attempt to shift attention away from minutiae and toward the broad purposes for which public money is appropriated. Whereas past practice has been to structure budgets largely in terms of so-called "objects of expenditure"—salaries, supplies, rent, and the like—the program budget highlights the services rendered by each state agency or institution.[9]

9 Another new budget technique, the performance budget, is based upon unit costs. Where projects can be broken down into unit costs, a performance budget is built as a "target" to which each cost element attempts to adhere. At the conclusion of the project, actual costs are determined and measured against the "target" budget to assess the degree of performance. For example, in paving a road so many needed cubic yards of asphalt are estimated and when the road is paved the actual yardage is compared to the estimate as a measure of successful performance. Because costs in many major services of government have never been fully computed, the performance budget is seldom used in public budgeting. Some qualified accountants are dubious if the major services of government can ever be realistically broken down into unit costs. In much of the literature and discussions of budgeting, program and performance budgeting are used almost interchangeably.

In the case of higher education, budgeting under the program method is cast in terms of the activities that colleges and universities carry on rather than the resources they happen to employ. Connecticut, for example, has introduced one of the most comprehensive systems of program budgeting, and its experience provides some indication of the changes that this device can bring about in budget presentation. Previously the university submitted its requests for an operating budget in terms of such objects as personal services, contractual services, commodities, and fixed charges. Under the program system, these requests are now presented within the more meaningful categories of things accomplished, such as administration, general services, educational and related services, operation and maintenance of physical plant, and operation of auxiliary enterprises and student aid. (The range of activities carried on under each of these categories is spelled out in considerable detail within the budget document itself.) [10]

Program budgeting has won increasing support in studies of fiscal management. In 1949 the first Hoover Commission strongly recommended the adoption of this system of budget presentation by the national government, stating that such an approach would focus attention upon the "general character and relative importance of the work to be done, or upon the service to be rendered, rather than upon the things to be acquired." [11] Several states have since moved to establish a program system of budgeting, including Maryland (1952), Connecticut (1956), and Pennsylvania (1957).[12] Unless current trends are reversed, the prospects are that more and

[10] Connecticut, Governor Abraham Ribicoff, *Budget Report,* 1957–59.

[11] See U.S., Commission on Organization of the Executive Branch of the Government, *Budgeting and Accounting* (Washington: U.S. Government Printing Office, 1949), p. 8.

[12] See Council of State Governments, *Book of the States,* biennial articles on "Finance Management."

more states will come to embrace this new device in their own fiscal operations.

Ultimately, of course, the impact of program budgeting depends very much upon whether or not it breeds a change of perspective on the part of budget officials, lifting their sights from the minor details of expenditure to the broad range of activities carried on by the institutions and agencies of state government.[13] For even under the performance system it is still possible for a budget examiner to focus all his attention upon details of expenditure. In both Maryland and Connecticut, for example, the budget under each program category is broken down into line items of expenditure.[14] And it is always possible for the review process to focus upon these details rather than the broad outlines of policy.

Another development which some observers believe can lower the temperature of dispute on matters of budget review is the increased use of formulas, ratios, and systems of cost analysis in the construction of budgets. The development of these more refined tools of measurement reflects the emergence of a new science, or at least a greater attempt at objectivity, in state budgeting. As applied to higher education this movement has derived its strongest impetus from the pressures upon state officials to find some objective device for appraising rival budget requests from institutions of higher learning in states in which several schools compete for financial support. The expectation has been that the development of quantitative measures of need will provide both budget officers and college administrators with an objective framework within which they can iron out their dis-

[13] The program budget approach may have significant impact upon legislative attitudes. See Chapter XI, pp. 10–11, 16–18.

[14] For recent discussion of the Maryland budget system, see George A. Bell, *State Budget Administration in Maryland* (College Park: University of Maryland, Bureau of Governmental Research, 1957).

agreements. The State Board of Regents in Oklahoma has used a formula as a means of justifying its consolidated budget requests and distributing funds among institutions under its jurisdiction. Kentucky has developed mathematical techniques for achieving these same goals.

California has made great use of formula in the construction of budgets for its state college system (though not for the university). The Department of Finance has played a leading role in developing these techniques, although the state colleges have also had a large voice in their formulation. Since the costs of personnel bulk so large in the operating budget of any institution of higher education, staffing formulas have played an important role under California practice. Each college uses a formula in determining its needs not only for faculty members but also for clerical, maintenance, and administrative personnel as well as groundskeepers. In the case of faculty staffing, the formula is a highly flexible device which gives careful attention to the varying needs of California institutions for teaching personnel in lecture, discussion, and laboratory classes.[15] The state colleges in California also rely upon formulas in justifying their requests for supplies and equipment.

One difficulty with the use of mathematical techniques of budgeting to this point has been a tendency on the part of some fiscal officers to misuse them in the appraisal of educational expenditures, especially in the easy but dangerous comparison of dissimilar programs such as teacher education and medical research. Particular fire has been directed against

15 The California formula is an interesting, though complicated, attempt at quantification. See California, Department of Finance, "The Faculty Staffing Formula of the California State Colleges," January, 1957 (mimeo.). As testimony to the way in which these ideas spread, a college official in West Virginia reported that his budget officer recently returned home from a convention on the West Coast and dropped this publication on his desk with the comment, "Why don't we try this?"

# The Oklahoma Formula

Criteria for determining number of faculty members needed 1959–61
(Based on full-time-equivalent students:)

*University of Oklahoma—Oklahoma State University*

For the first 6,800 students:
   a base faculty of 453 (15 to 1 base)
For all additional students:
   one additional faculty member for every 25 students.
Thus, for an enrollment of 11,000 students, a faculty of 621 (453
   plus 168) would be needed. This would result in a student-teacher
   ratio of 17.7 to 1 (11,000–621).

*Four-year colleges*

For the first 1,000 students:
   a base faculty of 59 (17 to 1 base)
For the next 500 students:
   one additional faculty member for every 30 students
For the next 500 students
      and thereafter:
   one additional faculty member for every 25 students
Thus, for an enrollment of 2,500 students, a faculty of 116 (59 plus
   57) would be needed. This would result in a student-teacher ratio
   of 21.5 to 1 (2500–116).

   Based on a mimeographed statement, Oklahoma State Regents
   for Higher Education

The Oklahoma formula is typical of those used across the country in
budgeting funds for higher education. The California formula (described elsewhere) is considerably more sophisticated, since it permits
adjustment to variations between lecture, laboratory, and discussion
classes. While the Oklahoma kind of formula may have greater appeal
because of its simplicity, many educators would regard the faculty-
student ratio it uses as too high.

the use of cost accounting techniques in budget analysis, where fiscal officers have been led to take a negative attitude toward certain educational programs merely because they reveal a high unit cost of operations. One authority in the field of accounting has levelled stringent criticism against this tendency to overextend the principles of cost accounting:

> . . . if the university accepts the responsibility for rounded curricula, islands of these high-cost courses may be numerous. Cost accounting can disclose which courses, departments or divisions are high cost per student hour, but cost accounting cannot decide whether the courses should be offered or abandoned. . . . The decision to offer such a marginal course needs to consider cost, but it should not be influenced or determined by the vague feeling that high student-hour costs are somehow reprehensible in themselves and should be discouraged.[16]

Of course, educators need to avoid developing any contrary attachment to the dogma that high-cost operations inevitably mean high-quality operations. The truth of the matter is that if mathematical techniques are used with discretion, they can be of value to both state officials and educational administrators in obtaining the maximum value from educational expenditures. Like splitting the atom, the costing of educational programs may be peacefully constructive or enormously destructive, depending upon the objective and skill of the technician.

One aspect of educational practice that has consistently impeded the development of improved relations between the campus and the capitol in the area of budget review has been a reluctance on the part of some institutions of higher education to submit budgetary information in all the detail that legislative and executive authorities think necessary.

16 Carl T. Devine, "Cost Accounting and Higher Education," A Memorandum submitted to the Committee on Government and Higher Education, February, 1958.

There is no more common complaint among state officials than the charge that they are continually frustrated in their efforts to obtain adequate information about university finance. In California, for example, the story is told of one meeting with a legislative committee at which the business officer of the university supplied information about the fiscal affairs of the school by referring to a little black book that he kept on his knees out of sight of the legislators present. Irritated by this procedure, one legislator finally demanded that the committee be allowed access to this hidden document. This request was rejected by the business officer on the grounds that it was the only copy he had. The University has long since abandoned this practice of secrecy and now spreads its records before the legislature in great detail. And it has had no reason to regret its adoption of this policy of complete candor.

Of course there can be no question but that the schools do have grounds for their reluctance to disclose information. In many cases their experience has been that information supplied in good faith has come home to roost in the form of control. There is an abiding fear among many college officials that if they submit budgets in detail it will lead legislatures to pass itemized appropriation acts. Others argue that disclosure brings control over areas of educational policy that have previously been immune from interference. One official in Colorado commented that supplying some legislators with all the information they requested on cost breakdown would be the same as passing out "burglar's tools" to enemies of the university. To these fears there is perhaps no adequate answer except the consideration that in the long run the costs of secrecy are so great in terms of suspicion and ill will as to justify the risk of candor.

## Administering the Budget

Some of the worst difficulties in the relations between the schools and the budget office are tied to the question of how much power this fiscal agency should have over the disposition of funds after they have been appropriated by the legislature. And here the variations in practice are enormous, with the clearest line of distinction lying not so much between states as between types of institutions. As a rule state universities are given considerably more latitude in spending the money appropriated to them by the legislature than state colleges or teachers colleges. Partly this is a matter of deliberate public policy. The universities, by constitutional or statutory declaration, may be explicitly assigned a position of independence. And partly it is a matter of tradition. The state colleges have grown up within the network of control, and the university has not. Difference in treatment is a legacy of history.

The least controversial of the controls imposed over institutions of higher education in the area of budget execution are those which a budget office applies in a general way to see to it that colleges and universities live within their financial means during the course of the year. Here the attention of the budget office is fixed upon the overall limits of expenditure rather than the specific items for which money is being paid out. Relations scrape the hardest when the budget office moves beyond this role of custodian of funds and begins to peer and tap at every line-item detail of expenditure made by a college or university. For this kind of daily patrol of each fiscal decision inevitably raises doubt as to whether it is the budget officer or a college president who is really running an institution of higher education.

GENERAL CONTROL OVER FUNDS

One of the most common controls imposed over the spending of funds is the periodic allotment system. The money appropriated by the legislature is parceled out to the schools in separate portions over the course of the year. This is designed to prevent the institution from overspending at the beginning of a year and having inadequate funds to meet expenses as the fiscal period runs out. It is also a technique that can be used to keep state expenditures, at any particular time, within estimated tax revenues. Only 43 out of 284 schools responding to a survey by the Committee were entirely free from this control over the rate at which they expended funds. A large number (139) of the institutions surveyed are subject to a system of quarterly allotments.

By and large this kind of generalized fiscal control has not been a source of sharp dispute across the nation. However, some schools do question the necessity or utility of the periodic allotment system in states in which institutions of higher education have an excellent record of living within their budget and not requiring deficiency appropriations. And in a state like Connecticut the complaint is made that while the schools are prevented from overspending their appropriations by a periodic allotment system, they are provided with no equivalent protection against having their appropriation suddenly reduced during the course of the fiscal year. The governor may in fact impose a 5 per cent or 10 per cent across-the-board cut on the expenditures of all agencies. This practice is usually justified on the entirely sound economic grounds that revenue collections are running behind original estimates. But of course it is also a useful political gambit for a chief executive who wishes to dramatize his zeal for frugality.

Perhaps the most troublesome of all general controls is the

power often vested in budget officials to control the transfer of funds from one budgetary account to another. Where it is rigidly applied to detailed accounts, this form of control can tie the hands of colleges and universities and prevent them from meeting unexpected emergencies. Of course, if it is restricted to broadly classified accounts, it may not be a real problem. In Delaware, for example, the Budget Commission retains control only over the transfer of funds between the six general categories in which university appropriations are made. To this date, the commission's power has not been a source of friction between the school and the budget office.

Control over the transfer of funds has been increasingly granted to central fiscal authorities as a means of restraining state agencies from receiving money for one purpose and then proceeding to spend it for another. It was reported in one state that money intended for salary increases had ultimately been used to build a new house for the president— complete with $5,000 barbecue pit. And in another state money appropriated for a badly needed heating plant at the university was diverted to other purposes. Out of 284 institutions covered by the Committee survey, 166 reported that it was necessary for them to obtain the approval of a state fiscal agency before diverting any funds from the purpose for which they had originally been allocated.

In many instances the receipt of approval for transferring funds is a fairly routine affair. But a literal-minded budget office can always use its general control over the release of funds to impede flexible administration at a college or university. At one school it was reported that the budget office refused permission to transfer funds to a depleted equipment account for the purchase of steel cabinets. As a result the school was forced to use funds from its personnel account to have laborers build wooden cabinets at considerably increased cost to the taxpayer.

In this instance as in others, the nub of the problem may well have been a failure in communications. The school may simply have failed to make clear to the budget office its need for new shelves.[17] But the question remains whether it is good management practice to require elaborate and time-consuming justification before any transfer of funds is allowed. The new director of administration in North Carolina found that the time of his staff was excessively taken up in handling the reshuffling of funds. One $5.00 transfer might take as much as two full pages of justification, and, by his estimate, $30.00 of the manpower resources of both the budget office and the state agency combined. As a result the director is now moving toward the view that every state agency should have discretion to transfer up to 75 per cent of the amount in each of its accounts.

In some states budget officers are also given the power to freeze surplus funds in each appropriation account. Sometimes this control extends down to specific items of equipment and personal services. The university is unable to use funds from these frozen accounts without prior authorization from the budget office. This approval is often difficult and cumbersome to obtain, for it is to the political advantage

17 One former state official has commented on the problem of adequate communications in a letter to the Committee: "Too many times in my experience purchasing officials have been blamed for purchases when there was a definite failure to indicate the specific reason for needing this particular brand or quality. I remember one time talking to a conservation officer in the field who was complaining about the kind of pumps that we were purchasing for him. I carried this complaint back to Lansing and found that our Purchasing Division had never received a complaint about the pumps. We were not interested in purchasing pumps that did not work in the field, but there was some responsibility on the part of the field personnel to report weaknesses in the pumps rather than to merely shrug their shoulders and damn the central purchasing office."

of a governor and a budget officer to be able to show savings at the end of each fiscal year. Thus, in Connecticut the schools are often kept from drawing money from a personal service account to hire needed personnel in cases where funds accumulate through staff vacancies. The same problem has occurred in North Carolina.

Ordinarily, the funds held in any frozen account revert to the treasury at the close of the fiscal year—along with any other unexpended appropriations that the university may have. This general practice of requiring the reversion of funds is the cause of a good deal of hurried and extravagant spending toward the close of each fiscal year, as schools and other state agencies seek to beat the clock before the closing of their books. But it is stoutly defended by fiscal officers as a necessary part of an adequate system of general fiscal control.

## FEES AND GIFTS

The control of fees and gifts—often referred to as free funds—promises to be one of the serious areas of controversy between the colleges and state agencies in the future. While many college administrators have yielded when pressured to deposit income from fees in the state treasury, they stoutly insist that the universities should retain full control over fees, income from auxiliary services, endowments, and private gifts. Otherwise, they contend, it will be difficult to finance certain activities that badly need financial support, such as lectureships and scholarship programs. In Wyoming it was recently suggested that the state should exercise control over a two-million-dollar endowment for an American Studies program at the university. From the viewpoint of the president of the University of Wyoming, this plan would seriously harm the very concept of private endowment.

However, fiscal officials are quick to point out that the state has a legitimate interest in the way in which free funds are used. One case in point occurred in Nevada, where the university received a generous gift from a private donor to construct a handsome new agricultural school. As yet the school has only been able to attract approximately one scholar per classroom, and its upkeep now and in the future will represent a substantial charge against state appropriations. One legislator commented with some bitterness that this state's money could be more usefully spent on providing students with better accommodations than the quonset huts in which they are now living.

The complaint is also heard that some schools use free funds to carry on activities that the legislature has not yet approved, or for which it may in fact have specifically refused to appropriate money. This was a point made with regard to the establishment of a division of music at a university in Florida. To this criticism many a college president would reply that without free funds they would be helpless to support many activities that are vital to a school's intellectual distinction, even though unappealing to the legislative and executive eye.

One point on which all agree is that the amount of university income from endowment and gifts is growing and will continue to grow. For there is a strong feeling that where universities are denied the use of public funds to embark on a project they definitely want to undertake, the way to salvation lies in having income from other sources available to accomplish these same ends. Taking their cue from this fact, several schools across the country are launched upon an active campaign to find sources of revenue other than state appropriations for the support of public universities. This may be a losing proposition, however, since legislatures may in turn begin reducing appropriations by the amount received from other sources.

Several universities with an eye to the future are creating research foundations as a method of protecting free funds from state regulation. This is the case in New York, where college officials believe that a research foundation tied to the university has been the salvation of medical research by avoiding entanglements with state fiscal agencies. The New York foundation was established with the co-operation of state officials, who recognized that a foundation could give a necessary flexibility to research and would allow higher education to receive grants from some sources which are reluctant to subsidize governmental agencies.

West Virginia University has also established a foundation to handle private gifts.[18] A powerful incentive here was the effort of the state auditor to require all schools to deposit such gifts in the state treasury. The state colleges in California, never backward on matters of this kind, have now moved to establish foundations allied with their own institutions.

## PINPOINTING CONTROL

In addition to a penetrating array of general controls over funds, some states follow the practice of requiring rather intensive budget-office scrutiny of particular kinds of expenditure by colleges and universities. Here the tenuous line between fiscal and educational policy is drawn very thin, as the weight of budget-office authority begins to make itself felt on such matters as the selection of individual faculty members and the purchase of equipment for specific research

18 For a discussion of the rationale and activities of the West Virginia foundation, see *West Virginia University, 1946–1958*, West Virginia University Bulletin, Series 58, No. 12–2, June, 1958, pp. 31–33.

projects. When control is carried this far, tension between the budget agency and the president's office may reach a high voltage.

One of the states which singles out certain types of expenditure for special supervision is Florida. Under the law of that state, the budget commission is given the power to approve the payment of all salaries in excess of $10,000 not authorized by legislative action. The approval of this agency must also be sought before any salary can be paid from two funds, as for example, when a professor's income is to be split between teaching and special research. Permission must also be obtained from the commission for the purchase of all passenger-carrying vehicles as well as trucks and machinery costing in excess of $5,000. And if any college or university employee intends to remain away from his desk for more than thirty days on per diem compensation, he must first clear this arrangement with the Budget Commission.

At the very least, the existence of these controls means that extensive and time-consuming negotiations with the budget office are required in the administration of colleges and universities. This has been a particular grievance in North Carolina, where the complaint has been heard that school administrators are required to "put their brains on the shelf" for a period of two years after the adoption of a line-item budget. However, in this state as in others, there are some college officials who feel that the close control exercised by the budget office is something of a blessing in disguise, since it relieves them of pressure from their own staff. This attitude provides a perfect example of one of the more "bureaucratic" effects of an extended system of controls—that it allows the less competent administrators to avoid basic managerial responsibilities by blaming the system instead of assuming initiative.

One thing is certain: disagreement between the schools and

the budget office over the question of legislative intent on appropriations can never be entirely eliminated. For there will always be ambiguities in this as in other areas of legal interpretation. One Michigan college, for example, sought $7,000 from the legislature for the purpose of repairing a greenhouse. The legislature, after much debate, finally appropriated $500 for this purpose. The school assumed that this money had been appropriated in order to get the repair job off to a start. And it forthwith proceeded to allocate the $500 for preliminary survey and planning operations. However, the budget office took a quite different view of the matter. It argued that the school was legally obliged to finish as much as it could of the actual repair work with the sum appropriated, and in this instance was finally successful in getting the school to see things the same way.

The Michigan Department of Administration conducted a survey of state budgeting and higher education in 1957.[19] Among the questions asked all state budget agencies was the following: "Please indicate the degree of budget control over spending of operating appropriations by educational agencies that you exercise." To this query, six states marked "none" as the appropriate response. Twenty states gave an answer that the Michigan agency categorized as indicating "some" degree of control. And ten states were classified as having a system of "strict" control. Admittedly, this method of classification has a number of defects, not the least of which is the fact that it relies upon the evaluation of the budget office rather than operating agencies as to whether its own control over expenditures is "strict" or not. But it serves as a rough guide to variations among the states in budget office control over the expenditure of funds for higher education.

[19] See "Selected Questions on State Budgeting and Higher Education," compiled by the Budget Division, Michigan Department of Administration, Lansing, Michigan, September, 1957, pp. 3–4.

There does seem to be a growing tendency among budget officials to look with disfavor upon detailed line-item supervision of all state expenditures. For some fiscal officials, the task of analyzing requests and putting together an executive budget is a formidable enough assignment, and if it is done well, many believe it can reduce if not entirely eliminate the necessity for close control over the expenditure of funds. Arthur Naftalin, Commissioner of Administration for the State of Minnesota, has recently given voice to this tendency in appraising the relations between the budget office and higher education:

I should divide the problem of fiscal control over state-supported higher education into two parts. First there is the initial question of what portion of a state's total economic resources should be devoted to higher education, and second the expenditure and internal allocation of the state support once it has been voted. With respect to the first stage I believe this is wholly, appropriately, and inescapably within the jurisdiction of the Governor and the state legislature. This determination is inevitably a political one and, under our constitutional system, must be made with responsiveness to the public will as expressed in our democratic elections.

But with respect to the second stage, once the elected representatives have spoken, fiscal control should become the responsibility of the academy itself, as represented and symbolized by the regents or trustees or college board. It should be their responsibility to determine how the limited resources available shall be distributed among the infinite number of competing academic needs. To impose upon this process the will and direction of state fiscal officers constitutes an encroachment that is potentially extremely dangerous.[20]

[20] "Fiscal Independence for Higher Education," A Statement Prepared for the Committee on Government and Higher Education, Baltimore, Maryland, September 27, 1957, p. 5.

The strength of this tendency toward de-emphasis of the importance of topside control over the execution of the budget is not as yet very great. The Naftalin position still remains very much the minority view among budget officers.[21]

## Summary

In theory and in practice centralized budgeting has sired a broader range of controls over colleges and universities than any other administrative innovation in the recent history of state government. Some of these restrictions have arisen as a by-product of attempts by budget officers to introduce more refined methods of weighing and appraising budget requests than the old system of whacking away at estimates with across-the-board percentage cuts. From the perspective of institutions of higher education, however, an equally onerous set of controls has followed from the tendency of budget officers to seek a voice not only in appropriations but also in the expenditure of funds by colleges and universities.

One distortion that often creeps into a discussion of a difficult administrative relationship is the impression that dealings between the people involved are invariably characterized by hostility and heated dispute. As far as the schools and the budget office are concerned, this is far from being the case. A good deal of their relationship is routine, matter-of-fact, and entirely amicable. Many of the disagreements that arise stem from friendly differences in interpretation of the law. Some of these differences may even bring a welcome note of

21 However, for an address which gives considerable support to the Naftalin position, see "Budget Policies of the Department of Administration," by Paul A. Johnston, Director of the Department of Administration of the State of North Carolina, March 4, 1958. Cf. also the speech by George W. Mitchell, cited *supra,* footnote 7.

humor into the bleak solemnity of administrative routine. In Oklahoma, for example, the budget officer questioned the purchase of a half-interest in an expensive Angus bull to be used for agricultural research. "Under law," he argued, "the state cannot be a mere partner in the ownership of property, and besides, which end of the bull does the university intend to buy?" This issue was eventually laid to rest with the aid of an attorney-general's opinion.

Many of the difficulties that have plagued the relationship between the schools and the budget office flow from the fact that the states are so hard pressed to find revenue with which to meet the mounting demands for public services. The slogan of "economy," overshadowed on the national scene by defense, foreign policy, and issues of domestic urgency, has loomed very large on the horizon of state politics. And the budget office has been under substantial pressure to justify itself as but one of several watchdogs over the state treasury. In a day when state elections often turn on the issue of taxation, governors and legislatures have been prone to measure the efficiency of a fiscal agency by the sole criterion of its ability to hold down expenditures.

In many ways state budgeting today, is reminiscent of the operations of the U. S. Bureau of the Budget back when it was first established in 1921. In the climate of opinion which prevailed at that time across the country, the bureau put all its emphasis upon saving money, seeing to it, as its first director proudly declared, "that coal is not wasted." In 1924 the bureau's annual report contained an item that would have a painfully familiar ring for many college presidents today:

> Pencils. The bureau has given special attention to economy in this direction. Only one pencil at a time is now issued to anyone and he is expected to turn in the unused portion of the last one received. The results justify the

practice. Our item of expense for pencils is materially less.[22]

Here as elsewhere, however, the states tend to lag far in the wake of national progress. For the Bureau of the Budget has long since abandoned its old-fashioned bookkeeper's approach to budgeting. It sees its role today as primarily that of assisting in the broad development of a sound and balanced program of public expenditures. And while there is still widespread criticism of the bureau's controls,[23] "positive" rather than "negative" budgeting is, in theory at least, the watchword of the hour.

In so far as some state budget officers are beginning to move toward this modern view of their role in the governmental process, there is ground for belief that considerably improved relations between the schools and the budget office may result. In North Carolina, Michigan, and Minnesota, for example, responsible fiscal officials have all given voice to the conviction that the budget office best serves the state when it refrains from attempting to substitute its own judgment for that of educators on how best to spend funds appropriated for higher education. In the states as in the national capital, verbal overtures may lead actual practice by several lengths, and there is not always as much administrative decentralization as official pronouncements might suggest.

The emergence of greater public confidence in the busi-

[22] U. S., Bureau of the Budget, *Third Annual Report* (Washington: U.S. Government Printing Office, 1924) p. 217. Quoted in Burkhead, *op. cit.*, p. 290.

[23] The Navy's chief of the Bureau of Ordnance, in a news conference remark about the operation of the Navy missile program, observed that he sometimes feels he is not really the chief of his operation, "but rather that some clerk in the Budget Bureau is." "It is not money," he is reported as saying, "but control of money. We don't see any of it until we have justified every item." Baltimore *Sun,* January 16, 1958. His comments would have a familiar ring in academic circles.

ness efficiency of the school might do much to speed the grant of autonomy elsewhere. One development that may go far to stimulate such confidence is the practice followed in California and Indiana of recruiting budget officials into high positions in college administration. Not the least of the advantages that can flow from this tactic is an improvement in communications between the colleges and the capitol. For one of the chief complaints levelled by budget officials in the past against higher education has been that it is impossible to find out what the colleges are doing with the money appropriated to them. But if the college official speaks the language of budgeting, he can translate estimates into terms that state officials can understand. And here it is important to note that the younger generation of college administrators is also becoming quite articulate in the vocabulary of budgeting. Familiarity with terms like "full-time equivalent student" and "footage per student station" may produce closer communion between the schools and the budget office, even if it shuts out the rest of the world altogether.

CHAPTER V

# Day-by-day controls

THE DAY-TO-DAY CONTROLS imposed upon spending by colleges and universities from the beginning to the end of each fiscal year easily represent the most controversial area in the range of contact between the state and higher education. Institutions of higher education may dissent from the judgments of budget officers and legislative committees on the proportion of the state's financial resources that should be allocated to higher education. And they may be resentful of such adverse comments as may crop up in the post-audit of a school's finances. But they cannot reasonably quarrel with the necessity of a state's exercising such appropriations control and post-audit control over the activities of colleges and universities.

Central purchasing, pre-auditing, and the other controls affecting the everyday disposition of funds—here is the area where the average college official feels that proper control most often translates itself into improper interference. For

103

state regulation here tends to pit the judgment of state officials against that of college administrators on questions of
equipment, supplies, the selection of staff and other matters
central to educational policy. This is a perfect recipe for conflict, and in some states it has stirred bitter controversy. But
in other states workable adjustments have been achieved,
partly because of the climate of confidence in the good faith
and technical skill of college officials and partly as a result of
a sense of restraint and proportion by both state and college
administrators in exercising their separate responsibilities.

*Central Purchasing*

The system of channeling all state purchases through a
single government agency has long exerted an irresistible
attraction for the economizer. It provides a means by which
substantial savings usually can be made through the discounts
obtainable on large quantity orders. Central purchasing also
cuts down sharply on the number of civil servants or university officials who are obliged to cope with vendors, and it
helps to preserve a high standard of administrative rectitude
in the purchase of supplies and the negotiation of contracts.
All of this—in theory at least—central purchasing can do without sacrificing the necessary quality of goods. Both economy
and morality are thus served by the establishment of a central purchasing agency as a standard feature of state administrative organization.

In 1958 the Council of State Governments reported that
"the purchasing function has now been clearly centralized in
thirty-nine states, and a marked degree of centralization is
noted in six others." [1] Of course, it is not uncommon for

[1] Council of State Governments, *The Book of the States, 1958–59*, (Chicago:
Council of State Governments, 1958), p. 132. Of course, purchasing systems

institutions of higher education (along with certain other state agencies) to be left free of purchasing control even after such agencies have been set up. Of the 284 schools responding to the Committee's survey of fiscal controls, only 164 reported that they were obliged to route purchasing through a central agency. Of the remaining schools, 34 did their own buying; 37 had the option of using the facilities of a central agency if they wished; and 56 reported that the school's purchasing was carried on independently although in accord with a uniform state purchasing law. Thus while a majority of these institutions reported themselves as subject to the requirement of clearing their purchases through a central agency, a strong minority of institutions are left with substantial freedom from purchasing control.

With expenditures on current state purchases standing at approximately $11\frac{1}{4}$ billion,[2] it is to be expected that the pressure for maximum economy and efficiency in this area of administrative operations will continue to be intense. In comparison to conventional state agencies, however, there appears to be no recent nationwide push to bring more colleges and universities under a system of central purchasing. As a matter of fact, there are some indications of a swing in the opposite direction. A bill passed by the Virginia legislature in 1958 gave the State Purchasing Director the authority to allow institutions with adequate purchasing staffs to handle all or a major part of their own purchasing.[3]

---

vary as to their comprehensiveness. In some states central purchasing applies only to a few standard items bought by the state, while in other areas it applies to some but not all state agencies. For a discussion and description of these variations, see Council of State Governments, *Purchasing by the States* (July, 1956).

[2] Council of State Governments, *loc. cit.*

[3] See Virginia, Auditing Committee of the General Assembly, and the Auditor of Public Accounts, *Purchasing for the State of Virginia*, pp. 38–39.

## TABLE 1

# Central purchasing controls over higher education

| | | |
|---|---|---|
| *No central purchases* (14 states) | ARIZONA [d] | LOUISIANA [c] |
| | ARKANSAS [c] | MISSISSIPPI [d] |
| | DELAWARE [d] | NORTH CAROLINA [c] |
| | FLORIDA [c] | OHIO [c] |
| | ILLINOIS [c] | OKLAHOMA [c, d] |
| | INDIANA | UTAH |
| | IOWA [d] | WYOMING |
| *Central purchasing optional with schools* (8 states) | ALABAMA | NEW MEXICO [c] |
| | IDAHO [c] | NORTH DAKOTA |
| | MAINE | SOUTH CAROLINA |
| | NEBRASKA | TENNESSEE |
| *All purchases (except emergencies) central* (14 states) | CALIFORNIA [a] | PENNSYLVANIA |
| | CONNECTICUT | RHODE ISLAND |
| | MARYLAND [b] | TEXAS |
| | MINNESOTA [a] | VERMONT [a] |
| | MONTANA | WASHINGTON |
| | NEW HAMPSHIRE [a] | WEST VIRGINIA |
| | NEW JERSEY [a] | WISCONSIN [a] |
| *Most purchasing central* (12 states) | COLORADO [a, c] | MISSOURI [a] |
| | GEORGIA | NEVADA |
| | KANSAS | NEW YORK |
| | KENTUCKY | OREGON |
| | MASSACHUSETTS | SOUTH DAKOTA |
| | MICHIGAN [b] | VIRGINIA |

[a] Major university is exempt from central purchasing control imposed on the other schools.

[b] The major university, exempt from control, has the option of purchasing through a central state purchasing agency.

[c] The schools do their own purchasing, but in accord with a uniform state purchasing law.

[d] State has no system of central purchasing.

## "THE TROUBLE WITH PURCHASING" [4]

In those states in which college and university requisitions are funneled through a central purchasing office, the complaint is frequently heard that the system causes annoying delays that are fatal to projects requiring equipment within a short space of time. Typical of this grievance is the case at a New York medical center where a man with a Public Health Service grant (good only for the fiscal year in which it was allocated) spent eleven months in continual correspondence with the state purchasing department before he finally acquired the precision scale he wanted for his research project.

A college official in New Jersey noted that on one occasion his school had placed an order for industrial art supplies as soon as the fiscal year began in July, with the expectation that the supplies would be available for a class that was to begin in the fall. Much to his disappointment, however, the supplies did not arrive until late December, when the fall semester was nearly over. This delay, which was by no means exceptional in the history of the college, proved to be a serious impediment to the school's academic program.

In Texas, reports on purchasing delays are legion. One teachers college reported that it was forced to order all books for the library through a bookstore in Dallas, after preliminary approval from the state purchasing agency.[5] Here the

---

[4] Aside from technical difficulties, there is also a political side to the purchasing story. While state purchasing offices are becoming more professional, the spoilsman has left his mark in several states. Here is a report from the midwest: "[Our] state purchasing is done by a group of political appointees. There is no continuity to these positions nor is selection based upon qualification or training. . . . Vendors have complained in the past about the fact that they are expected to make contributions to the 'war chests' of the political party in power—this would increase the costs to colleges and universities." A college official's letter to the Committee, November 20, 1958.

[5] This is an uncommon requirement. In Massachusetts and other states

procedure requires that books requested for the teachers college be first submitted to the purchasing office, which works on the lists for 3 to 5 weeks before sending them on to a bookstore in Dallas with which the state has contracted to purchase all books needed for official use. Due to the cumbersome procedures followed at both the purchasing agency and the bookstore, orders often take from 3 to 5 months to be partially filled. And since the college seldom gets all the materials that are needed, it must repeat the same process to reorder. Ironically, the same books could be purchased at the same price from local distributors in five days.

Of course any alert purchasing official will have a ready reply to many of these complaints. Delays occur when the schools like other state agencies are guilty of poor management. They should keep their inventories so well stocked that they are not continuously running out of essential supplies and equipment and they should order replacements on goods well in advance. But in Rhode Island it was observed that the practice of scheduled purchasing and the requirement of extensive advance notice by the university on all anticipated requisitions does not work for an institution of higher education. As one college official commented: "Here is a professor delving into the unknown, and under current purchasing procedures he is expected to know his needs as much as a year in advance." (The reference here is to the fact that anticipated purchases must be budgeted a year ahead of time.)

Along with the problem of delay that has arisen from central purchasing, some university officials question whether the system always achieves the economies that are claimed for it. To be sure there are institutions like the University of California which have found it highly advantageous to

which have a system of central purchasing, the purchase of books is exempt from control.

purchase standard commodities such as gasoline through the state purchasing system even though they are under no legal obligation to do so. But these same schools point out that, as educational institutions, they are able to purchase many other items more cheaply on their own. This is particularly true in the case of scientific equipment. Ordering through their national association, the college and university purchasing officers gain advantages of bulk order discounts that are unavailable to any single state purchasing office ordering one or two similar items.

Perhaps the heaviest broadside university officials level against central purchasing is the charge that the needs of institutions of higher education are often inadequately filled due to arbitrary decisions on brands or specifications by the purchasing agent. In Connecticut it was alleged that the purchasing department introduced excessive standardization in the purchase of syringes, beakers, and other laboratory equipment. As a result professors were prevented from obtaining the type of equipment needed for unusual experiments.

Arbitrary revision of specifications is another source of discontent. In Massachuetts the School of Agriculture needed cattle feed of an approved quality in connection with some experiments it was running on animal nutrition. But when the feed finally came through the purchasing office, it was found to be of a lesser grade. In the absence of any alternative, the agricultural staff was forced to use the inferior substitute. But this failure to obtain the feed that had been requested meant that the whole experiment was thrown off course, and the results were virtually worthless.

From an Eastern medical college comes a similar report:

> On two occasions the state purchasing agency changed our specifications for microscopes because they did not consider a variable focus condenser a desirable feature even

though our professors of biochemistry and bacteriology explained why they considered this feature highly desirable for their special work. Because of the urgent need for the equipment we agreed to accept microscopes without the special features. The next microscopes purchased, however, must have variable focus condensers. Meanwhile the departments have not had the benefit of this improved equipment.

In this case as in others, the purchasing agency was apparently motivated in its decision by a desire to keep the way open for competitive bidding. The "variable focus condenser" was a feature peculiar to one make of microscope, and by including this specification the university was in effect ruling out the possibility of alternative bids. From the viewpoint of a purchasing officer, such a specialized requirement usually reflects a professional idiosyncrasy; the professor can get along just as well with some other type of equipment.

To be sure, a certain element of irrationality may enter into a preference for one kind of equipment over another. But the position defended by the university in these disputes is that on matters of judgment the purchasing officer should yield to the professional on whether a specific type of equipment is necessary for the conduct of a research project. The man responsible for results should be entitled to choose his own tools for the job.

Purchasing offices sometimes argue that much of the difficulty in matters of this kind springs from a failure on the part of those in charge of research projects to write adequate specifications for the equipment they need. The purchasing officer is often given no explanation for what appears to be a purely arbitrary preference for an expensive type of equipment when there are competitive brands that seem adequate for the job. But college officials reply that the task of writing specifications that will satisfy a purchasing officer consumes an inordinate amount of time and energy that could be better invested elsewhere.

A great deal of the time, friction on purchasing is centered on matters that many people would regard as tangential to educational activity itself. Paint, stepladders, desks, chairs, typewriters, paper towels, floor wax—these are everyday grist of administrative dispute. Sparks flew in Texas over the poor quality of light bulbs supplied by the central purchasing agency. It was alleged that the Board of Control obtained the cheapest light bulbs available for use in campus buildings. As a result the custodial staff of the college was kept busy constantly changing bulbs.[6] And in South Dakota controversy developed over whether a particular make of truck was suitable for use on a special project by the School of Agriculture.

Many of these minor irritations are inescapable in any bureaucratic setting—public or private. And colleges and universities are not always in the right in these disputes. One New Jersey college complained bitterly that an organization specializing in the painting of water towers contacted the college at a time when the school's water tower needed painting and offered to do the job for $1,800. However, the firm in question refused the purchasing department's demand that it submit a formal bid, and the contract was awarded another company at a total cost of $3,600. Although the school was here the apparent victim of bureaucratic red tape, the bane of the existence of any purchasing office is the fly-by-night operator who makes offers upon which he later reneges. (Upon closer inspection the traveling organization might well

6 This case further illustrates the crucial role that communication plays in a central purchasing system. The Board of Control in Texas regards the problem as a failure of requisitioning agencies to specify the voltages in operation in their area. The supplier of the bulbs assumed that standard voltages were used and supplied bulbs on that basis. The bulbs, operating on voltages higher than that for which they had been designed, naturally burned out rapidly.

have discovered that the water tower was in much worse shape than had been originally estimated.)

But while these criticisms of central purchasing are widespread, there are some smaller colleges which speak up very strongly in favor of the system. As a college official in Kentucky puts it:

> Central purchasing has been helpful to us here, and on the whole we like it. It relieves us of a great deal of bothersome detail in taking bids and dealing with salesmen. Our experience is that we usually get what we want and at a lower cost. Arrangements are made for emergency situations that are bound to arise and for the purchase of perishables. We have found that the state is willing to make any arrangements that our needs require.

And the president of a Texas college was of much the same view:

> As we see it, technical agencies, such as central purchase offices, state auditors, etc., have relieved the colleges of many troublesome tasks that would otherwise divert them from the main tasks of education.

But not all college presidents in either state are so well satisfied. A sample of the more critical view of central purchasing, came from Kansas:

> Central purchasing has been of no particular help to our college. In most cases the delays involved in processing a purchase order have far outweighed any advantages that might have been secured from lower prices due to volume purchases. It should be pointed out that the college purchases many items which do not lend themselves to central purchasing procedures, since there are so many specialized departments and fields for which purchases must be made. Our biggest complaint probably should be that the central purchasing office too frequently has awarded purchases on the basis of price alone and we have received shoddy and inferior merchandise which has again hampered the college in its most efficient operation.

PATHS TO REFORM

This catalog of complaints should not convey the impression that in states where central purchasing exists, school officials and purchasing agents are forever at sword's point. Many local ground rules have been developed which ease relations between the campus and the capitol in the area of purchasing. Some schools have been delegated the right to purchase items such as perishable foods without clearance through the central office. And it is common practice for purchasing offices to allow schools to do their own purchasing for items costing less than a specified amount, such as $50.

Competitive bidding requirements have been waived in Wisconsin and Kentucky for the purchase of scientific equipment.[7] The only reported difficulty that cropped up in the latter state came when the university purchased specially selected heifers and Hampshire rams for experimental purposes and had the purchase immediately questioned by the Purchasing Division. It was only after a long fight that the school was able to convince state officials that a heifer or a ram was, at least for experimental purposes, a *bona fide* piece of scientific equipment.

Michigan provides illustrations of procedures that have gone a long way to promote harmony. The purchasing division in that state keeps a man in the field who is assigned to the task of visiting the state colleges to ascertain whether or not central purchasing is meeting their needs. And although the three major universities, Michigan State, University of Michigan, and Wayne State University, are legally exempt from central purchasing control, an informal arrangement has been developed that works to the advantage of both sides.

[7] The Kansas Legislative Committee on Economy and Efficiency has recently recommended that scientific equipment up to $2,000 in value be exempted from central purchasing.

The three big schools join with the state purchasing division in buying items such as light bulbs to get the increased discounts that come from quantity orders. These schools also purchase some of their supplies from firms holding regular state contracts with the purchasing division. Tires, batteries, and other automotive equipment are examples. Good relations in this state are largely the product of a purchasing division which regards itself as an instrument of service rather than control. Its general philosophy is that it should do a better job of purchasing than the schools, or it has no business trying to do it for them.

The practice of leaving it up to the schools to decide whether or not to avail themselves of the facilities of a central purchasing office is the key to harmony in other states where central purchasing exists. Experience has shown that schools do in fact take advantage of central purchasing where it has proven economical to do so. This arrangement is complemented in states like New Mexico by the requirement that where schools do their own purchasing, they must follow procedures outlined in a standard purchasing act. Under a voluntary system the schools are able to buy standard items at the discounts obtainable through bulk purchasing by the state. At the same time they are left free to meet their specialized needs without the twin problems of delay and inferior substitution that often crop up when all purchasing must be carried on through a central agency.

## Travel

Traveling by government employees has always been a sensitive subject in state politics. There is widespread suspicion that much of what passes for official travel is actually junketing at public expense. As a result the state usually imposes close restrictions upon such trips, and it is not uncommon for the governor's office itself to pass on all applications for travel outside the state.

These restrictions tend to be burdensome for professional employees in all areas of state government. In so far as such rules limit contact and communion with colleagues in other states they are regarded as a handicap to professional development.[8] But institutions of higher education feel themselves at a particular disadvantage in this regard, given the range of professional interests represented on a university faculty. The somewhat special need of college personnel for travel is graphically illustrated by the situation of the University of Hawaii—separated as this institution is from the mainland. As a college official there pointed out:

> One of our most serious morale problems in the faculty results from a feeling of isolation from professional associates, periodic attendance at scientific meetings, etc. . . . No agency of the Territory with which I am familiar has this problem to anything like the extent the university faces it. . . . The Department of Public Works, for instance, has a very large technical staff at work on buildings, roads, and other physical projects in the Territory. There is very little reason for staff members other than the chief and one or two department heads to make visits to the mainland.

In Colorado one state college encountered so much difficulty in securing approval for out-of-state travel by members of its staff that it abandoned these requests altogether. Instead it decided that faculty members themselves would

---

[8] In Kansas a unique double standard exists which adversely affects higher education. The need to maintain professional contacts is recognized for all the major regular operating agencies of the state, and payment is made without question for all expenses to professional meetings for personnel of these agencies. But educational personnel, in contrast, merely receive the equivalent of first-class rail fare to defray costs of their professional meetings.

have to bear the burden of expenses for all official trips. Staff travel at this institution had been criticized on the grounds that much of it was designed to recruit students from other states for the school's teacher training program. This was held to be a form of empire building which added to the already swollen costs of the state's higher educational system. But the school remains convinced that this practice was amply justified by the need for teachers in Colorado.

Where governors are authorized to pass on travel applications, they may use this power with telling effect. In Kansas the governor exercised his discretion by personally deciding which members of the anatomy department at the medical institution he would allow to travel to an out-of-state conference. But most governors do not appear to covet this prerogative. In New Mexico, for example, the governor found the duty of passing on all applications for faculty travel so burdensome that he eventually passed it on to the Board of Educational Finance—the co-ordinating agency for educational institutions within the state.

A good part of the difficulty in out-of-state travel springs not so much from arbitrary rulings by state officials as it does from outmoded laws and regulations governing official reimbursement for travel on official business. Per diem allowances, for example, tend to lag far behind the rising cost of living on the road. Here as elsewhere, there is much to be said for an up-dating of state fiscal regulations and procedures. In Michigan, for example, the state Department of Administration is relinquishing control over travel expenses to the responsible agency heads who are assuming authority over such costs within budgetary allotments.

## Publications and Censorship

For many observers, the existence of any state control over university publications has seemed inherently incompatible with academic freedom. Strand's 1953 survey of controls over higher land-grant institutions was quite explicit in its condemnation of this practice:

> In our judgment, the most serious control that has been enacted over higher education . . . has to do with publications. We do not mean the printing of publications, which is usually handled by institutional presses or by State contract. We refer to cases where it has become necessary to get the approval of a non-educational state official before material on any subject can be published by the institution. This abrogates the most vital power vested in governing boards, usually by constitutional enactment. It is not done in the name of censorship but could easily result in such an objective. It is done in the guise of saving money for the State by eliminating unnecessary publications.[9]

This view is shared by others. Morey, for example, describes state control over publications as "particularly unjustified and burdensome."[10]

Actually, however, the question of publications has not to this point been a serious issue in the relations between the state and higher education. Only 49 of 284 institutions responding to a Committee survey were covered by such control, and if significant cases of actual censorship have occurred in those areas in which educational publications must receive

[9] A. L. Strand, "Land-Grant Colleges and the State," *Proceedings of the Association of Land-Grant Colleges and Universities,* Columbus, Ohio, Nov. 10–12, 1953, p. 224.

[10] Lloyd Morey, "Governmental Control of Public Higher Education," *Transactions and Proceedings of the National Association of State Universities,* LIII (1955), p. 34.

the approval of a state official prior to printing, they have been well concealed. Purchasing agents and other officials who enjoy the right to pass on all state publications have ordinarily used this power merely to curb the releases of material they considered to be frivolous or publications designed to inflate the public prestige of a state agency.

State officials contend that their disapproval of publications most frequently involves manuscripts that bear no very close relation to higher learning. One state official turned down a pamphlet on the home preparation and care of brassieres and girdles. Others have rejected manuscripts dealing with apple farming, honey bees, and the hatchability of eggs. These latter topics may seem ludicrous to an outside observer, but may be of extreme importance to specialists in the field. More important, some college officials argue that the mere existence of this censorship power puts a dangerous instrument in the hands of the state and that it could be used to cut deeply into the intellectual freedom of a university.

And while it is true that many trivial pamphlets deserve to be turned down by the university itself, there is doubt whether a fiscal official has the competence to pass on the scholarly significance of a proposed publication or whether he should have the authority to do so. In the context of budgetary rather than publications control, college officials recall the time when fiscal officials in New Jersey wanted to cut off funds for what appeared to be an esoteric study of fungus by a professor at Rutgers. The project was, however, continued, the fungus produced streptomycin, and the professor, Dr. Selman Waksman, was eventually awarded the Nobel Prize for one of the most significant contributions to science in this century.[11]

11 *Time Magazine*, Nov. 7, 1949, p. 70.

Although not directly related to the issue of academic freedom, the necessity for channeling standard university publications such as catalogs through a state printing office has caused considerable concern among college administrators. College executives complain most frequently of the delays encountered in the publication of directories and of other materials and of the slipshod quality of much of the work that is turned out. State officials agree that the work of many printers with government contracts has been unsatisfactory, but they also argue that universities like other state agencies often tend to be unreasonable in their demands upon a printer.

## Auditing

The purpose of auditing in state government is to insure that public agencies spend money only in accordance with the constitutional and statutory provisions that govern the revenue they receive. In any given state, an auditor may discharge this duty through either or both a pre-audit and a post-audit. A total of 198 of the 284 institutions responding to a Committee survey are subject to a pre-audit covering all or most of their expenditures. (Tuition and fees, as well as the income received from auxiliary enterprises, are sometimes exempt from this control.)

A far larger number of institutions is subject to post-audit by the state. No fewer than 257 out of 284 institutions reported themselves covered by this method of state surveillance. In the case of 29 other institutions the post-audit is conducted by a private firm employed by the school. Since the earliest a post-audit is held is at the end of the fiscal year in which funds are expended, it has not ordinarily threatened any serious infringement upon the day-by-day operational authority of college officials.

As a matter of fact, even the most staunch defenders of university autonomy freely acknowledge that the post-audit is an entirely legitimate and highly desirable form of state control over institutions of higher education. Richard Plock, who has been at the forefront of efforts to defend the authority of governing boards from encroachment by the state, has pointed out that "in the expenditure of public funds there should be no secrets and such expenditures should be subject to continuous and rigorous post-audit." [12] Other educational spokesmen, including Lloyd Morey [13] and Edgar Smith [14] have taken a similar view regarding the necessity of a thorough review of all university expenditures.

Of course even the post-auditing process has its moments of dispute. In Texas, Utah, and other states, auditors have leveled stringent criticism at university bookkeeping. And college officials themselves are outspoken in their opposition to post-audits which inquire into not only the legality but also the wisdom of university expenditures. State auditors, they contend, have no particular competence to question the business judgment of educational officials on matters of policy. Sometimes it is felt that auditors engage in this practice as a method of dramatizing their vigilant defense of frugality in government. In Florida, for example, considerable resentment was expressed against an auditor's report that gave the university a public reprimand for the methods it employed in running a dairy farm (although more than

[12] "Facing the Critical Decade," *Proceedings of the Western Regional Conference on Education beyond the High School*, April 9–11, 1957, p. 159.

[13] Morey, *op. cit.*, p. 40.

[14] "The Government of Public Education," *Proceedings of the Association of Governing Boards of State Universities and Allied Institutions*, 1954, p. 71.

one college official confessed privately that the criticism was not without foundation).[15]

The charge is also heard that auditors sometimes require reports in excessive detail. In South Dakota, for example, every toll charge phone call requires a memorandum which identifies the names of both parties and includes a synopsis of the conversation. This, in turn, must be filed with the business manager of the university and ultimately submitted to the state auditor for his inspection.

Perhaps the chief criticism leveled at the post-audit in many states is its inefficiency. In Oklahoma, for example, the state auditor has only two examiners to audit the books of eighteen colleges and universities, not to mention the twenty correctional and mental institutions also placed under their jurisdiction. Two men are thus given the impossible assignment of keeping tabs on thirty-eight separate institutions. Under these circumstances, the post-audit may become little more than a perfunctory affair and auditors may fall years behind in their work. But events in Arkansas, Maryland, Michigan—where embarrassing shortages of college funds have appeared in recent years—suggest that even a belated post-audit can have a telling effect in revealing instances of fiscal mismanagement when they occur in higher education.

[15] As a means of obtaining smoother university-state relations one state auditor writes: "I would say that audit reports should be made and then evaluated by a conference attended by both the head auditor and the college deans before the final draft is made public or the final reports are published. The public is justified in wanting audits, but the public can't be expected to fully digest the audit of a college or any other governmental agency." William J. Dodd, State Auditor, State of Louisiana, letter to Committee, November 17, 1958.

## PRE-AUDIT AND CERTIFICATION

It is the pre-audit and the allied process of certification, however, that brings institutions of higher education their most serious problems with auditors and state controllers. In the pre-audit the state official has the power to make his voice heard even before a college or university is able to spend any money. Where he is required to certify expenditures for their legality, the official is able to refuse payment for obligations already incurred by the institution. In some states it is the pre-audit that is particularly troublesome, while in others it is certification, but the problems with which institutions of higher education are presented are essentially the same.

By far the greatest of these problems is the tendency of both auditors and comptrollers to make judgments on educational policy under the guise of making decisions on the legality of expenditures. In Arizona, for example, the state auditor refused to issue warrants authorizing payment of expenses incurred in connection with the inauguration of a new president of the university.[16] These expenses were for such items as the rental of caps and gowns, programs, direction signs for the guidance of visitors, announcements, invitations, information folders, and a public address system. This was the same auditor who had refused earlier to certify claims of the Board of Regents for the payment of dues and fees in professional societies and organizations, or to reimburse university personnel for their travel expenditures when they attended professional meetings.[17] In each of these cases the auditor claimed that the expenses involved had not been

[16] Overruled by the courts in *Board of Regents of University and State Colleges* v. *Frohmiller,* 69 Ariz. 50, 208, Pac. 2d 833 (1949).

[17] Also overruled in *Frohmiller* v. *Board of Regents of University and State Colleges,* 171 Pac. 2d 356 (1946).

**TABLE 2**

# Pre-auditing controls
# over higher education

| | | |
|---|---|---|
| *No funds pre-audited by state (15 states)* | ALABAMA | MONTANA |
| | ARIZONA | NEBRASKA |
| | GEORGIA | NEW MEXICO |
| | INDIANA | NORTH DAKOTA |
| | IOWA | SOUTH CAROLINA |
| | MAINE | TENNESSEE |
| | MISSISSIPPI | UTAH |
| | MISSOURI | |
| | | |
| *Part of funds (including all appropriated funds) pre-audited by state (14 states)* | CALIFORNIA [a] | OHIO |
| | COLORADO [a] | OKLAHOMA |
| | IDAHO | OREGON |
| | ILLINOIS | PENNSYLVANIA [a] |
| | NEVADA | RHODE ISLAND |
| | NEW HAMPSHIRE [a] | SOUTH DAKOTA |
| | NEW JERSEY [a] | WASHINGTON [a] |
| | | |
| *Most funds (including appropriated and auxiliary enterprise funds) pre-audited by state (6 states)* | ARKANSAS | MICHIGAN [a] |
| | LOUISIANA [a] | TEXAS |
| | MARYLAND | VIRGINIA |
| | | |
| *All funds pre-audited by state (13 states)* | CONNECTICUT | NEW YORK |
| | DELAWARE [a] | NORTH CAROLINA [a] |
| | FLORIDA | VERMONT [a] |
| | KANSAS | WEST VIRGINIA |
| | KENTUCKY [b] | WISCONSIN |
| | MASSACHUSETTS [b] | WYOMING |
| | MINNESOTA [a] | |

[a] Major university is exempt from pre-audit while other schools are not.
[b] Major university *partially* exempt from pre-audit.

made for a legitimate educational purpose, thus substituting his own judgment on the character and purpose of higher education for that of responsible college authorities. Only through the intervention of the courts was the supremacy of the university on matters of educational policy eventually re-established.

In Texas, complications have arisen over the interpretation of a constitutional provision which prohibits state employees from holding more than one office of honor, trust, or profit in the government. In the eyes of the state comptroller, the provision means that the president of West Texas State College cannot make an expense-paid speech at East Texas State College, because he would be holding more than one place of honor, trust, or profit. A dean at the University of Texas gave a commencement address at another Texas college only to have his expense account rejected as an illegal expenditure.[18]

Following an administrative survey in Iowa by a "Little Hoover Commission," the state legislature applied a system of pre-audit control to all institutions of higher education and provided that representatives of the comptroller's office would be stationed on each college campus to approve all requests for expenditures. Although in theory the pre-auditor

[18] The Texas comptroller bases his opposition on an opinion of the state attorney-general (vol. 65, copy No. 2933, Oct. 1, 1933) which rules that although the university trustees may prescribe the duties of university personnel, such duties, to be reimbursable, must not only be public in aim but governmental in nature and, further, that the duties be in connection with the government or operation of the university. Under this line of reasoning the attorney-general denied the right of the comptroller to refuse payment to the dean of the law school for expenses in attending a meeting of the Association of American Law Schools (as this organization is designed, in the attorney-general's opinion, to directly improve a division of the university— the law school) but upheld the comptroller's refusal to pay the dean's expenses to the American Law Institute (which is in no way, said the attorney-general, concerned with the betterment, management or direction of a school of law).

was there only to perform a purely ministerial check of expenditures before they were made, he was actually in a position to exercise considerable influence over educational policy by means of delay or outright disapproval of requisitions.

On one occasion, for example, the auditor in residence at the university refused to approve the requisition of funds for the operation of the state bacteriological laboratory on grounds that a major purchase made by the university was actually an attempt to use up funds in the last month of the fiscal year. Although the university was able to demonstrate that the purchase in question had been planned for a long time, it was able to win its case only after an extensive negotiation with the comptroller's office. Finally in 1957 the schools were able to persuade the legislature to exempt higher education from the system of pre-audit control.[19]

In West Virginia the university and other institutions of higher education have been involved in a marathon conflict, dating back to 1932, with the present incumbent in the office of state auditor. One college official complained that there is virtually no morning mail that does not bring a refusal from the auditor's office to honor a requisition made by a school upon the public treasury. Perhaps the most famous of all the auditor's decisions was his refusal to pay the salary of a professor at Shepherd College while the faculty member was on sabbatical leave. His argument was that a sabbatical leave is of benefit only to the individual and not to the educational institution.[20] But the actual range of problems with which the auditor has presented institutions of higher education in West Virginia is very broad. Fiscal

19 Iowa, *House File 81,* Fifty-seventh General Assembly, amending *Iowa Code* (1954).
20 The state Supreme Court overruled the auditor in *State ex rel. West Virginia Board of Education* v. *Sims,* 81 S. E. 2d 665 (1954).

standards are always open to abrupt amendment at his hands and a school is liable at any time to find that a bookkeeping procedure it has been following for decades has suddenly become unacceptable. This serves to make both long-range planning and day-to-day operations very difficult, and it consumes a great deal of the time of university officials in negotiations with the auditor's office.

Until recently West Virginia University was locked in a dispute with the auditor stemming from his decision that the university could no longer purchase supplies from its own bookstore unless the supplies were furnished the institution at their actual cost to the store. Under this system, no allowance would be made for indirect costs, clerical, and housekeeping expenses involved in running an operation of this kind. Another recent dispute involved bequests left to institutions of higher education by private citizens. A former student of Bluefield State College left his estate to the college upon his death. The auditor ruled that all such monies should be deposited directly in the State Treasury to be appropriated to a college only through ordinary legislative act. This ruling was eventually reversed upon resort to the courts, but for a time it threatened to dry up private gifts for public colleges in West Virginia altogether.[21]

Parenthetically, it should be noted that the state auditor's flair for disagreement is not confined to higher education. During the summer of 1957 all the other agencies of state government shifted over to daylight saving time, but West Virginia's auditor kept his employees working on a schedule based on standard time. As a result they came to work at 10:00 A.M. and left their offices at 6:00 P.M., an hour later than all other state employees. Here the human factor has worked to aggravate conflict, as contrasted with the situation

[21] State ex rel. West Virginia Board of Education v. Sims, 101 S. E. 2d 190 (1957).

in many other states where this factor has helped to smooth over the sharp edges of a difficult organizational system.

Part of the problem faced by institutions of higher education in West Virginia may also be generated by the state auditor's conception of what it takes to keep getting re-elected to office. The auditor has made his reputation in West Virginia as a guardian of the public purse, and he has run all his political campaigns with the aid of publicity designed to refurbish his statewide reputation as an economizer—a reputation he has earned in good part at the expense of the schools. But, of course, the auditor himself can trace his decisions to his basic constitutional obligation to safeguard the public treasury.

The state colleges of California are under a system of pre-audit control which obliges each institution to secure approval twice for many items of equipment that it purchases. The procedure follows these steps:

1. The state colleges submit lists of proposed equipment purchases for the advance approval of the Department of Finance.

2. The department approves most of these items without further ado, but tags other items for further justification. These are usually specialized and expensive items such as vehicles and electric typewriters.

3. These tagged items cannot be purchased by the state Purchasing Division until the Department of Finance has pre-audited the requests. Similarly, items not included in the original list must also be pre-audited before purchase.

The pre-purchase device has been refined considerably in California, but at one time this double-edged system of control had peculiar results:

> There have been cases when at the time of this pre-purchase audit the Department of Finance has rejected items for which it had presumably given approval when

formulating the Governor's budget. The colleges must then repeat the whole process of trying to justify the item. A two-to-four-day trip of one or two college representatives to Sacramento is often required. In recent years some colleges have been unable to give sufficient justification to the Department of Finance to obtain approval of certain necessary music, psychology, engineering, and business instructional equipment even though they had been included in the proposed budget.[22]

As is true of budget execution controls, a good deal of the pressure for a cumbersome pre-audit of this kind comes from the fear that a college will obtain money on one pretext and spend it for another.

*Summary*

Public support for each of the day-by-day controls considered in this chapter rests on the assumption that it contributes to economy and efficiency in government. Central purchasing in many situations provides an obvious means of saving money through bulk buying. The pre-audit may nip illegal spending before it can even occur. Close control over travel and publications serves to hold a tight rein on at least two important categories of state expenditure. Operating, as state government does, under relentless pressure for economy, it is easy to understand the widespread appeal of these and other devices of detailed fiscal supervision.

The value of central purchasing to institutions of higher education seems to vary inversely with the size of the school concerned. Small colleges, with a limited business staff, often report themselves as well served by the state purchasing

22 T. R. McConnell and staff, *A Restudy of the Needs of California in Higher Education* (Sacramento: California State Department of Education, 1955), p. 269.

system. But the larger schools tend to find central purchasing of very limited utility, save perhaps in the case of a few standard items of supply. Because of their size, the larger schools are able to reap the benefits of bulk purchasing without the intervention of a central purchasing agency.

The pre-audit is perhaps the most profoundly disliked of all avenues of state control. In some areas, where it is merely a check upon the availability of funds for contemplated expenditures, it is looked upon as an unwieldy fifth wheel in the administrative process. But in California the pre-audit has brought a system of double jeopardy under which the state colleges may be denied the right to purchase equipment that has already been authorized in their budgets. And in Arizona and West Virginia, where the pre-audit power has been pushed to its furthest limit, substantial intervention in the internal affairs of higher education has occurred.

CHAPTER VI

# The building division
# and the ivory tower

UNIVERSITY BUILDING BOOMS in the last fifteen years have
fostered new controls over nearly every phase of capital outlay projects, and centralized state building agencies have
appeared as increasingly important elements in the story
of college-state relations.[1] To the state official, the reason
for this ascendancy of the central building office is ob-

1 Various names are used to designate these control agencies: State Planning Commission; Building Division; Public Works Council; State Building
Commission or Council; State Architect's Office; and Capital Improvements
Division. Controls over capital outlay may also be wielded by budget officers
and governors. At present, public administrators have not defined the precise
scope and jurisdiction of the different types of building agencies. Some agencies merely co-ordinate capital requests, others have additional power to
supervise expenditures and construction, and still others (outside the scope
of this study) are such special corporate agencies as toll-road authorities.

130

vious: the way to preserve orderly, balanced development in a period of uncommonly fast expansion is for a single state agency to hold a restraining hand over the construction of buildings and the acquisition of land for all projects, including in most states, self-liquidating ventures financed by the individual schools. And the presence of a central agency can help reduce architectural and other fees connected with construction.

College officials are divided on the question of central control of capital outlay and construction. In states where supervision amounts to little more than formal approval of plans originated by the college itself, friction seems to be at a minimum. Actually some of the small colleges welcome the technical aid of specialized engineers and architects in a central agency. But tensions climb in states where building agencies are given broad power to control the planning, contracting, and construction of educational buildings. In Kentucky, New York, and to a lesser degree in other states, the universities have felt themselves the victims of administrative pitfalls and what amounts to policy control through the device of controlling expansion. College officials are convinced that a university which cannot control its own capital outlay cannot determine its academic program. But state officials are quick to reply that the huge expenditures for college building activities must, in the name of sanity, be balanced in the light of the over-all needs of the state. And so the conflict has grown amidst rejoinders and counter-rejoinders, but there are clear indications that most states are adding rather than deleting controls in all stages of capital outlay and construction.

## The Rise of Building Controls

Although central control over capital outlays has for years been a feature of government in several states, it was not until the immediate post-World War II era that the idea of a centralized building agency attracted wide support. Legislators, hardpressed by debt ceilings, limited resources, and mounting demands for capital funds, sought to bring a semblance of order and priority into the system of capital expenditures by public agencies. The centralized building agency has been one solution to their problem.

These agencies have ordinarily been established as a regular staff unit under the immediate direction of the governor or the commissioner of administration, standing alongside centralized purchasing, personnel, and accounting offices. Their authority is varied, but normally they supervise the planning, design, and often the construction of buildings for all state agencies. But not all building control is confined to specialized building agencies. The state budget office also oversees the development of the capital budget and often has authority over priorities in planning and construction.

State building officials usually stress the practical value of their role: the co-ordination and technical evaluation of requests, the comparative assessment of competing demands, and the specialized supervision of engineering problems involved in construction. And yet, state control over capital funds has often provided tremendous political leverage for those bold and skillful enough to grasp the opportunity. In Kentucky, governors have been known to speed up or slow down progress toward capital improvement at public institutions on the basis of partisan political signals. Until 1956, supervision of all state building programs was vested in the Kentucky State Property and Buildings Commission, headed and dominated by the governor. (In 1956 the legislature shifted most of the responsibility for capital construction to the Department of Finance.) Officials at some schools allege that governors often played politics with their power to determine which buildings should be built. One official charged the old buildings commission with hiring an "incompetent" as architect for a multimillion-dollar construction project, and contended that improper planning had marred the project from beginning to end.

Current trends suggest that the movement for central building controls will continue to gain adherents. New Jersey now has a bureau of construction with authority over all state capital outlays except highways. All institutional programs for capital expenditures in Alabama have been brought under the jurisdiction of the state building commission. Maine, in 1956, and Missouri, in 1958, set up special offices to review all state building programs.

In Wisconsin, a recent statute required the chief engineer and the governor to approve all contracts for engineering or architectural services and every contract involving an expenditure of one thousand dollars or more for construction work. Moreover, the chief engineer now supervises all engineering and construction activity. In addition, the 1957 Wisconsin legislature tacked on another provision: the state buildings commission, composed of the governor, three senators, three assemblymen, and one layman, is now required to approve plans and contracts for all construction projects costing more than fifteen thousand dollars. This includes projects financed from gifts as well as self-liquidating projects such as dormitories and dining halls.

## The Range of Dispute

In some states higher education has been at the center of controversy over capital outlay, and building practices on the campus have been the primary target of state officials. Unlike much ordinary state construction, campus building has developed to meet the need for a quiet, self-sufficient community geared to creative learning—a need which is antithetical to mass-production concepts involved in some office construction. Yet partly because of this difference, economy-minded state officials are quick to criticize higher education for unorthodox building procedures. Some of the criticism has led to increased control, while in other cases the institutions have been able to vindicate their positions.

In Kansas, state officials reported that a teachers college took funds from its operating expenses to build a "glamorous" building, leaving a science laboratory inadequately equipped. In Nebraska another official charged that the schools "want to build monuments instead of functional buildings." While the university and colleges of Nebraska have ready answers to these charges, their replies do not allay the critical attitude of public officials.

The governor of one state, while acknowledging a long history of efficient management at the state university and colleges, feels deeply disturbed over certain practices that have developed at the schools. Construction of buildings represents, in his opinion, a current problem. "I don't expect to tell them what buildings to build, but if one has a lot of ginger on it, I'm not going to go for it," said the governor (who has recently been given power to approve all capital projects). This chief executive balked, for example, at a proposal to build an $850,000 gymnasium at one of the state schools after he had seen a comparable building put up at one of the private colleges in the state for $350,000. At present the governor is pressing for a complete survey of the entire state building program to eliminate what he regards as slipshod business methods in planning and construction.

Until a short time ago the University of Nevada was severely criticized by government officials, educational consultants, and even members of its own faculty for expanding its physical plant beyond the immediate requirements of pending enrollments and at the expense of other academic needs.

Of course, colleges are not without grievances of their own. In Kentucky the state building commission authorized one city government to extend its sewer lines across the local state college campus without consulting or even notifying the school. As a result, the line was laid and covered before the college had a chance to connect its own facilities to the line. But more disturbing in the long run to college officials was the presumption that the building commission had the right to do what it pleased with campus property; the state agency had, so to speak, "dispossessed" the college of its property trusteeship. It was even reported that the building commission was planning to sell large tracts of one college campus to private interests—again without consulting educational officials whose campus was involved.

When a building agency makes final decisions about the use of campus property, it thereby raises a new set of difficult legal and practical problems for institutions of higher education. Traditionally, the colleges themselves have been the trustees of campus property. Acting in the name of the state, they have been responsible for the construction, maintenance, and alteration of buildings and grounds. But now a countervailing theory has challenged the trusteeship of the colleges, and asserts that the building division of the state is the proper trustee of all state properties. With a few out-standing exceptions,[2] the problem is so new that no clear lines of law or opinion have been established, but it is certain that the issue will arise in other states.

## PLANNING THE CAPITAL BUDGET

One of the important tasks of the building office is to co-ordinate capital requests from all state agencies. To accomplish this task, most offices have field staffs of engineers who visit each institution to assess relative needs.[3] The Vermont State Building Council fulfills the co-ordinating function by separating all requests into two lists labelled "Recommended" and "For Consideration." Similar lists prepared by the Massachusetts State Construction Division list projects within each category in order of priority.

While every college must expect to have its over-all capital needs critically appraised, educational administrators are disturbed when state officials attempt to rearrange the priority of projects within the college's own capital program. In one state where this has occurred rather frequently, the state building officer justifies his action by declaring that the college gives high priorities to residential construction rather than instructional facilities. Since the college is primarily an instructional institution he feels that it is his duty to put classroom buildings first in all construction plans. Other state building officials protest that college administrators fail to consult their faculties in setting priorities, with the result

[2] In 1903 the Washington State Board of Land Commissioners sold a tract of land belonging to the University of Washington and was upheld in its action by the state supreme court in *State* v. *Hewitt Land Company*, 74 Wash. 573, 134 Pac. 474 (1913).

[3] In states where co-ordination of capital outlay is directly in the hands of the governor or a legislative committee, the full benefits of field inspection may be lacking.

that administration buildings are rated higher in priority than needed classroom space.

In states like Nebraska the capital budget is developed directly by the governor. Other states such as Wisconsin use an interim legislative committee to prepare this budget. Whatever form is used, educators accept the necessity of the legislature's having an over-all picture of the total capital demands being made on the public treasury. But they often fear that a powerful building authority may become a substitute for legislative consideration of capital planning. And they feel that assessment of educational building needs is a difficult chore for officials who are not in intimate contact with an institution's development. Gains in greater objectivity derived from being removed a distance from the educational scene are frequently more than offset by dependence upon mechanical methods of evaluation as a substitute for understanding and knowledge.

SPACE UTILIZATION

Maximum utilization of space—either on hand or planned in future construction—is a central problem in modern building administration.[4] Questions frequently arise over the use of existing space facilities. Such attention never fails to stir doubts as to the effective use of plant under the customary patterns of university operations. An object of particular criticism is the fact that lecture halls tend to be used ex-

[4] The outstanding reference for space utilization is John Dale Russell and James Doi, *Manual for Studies of Space Utilization in Colleges and Universities* (Athens, Ohio: American Association of Collegiate Registrars and Admissions Officers, 1957). See also Donald A. Jones, *Physical Facilities Analysis for Colleges and Universities* (Oneonta, New York: American Association of Colleges for Teacher Education, 1958); and Michigan Survey of Higher Education, *Space Utilization and Value of Physical Plants in Michigan Institutions of Higher Education,* Staff Study No. 9 (June, 1958).

clusively in the morning and stand empty in the afternoon. The use of laboratory space is similarly unbalanced, tending as it does to be concentrated in the afternoon periods. This uneven loading of plant facilities leads to a familiar complaint: Why are large facilities needed to meet peak demands when such capacity remains idle or under-used the balance of the time? [5]

In an effort to deal with these complaints, there is a movement afoot in many states to smooth out the peaks and valleys of fluctuating daily use of university facilities. Space surveys initiated by the Kentucky state building commission have been found useful by educational institutions in that state. In 1948–49 the commission, in consultation with the schools, engaged an educational expert from outside the state to direct these surveys. The commission's architects and engineers worked closely with college officials and faculty on plant needs. This co-operative approach, with the state central office providing a technical service to the operating agency, has been the key to successful building programs in many states. Later, when a more dominating and aggressive personality took charge of the Kentucky building commission, friction and conflict rapidly developed between the authority and the colleges and universities.

The state of North Carolina has also engaged professional consulting firms for space studies in connection with capital outlay budgets. The university has questioned the value of this service when the work duplicates studies made by the university in developing its own building program. In the case of smaller colleges in North Carolina, the state budget officer has taken on the power to prescribe the use of space

[5] The parallel criticism of having a large educational plant idle during three months of the year has abated considerably as public institutions have continued to develop summer sessions, institutes, and conferences to fill the campus during "vacation" periods.

at these institutions. While the smaller schools appreciate the benefit of professional advice on such matters, they are apprehensive about the rigidity which this procedure injects into the management of their institutions.

It would be wrong to leave the impression that public institutions inevitably require the whiplash of central direction in order to take action on space utilization. Many universities have taken the lead in instituting space surveys of their own plants. In states such as New Hampshire, the university (in the absence of a state building authority and in advance of many other agencies) initiated space utilization studies that are constantly brought up to date. Professional educational personnel at both the University of Colorado and the University of Minnesota have been active in developing workable standards of space utilization for their institutions.[6] The University of California, the California state colleges, Purdue University, and Indiana University also deserve mention for their leadership in space utilization and plant planning.

University trustees and officials offer strong warning against one fallacy to which many space utilization studies are subject: not all the uses of the physical facilities of a university are comparable to space utilization in factories or offices. The research laboratory with virus cultures growing in quiet solitude does not need to be as crowded as a warehouse in order to achieve maximum usefulness of plant. The special needs of higher education do not serve as an excuse for ineffective plant use, but they are certainly factors which deserve adequate consideration in any system of space planning.

6 See W. T. Middlebrook, *How to Estimate the Building Needs of a College or University: a Demonstration of Methods Developed at the University of Minnesota* (Minneapolis: University of Minnesota Press, 1958).

ARCHITECTURE AND CONSTRUCTION

The selection or assignment of architects by a state building agency has been a source of contention in some states. Charges are sometimes heard that politics plays a large part in the selection process. Kentucky and Massachusetts, to cite two examples, have had noticeable changes in architects when changes occurred in the political administration at the statehouse. In Massachusetts the university was authorized by the General Court to add a wing to a building that had recently been completed. To the chagrin of the university the firm which satisfactorily designed the original building was passed over in favor of another company (believed to be in better grace with the statehouse powers). Officials at the school had no choice but to go along with the switch in architects.

A further disadvantage to the university of having an architect appointed by the state rather than by the school is the latent possibility that such an arrangement may bring an explosion over architectural style. Frequently the charge is made that many of the "ivied" frills associated with the campus are detrimental to efficiency. But Glen C. Turner, controller of Colorado State College, has pointed out that the pressure toward functionalism in university architecture has come at a time when industry and business are moving in another direction:

No self-respecting giant corporation would now be without its research center where neat laboratories are intersperced with fountains, boxwood-bordered avenues and flowering crab. Camshafts are designed by General Motors where the view of the worker is out toward rolling knolls; glass technology is demonstrated by Corning to executive workshoppers who meet in sumptuous surroundings; groceries are bought in huge Safeway shopping centers where trading is done just off multicolored patios; Connecticut General's insurance workers check their electronic computers in an atmosphere open to an eye-inviting country-side. About the time when it grows suspect for higher education, adapting natural beauty has become good business for industry.[7]

Some institutions find the state architectural authority involving itself in the smallest details of construction. The Connecticut Public Works Department has a voice in the selection of sites, design, room sizes, laboratory layout, construction and even some equipment needs of public institutions of higher education. The small colleges must also accept uniform construction designs developed by the Public Works Department (e. g., all dormitory rooms are a standard size). And colleges often find the department substituting furniture, equipment, and instructional apparatus for the type requested by the institutions.

Construction delay is another characteristic of building programs run under the authority of a central building agency. Perhaps the classic case of delay occurred in New Hampshire. There the state university has autonomy over its own capital development while the state teachers colleges are under state building controls. They are required to clear their programs—both before and after appropriations have been made—through an assistant commissioner in the State Department of Education, the State Board of Education, the Governor and Council, and the Department of Public Works and Highways. One of the teachers colleges managed to obtain an appropriation for a building project at the same legislative session at which the university received authorization to build a dormitory. Pushing hard, the college finally managed to get its building plans through the elaborate system of control and was able to hold ground-breaking ceremonies

---

[7] *In Defense of Ivied Towers*, Address to the Western Association of College and University Business Officers, April 21, 1958 (mimeographed).

simultaneously with the university's dedication of its newly completed dormitory.[8]

Delay in payments can be expensive to construction. With many states having reputations for slow payment on construction work, contractors naturally anticipate this cost in their bids. In both Ohio and Massachusetts, informed sources have stated this was definitely the case on state construction let out on contract. The delay in payments in Ohio has been calculated at two to three months. One Ohio institution of higher education tried to slash the pay period delay down to ten days but was unable to get checks out of the state auditor's office any faster than usual. After futile attempts to cut the "red tape," the institution had to reconcile itself to lost discounts and the embarrassment of overdue bills.

Since Kentucky centralized its control over educational building, school officials estimate that it requires 50 per cent more time to construct a building than it did when the institutions were responsible for their own work. Similar lags in construction developed in Louisiana with the advent of the central building authority. The state colleges were brought under the central system, despite the good record of the State Board of Education in handling previous building programs at the colleges.

Taken together, a network of building controls may be enough to de-energize a program of building maintenance on a college campus. The case of New York is illustrative. One official at a teachers college in that state remarked that he

8 Different treatment of universities as compared to smaller colleges is prevalent in state control of capital development. In California, for example, the state university enjoys a large measure of responsible freedom in developing its capital plant. The small colleges, though, must proceed through the State Department of Education, State Department of Finance, State Division of Architecture, and the Public Works Board for their capital projects. See Chapter VIII for a further discussion of the double standards of control over public higher education.

had tried for six years without success to correct damaging water seepage in the basement of a school dormitory. The authority which built the building and leased it to the state university would not make the repairs because it insisted this was the responsibility of the Department of Public Works. But the latter, in turn, refused to undertake the repairs because technically the building was not state owned. Finally the legislature resolved the issue in 1957, and officials then began negotiation through channels in Albany to correct the matter.

## New Campus Procedures

A development on some campuses that deserves attention is the emergence of the special building authority as a device for financing college construction programs. While these building authorities have been established mainly to circumvent legal limitations on the borrowing power of state agencies,[9] their presence may also serve to eliminate capital outlay as an area of conflict between the state and higher education.

A special building unit was created in 1949 in Georgia with sole responsibility for constructing libraries, dormitories, laboratories, and classrooms for the university. The board of regents rents completed buildings from the University System Building Authority and assumes maintenance costs. When the bonds used for the building costs are retired the university receives title to the structure.

The colleges of New York have succeeded in establishing a dormitory authority which legally permits borrowing for

[9] See Gilbert Y. Steiner, "A State Building Authority: Solution to Construction Needs?" *Current Economic Comment*, XVII (February, 1955), pp. 22–30; and Council of State Governments, *Public Authorities in the States* (Chicago: Council of State Governments, 1953).

self-liquidating buildings (the New York constitution otherwise prohibits such borrowing). In addition, the authority
circumvents many of the delays experienced under regular
state building controls. College officials are unanimously of
the opinion that the dormitory authority has speeded up residential building and saved the institutions from falling hope-
lessly behind skyrocketing enrollments.

## THE CO-OPERATIVE APPROACH

Indiana institutions co-operate in submitting a ten-year
educational building program as the basis for their biennial
capital requests. Funds are allocated among the institutions
through an agreed-upon formula. Individual projects are
subject to approval by the State Budget Committee, but this
has not been a source of serious difficulty for the schools. The
institutions themselves are responsible for plans and construction.

Co-operation is also the key to the successful role of the
Ohio Inter-university Council in building programs. Joint
budget requests of the member institutions include capital
outlays developed on the basis of student enrollment and the
basic needs of each participant. However, four universities in
Ohio are still under the authority of the State Department of
Public Works, which assigns architects, receives bids, and
advises on contract awards. In practice, the department gives
great weight to the views of the schools in making decisions.

All eighteen state institutions of higher education in Oklahoma have their building programs co-ordinated by the
Board of Regents for Higher Education, but each institutional governing board has control of its own building activity. Oregon colleges have developed excellent technical
services on construction under the supervision of the Oregon

Board of Higher Education. The experience and training of the staff of the central board have assisted the various institutions to become more effective in their building programs, especially in dealing with architects and contractors.

*Summary*

From the initiation of every capital outlay project to the dedication of the completed unit, the state building agency may exercise a decisive voice in the physical development of a college campus. Where the building agency acts in a service capacity and confines itself to co-ordinating requests for financial support and to advising colleges on building administration, the relationship between statehouse and campus is likely to be harmonious.

Small colleges are particularly appreciative of the specialized technical services that central agencies may provide. The Office of Institutional Engineers in the Virginia budget office has been extremely helpful to the smaller colleges in the state with its advice (available on request) on construction and maintenance problems.

The building agency may also play an important role in reconciling competing demands for capital outlay funds. The need for co-ordination in a state building program is an accepted fact, and does not create serious problems except where the process threatens to cut off a college's access to the legislature. Of course there are states where no central building agency exists and where alert educational administrators have developed effective methods of their own for developing college building programs on the basis of needs. Experience indicates that where a number of colleges require capital funds from a state, the voluntary co-ordination of requests among the institutions leads to greater confidence in their validity and insures a program related to educational standards.

Space utilization studies have proven valuable tools when they give adequate recognition to the special needs of educational institutions. There is some danger that, when space studies are made by a central state office, an attempt will be made to force higher education into a mold it does not fit.

Central state control over construction is far and away the greatest source of friction in building administration. Designed in theory to supply technical expertise on engineering and fiscal matters, the activities of many control agencies clearly violate the cherished maxim that "experts should be on tap, not on top." Delay under a centralized system is also prevalent and combined with the unreasonable exercise of authority in the central office leads to widespread dissatisfaction with the role of the building agency.

An emerging trend is the establishment of special university building authorities to aid institutions of higher learning in time of pressing demands to escape legal barriers to their long-range financing and physical development.

Somewhat further down the road, it can certainly be anticipated that university building programs will gradually assume greater responsibility for the living conditions of students as well as their academic training. Dormitories, married student apartments, and dining halls, primarily built as self-liquidating projects, may thus proliferate even more rapidly than such traditional projects as classroom buildings.

It should be noted that the principal sources of difficulty in capital outlay controls arise from technical requirements of central state agencies, not from political pork-barreling among legislators and elected officials. College officials generally agree that politics plays much less a role in building programs today than was the case in the past, when construction projects were associated with widespread corruption. This fact speaks well for the integrity of state officials as well as college administrators.

# CHAPTER VII

# The academy under civil service

ONE OF THE enduring tenets of higher education is that faculty and staff should be governed exclusively by the educational institution they serve. Underlying this arrangement is the belief that the unique and sensitive responsibilities of both professors and administrative staff justify such autonomy. But this idea has been challenged in recent years by the extension of state control over the academic and non-academic personnel of higher educational institutions. And while many states remain solidly in the tradition of leaving matters of personnel to the officials in charge of colleges and universities, the intense concern generated by this recent challenge has made personnel administration a critical subject in academic affairs.

Historically, the idea of institutional freedom in personnel matters goes back to the very laws that founded colleges and universities in the American states. These laws vested the

148

academic institutions with full authority over all appointees.[1] In the absence of centralized state personnel agencies, early leaders in state government without exception entrusted the principal tasks of personnel administration to the educational institutions themselves. Clear precedents for this move were found in the practices of European universities, where faculties maintained full control over personnel, and in the early private colleges of America, where the tradition of control by lay boards was firmly established.[2] In both Europe and America, the underlying assumption was that the educational institution itself was best qualified to select its own staff. Today, more than half the states still leave all college and university personnel under the sole jurisdiction of the institutions themselves.

A primary reason for removing educational personnel from the supervision of state government was to protect the schools from being used as dumping grounds for patronage appointees and to bar political officials from firing professors for their views on controversial issues.[3] Clearly the possibility of bold political intrusion on the educational system affords clear justification for protecting educational personnel from outside interference.

Much later a grass-roots movement arose in all parts of the

[1] An act creating the Board of Regents in Arizona (Arizona, *Code,* sec. 54–1602 and 1602 a–d) is illustrative: "The Board shall appoint presidents and other officers and employees as it deems necessary, fix their salaries, provide for their retirements and remove them when in its judgment the interests of education in Arizona require it."

[2] See Chapter XII for a discussion of the tradition of lay control and institutional autonomy in the United States.

[3] One of the most memorable cases was the attempt of Governor Talmadge of Georgia to remove Professor Walter D. Cocking from the University of Georgia in the early 1940's. Professor Cocking was known as a liberal on racial issues and incurred the wrath of the segregationist governor. See Robert Preston Brooks, *The University of Georgia, 1785–1955* (Athens: University of Georgia Press, 1956), pp. 186 ff.

country to bring every state agency within the scope of a merit system.[4] This general civil service movement for states was aimed at the destruction of political interference and favoritism in the hiring and promotion of all civil servants. And its overriding purpose was to inject into public service the multiple principles of employment on the basis of merit, protection of the able employee, and the establishment of a professional career service. In this regard it is worth noting that colleges and universities in many parts of the country were already free from the spoils system that the civil service movement was now attempting to abolish in state government generally.

New York led the way by establishing a department of civil service in 1883—the same year the federal government began its own merit system. Massachusetts followed in 1885, and Illinois and Wisconsin in 1905. Thereafter, the ideas of civil service reformers spread rapidly. By 1958, twenty-eight states had a state personnel agency that administered a personnel program covering the general run of state employees. The remaining states had established at least some variety of merit system, usually in response to federal grant-in-aid requirements for employees working under programs administered by the federal government.[5]

With the general growth of merit system programs, it is not surprising that some reformers should rationalize the

[4] The terms "civil service," "merit system," and "personnel system" are frequently used interchangeably. A few states have both a civil service agency which screens applicants for public employment and a personnel division which regulates "on-the-job" conditions such as position classification, salary scales, and promotion. A merit system is based on competitive examinations or proved ability as a basis for entrance and promotion, and is usually a feature of a comprehensive civil service system. In this study the term "personnel system" refers to formal programs of personnel administration, including civil service and merit systems where they may exist.

[5] Council of State Governments, *The Book of the States, 1958–1959* (Chicago: Council of State Governments, 1958), pp. 140–43.

extension of the system into the phases of academic life that seemed to fit the orthodox pattern of state-controlled personnel. By 1958, twenty-three states had moved personnel controls (usually over nonteaching employees) to the state college campuses. It is here that the movement for civil service reform came into conflict with the tradition of freedom in the management of the personnel of higher education.

The exact nature of the tension over personnel controls varies from state to state. In broad terms, difficulties arise where a state personnel agency is given the authority to regulate phases of the hiring and promotion of personnel in the educational institutions, rather than leaving discretion in the hands of the institutions themselves. For many of the rigid rules and procedures laid down by state personnel agencies have no legitimate relation to the actual needs of the institution.[6] Cumbersome policies, lack of concern for unique jobs, and unrealistic salary scales are particularly upsetting to college authorities.

But there are other tensions that involve more fundamental issues of academic life. As state personnel systems extend their influence beyond the purely nonacademic employees to include professional, administrative, and even teaching personnel, college governing bodies may lose power over a precious area of discretion—the selection and direction of the personnel who carry out the main program of the institution. Nor is this mere conjecture; the University of

6 "Very frequently rigid rules and procedures are expressed in legislative enactments, or are made necessary by the provisions of law. Very often these rigid rules and procedures represent legislative reactions to actual or alleged excesses on the part of administrative officials. Many times they come about through the efforts of employee groups in seeking redress through the Legislature from what they consider to be administrative abuses, and many times the attempt at correction creates a condition more intolerable than the original grievance." John F. Fisher, Executive Officer, California State Personnel Board, letter to Committee, September 11, 1958.

Massachusetts, to cite the most prominent example, engaged in open combat for several years with state agencies over the right to control the salaries and promotions of its own faculty members.

The battle line on personnel was drawn clearly by the President of the University of Massachusetts in an address to his own faculty when he said:

> As long as the number of positions, professional or non-professional, the job specifications that determine salary rates, the downgrading or elimination of positions, even the assignment of specific jobs to activities within the entire university educational program; as long as all these activities are controlled and directed by civil service clerks on a Boston commission who have no experience in either education or educational administration; then . . . the total university program is slowly deteriorating. . . .[7]

## A Profile of Personnel

In twenty-seven states there are no state personnel controls over colleges and universities.[8] This figure, however, is somewhat deceptive. For of these twenty-seven states, nineteen do not even have a comprehensive personnel system.[9] Rather, they have a minimum merit-system program to meet federal grant-in-aid requirements (Delaware is an example), or else they have a limited merit system that applies to a small seg-

[7] J. Paul Mather, "Not as a Facsimile," (mimeographed), September, 1955, p. 3.

[8] Alabama, Arizona, Arkansas, Delaware, Florida, Georgia, Idaho, Illinois, Indiana, Iowa, Kentucky, Maine, Michigan, Mississippi, Missouri, Montana, Nebraska, New Mexico, North Dakota, Oklahoma, South Carolina, South Dakota, Texas, Utah, Washington, West Virginia, Wyoming.

[9] Arizona, Arkansas, Delaware, Idaho, Indiana, Iowa, Mississippi, Missouri, Montana, Nebraska, New Mexico, North Dakota, Oklahoma, South Carolina, South Dakota, Texas, Utah, Washington, West Virginia.

## TABLE 3

# Personnel controls over higher education

| | | |
|---|---|---|
| *No personnel control* (27 states) | ALABAMA | MONTANA [b] |
| | ARIZONA [b] | NEBRASKA [b] |
| | ARKANSAS [b] | NEW MEXICO [b] |
| | DELAWARE [b] | NORTH DAKOTA [b] |
| | FLORIDA | OKLAHOMA [b] |
| | GEORGIA | SOUTH CAROLINA [b] |
| | IDAHO [b] | SOUTH DAKOTA [b] |
| | ILLINOIS | TENNESSEE |
| | INDIANA[b] | TEXAS [b] |
| | IOWA [b] | UTAH [b] |
| | KENTUCKY | WASHINGTON [b] |
| | MICHIGAN | WEST VIRGINIA [b] |
| | MISSISSIPPI [b] | WYOMING |
| | MISSOURI [b] | |
| *Partial control of non-academic personnel only* (4 states) | CALIFORNIA [a] | OHIO |
| | NORTH CAROLINA | PENNSYLVANIA [b] |
| *Extensive control of non-academic personnel only* (14 states) | COLORADO [a] | MINNESOTA [a] |
| | CONNECTICUT | NEVADA |
| | KANSAS | NEW YORK |
| | LOUISIANA | OREGON |
| | MAINE [a] | RHODE ISLAND |
| | MARYLAND [a] | VIRGINIA |
| | MASSACHUSETTS | WISCONSIN |
| *Control of both academic and nonacademic personnel* (3 states) | NEW HAMPSHIRE [a] | VERMONT [a] |
| | NEW JERSEY [a] | |

[a] The major university in the state is exempt from central personnel controls while other institutions are not.

[b] The state has no fully developed civil service system although all states have a minimal civil service program to conform to federal grant-in-aid requirements.

ment of the state employment force (South Dakota has a merit system for the state police in addition to its grant-in-aid program). The remaining eight states with general personnel systems, however, do not extend their coverage to any state colleges and universities. Here they are permitted to work out their own personnel program within the limits of budgetary and legal restrictions.[10]

Several of the other states have the smaller state colleges partly controlled by a state personnel system, while exempting the major university or universities. A conspicuous example of this group is California, where the university is not subject to Personnel Board regulations that are imposed on the state college system. Altogether there are eight states which exempt the major university but leave the smaller colleges under the state personnel system.[11]

Thus, either by specific legal exemption, as in Florida, or through lack of a thoroughgoing personnel program, a majority of educational institutions are left free of personnel controls. This includes not only the faculties, but all other employees on the college and university campuses.

Where state personnel controls do touch college appointees, the type of regulation varies considerably. Out of 284 educational colleges and universities in a forty-eight-state survey, 119 institutions have their nonacademic positions classified by a state personnel agency. But only 18 institutions are compelled to have academic positions classified by a state agency. The overwhelming emphasis of personnel control has been on the nonacademic side of the educational staff.

Greater control over nonacademic personnel is also followed throughout other phases of personnel administration.

10 Alabama, Florida, Georgia, Illinois, Kentucky, Michigan, Tennessee, Wyoming.

11 California, Colorado, Maine, Maryland, Minnesota, New Hampshire, New Jersey, Vermont.

Thus 95 institutions cannot recruit their own nonacademic personnel, but must select their employees from lists established by a state agency. And in Vermont and New Hampshire, the professors at smaller colleges are selected from state eligibility lists, although in practice the schools have some discretion in picking their new teachers.

One hundred twenty-six institutions have no power to set their own salary scales for nonacademic employees and must accept the state personnel scales. And in 29 institutions, the salary scales of academic personnel are set by state personnel agencies. Finally, 88 institutions are not permitted to give raises to their nonacademic employees except in accord with a fixed plan laid down by the state personnel office, and raises for faculty are controlled by a state personnel agency for 26 colleges or universities.

In brief, the personnel of academic institutions remain under campus control in over half of the states; in the remainder, faculties are rarely regulated except in a few instances of job classification, salary scales, and raises. But in the category of nonacademic employees, state personnel controls have been threaded into the personnel programs of a number of state colleges and universities.

## The Faculty under State Regulation

If there is one steel bond of agreement among college and state officials, it is that faculties should not be subject to the controls of civil service. Frank Bane, former Executive Director of the Council of State Governments, summed it up handily in an address to the Association of Governing Boards of State Universities and Allied Institutions in 1954. He agreed with governing board members that the "usual personnel or civil service system is not applicable to the ma-

jor problems confronting a state university or college. . . .
The major personnel problems in a university or college have
to do with faculty and specially-trained, technical personnel
in various fields." "These," added Mr. Bane, "are not at
issue," nor did he know of a single state government or administrative agency "that contends it should have anything
to say in selecting that which is the heart of our universities
and colleges . . . namely, the faculties." [12]

It is true, of course, as Mr. Bane reports, that no state literally selects the faculties of any state institutions of higher
education, and that the principle of freedom for faculty personnel is well accepted in governmental practice. But a few
states have experimented with civil service controls over
faculties, and the results of those isolated instances deserve a
prominent place in the analysis of personnel practices.

Eighty years ago a college president said, "Professors are
sometimes spoken of as working for the college. They are the
college." [13] It follows, therefore, that when the state personnel
agency or any other agency of state government regulates the
hiring, promotion, or firing of professors, it tampers with
the hairspring of the university. What happened in Massachusetts highlights the dangers in such interference with
faculties.

[12] Frank Bane, "Government Control of State-Supported Institutions of
Higher Learning," *Proceedings of the Association of Governing Boards of
State Universities and Allied Institutions*, Thirty-Second Annual Meeting,
1954, p. 36. Mr. Bane went on to say that personnel systems in many states
can apply with validity to "employees of colleges and universities with the
same qualifications, duties and responsibilities that exist in other state institutions, departments, and activities." This view is commonly held among state
personnel officers.

[13] President Paul Ansel Chadbourne, inaugural address at Williams College,
1873, quoted in Richard Hofstadter and Walter P. Metzger, *The Development of Academic Freedom in the United States* (New York: Columbia University Press, 1955), p. 274.

## THE MASSACHUSETTS CASE

Until enactment of the Massachusetts "Freedom Bill" in 1956, faculty members at the state university were primarily under the jurisdiction of the state personnel agency rather than the university department to which they belonged. This was because the state agency had the power to control academic personnel through its power over the grade, title, and salary of faculty positions.

Whenever the University of Massachusetts wanted to hire a faculty member to fill a vacancy (legislative approval was required for all new positions), the university submitted a requisition to the state Division of Personnel and Standardization for approval or revision. At this stage the state agency had the authority to downgrade a position—a vacant professorship, for example, could be reduced to an assistant professorship if the division of personnel thought it appropriate—or to revise the salary scale for that position. The division was also empowered to abolish the position altogether. But if the requisition found its way through the state offices, the university could then nominate a person to fill the job, and this step again was subject to certification by the state agency.

Complicating matters further, if replacements were to be made, the university was prevented by law from offering a prospective faculty member anything more than the minimum salary in his grade, irrespective of his merit or distinction. Oddly enough this regulation prevailed even though professors already in residence received automatic salary increments no matter how indifferent their performance may have been. It was this situation that led Massachusetts' President Mather to declare that personnel administration by the Division of Personnel and Standardization doomed the university to "increasing mediocrity."

The power of the state agency to abolish a permanent position or reduce it in rank sometimes led to bizarre results. The story is told that the division once conducted a classification survey to see if all individuals holding a given rank were entitled to enjoy that status. In canvassing the university, a classification official came across a professor nailing together some laboratory equipment with a hammer. "What are you doing?" asked the classification officer. "What do you think I'm doing?" barked the professor, "I'm using a hammer." Whereupon the personnel officer returned to the state capitol in Boston and reclassified the professor as a carpenter.

Serious morale problems developed when the personnel division moved through the university reclassifying positions, since it often upgraded individuals not in high repute with the university and demoted others the institution held in great esteem. With the division of personnel making the ultimate determination of a faculty member's worth, it was of no little value for a college professor to ingratiate himself with the personnel agency.

Other complications harassed university officials who were attempting to develop a balanced faculty. Once the university decided to split the activities of a faculty member into two parts—he was to work part time on research on a twelve-month basis, and teach part time on a nine-month basis. This procedure, a relatively common one in educational practice, was rejected by the state personnel agency on the grounds that it would not be possible to calculate vacation time under the proposed arrangement.

Most disturbing of all to trustees and administrators alike was the inability of the University of Massachusetts to select and promote their faculty in a manner followed by major universities in other states. Lively competition for teachers and scholars took away a number of its outstanding academicians while the university stood by helplessly unable to grant merit raises that could have retained them. Meanwhile, the system of automatic salary increments rewarded some faculty members who were not fully deserving of the raise. Further difficulty occurred under provisions of the Massachusetts veteran's law, which provided that academic personnel with veteran's status automatically achieved tenure at the university after three years' service. This forced the university into early and in some instances prematurely adverse judgment on its young faculty members, or in other cases saddled the institution with individuals who had no further incentive to produce either as scholars or teachers.

Finally, in 1956, the issue came to a political climax. Friends and officials of the University of Massachusetts mobilized their forces for a major legislative revision of the personnel law. Speeches, pamphlets, and personal persuasion cleared the way for a change, and after extensive public debate the state legislature passed a "Freedom Bill" that granted to the university trustees full authority with respect to appointments, dismissals, and promotions.[14] The "Freedom Bill" retained the salary increment system established by the state, but authorized the university to hire faculty members above the minimum rate specified within the classified salary scale of a given rank. It also gave the trustees full authority to grant special step-rate pay increases to faculty members.

The "Freedom Bill" removed the great bulk of controls that harassed the university's efforts to develop a free and competent faculty along the lines followed by other state universities. But the victory was not yet conclusive, for the state Division of Personnel and Standardization objected to multiple merit increases that the administration granted to particularly able faculty members in order to retain their

14 Massachusetts, *Statutes* (1956), Ch. 556.

services. "If we can't do this," countered the president, "we are stripped of our best professors and left with only mediocrity." [15]

On February 13, 1958, the attorney general of Massachusetts gave an opinion which upheld the right of the university to grant the salary increases under the language of the new law.[16] And so, after years of extreme difficulty, there are indications that this particular phase of state control has been resolved into a form that is acceptable to all concerned.

While it is too early to judge the full significance of the removal of rigid controls over the faculty (nonacademic personnel are still fully regulated) at the University of Massachusetts, President Mather's comment underscores the profund difference in atmosphere now found on the campus. "The impact on morale as well as the noticeable improvement in caliber of candidates selected . . . is almost unbelievable. I can only say that the Bill is working, and it certainly was worth fighting for." [17]

## FACULTY CONTROLS IN OTHER STATES

Teachers' colleges in New Jersey labor under tight restrictions governing faculty recruitment and promotion, but here there has been a greater spirit of co-operation between state and educational officials. Although the state Civil Service Commission sets up the classifications for all professorial ranks, the agency generally follows the recommendations of the State Department of Education in writing its job descriptions. Even so, the head of a college is deprived of al-

[15] University of Massachusetts, *News,* (mimeographed) December 17, 1957, p. 2.

[16] *Opinion of Attorney General George Fingold,* February 13, 1958.

[17] Letter from J. Paul Mather, President, University of Massachusetts, to Committee on Government and Higher Education, December 5, 1957.

most all flexibility in dealing with faculty members. All salary scales are determined by the personnel agency. And all new faculty members normally must start at the lowest pay level in their rank and move up through pay increments that are given automatically. Exceptions may be made to the rule of starting at the bottom if the institution makes a special plea to a Salary Adjustment Commission composed of the state treasurer, the budget director, and the president of the Civil Service Commission. But the exception can be made only after the faculty member is hired, and it prevents the college president from making a definite commitment to a talented prospect. Similarly, college administrators are powerless to offer raises to retain faculty members who have been offered higher salaries by other institutions.

In New Hampshire a prospective faculty member for the teachers' colleges must submit a standard employment application to the state personnel agency. If the applicant meets the job specifications established by the personnel division, he is then placed on an eligibility roster. Thereafter when a college needs an assistant professor, he requests the names of the applicants on the eligibility list of the personnel division, and chooses from the top eight applicants. From this point on, promotions and raises follow rigid schedules just as in the case of employees in secretarial or custodial positions in any agency of state government. Under such circumstances it is conceivable that basic instruction can be given to students, but the method of control gives the institution the character of a rigidly operated high school rather than that of an authentic institution of higher education.

Faculties stand outside the orthodox bounds of public employment for reasons that cut deep. By nature academic work is creative and ill-adapted to packaging by personnel classification. "Standards in education," observed one college president in a letter to the Committee, "are always relative. You cannot measure the end product of education. . . . The setting of arbitrary standards to compare education to state agencies which render service is . . . a pitiful attempt to curtail and control education." And as another president remarked, "What is acceptable environment for the practitioner in government is not acceptable for his university counterpart, because the functions are not the same."

Nor can one ignore the true dimensions of the personnel market when thinking about faculties. Faculties of educational institutions operate in a national market, not within the rims of state boundaries. As one report phrased it,

> . . . *every university that seeks distinction is in national competition* for faculty, students, and important segments of financial support, and must adapt to prevailing conditions of national university life. Each member of a faculty is in addition a member of a national profession. As such, he has duties, aspirations, and opportunities outside his university that are part of his job inside his university. This is one reason that the movement of skilled personnel in and out of particular institutions is a normal characteristic of university life.[18]

And where general state personnel controls constrict the freedom of a university to compete for quality in the national pool, the caliber of a state's educational program is bound to suffer. Admittedly the limited financial resources of the state must always carry heavy weight in every decision, but it is folly to hope that a state with leaner revenue prospects can expect to improve the quality of its higher education by tightening the personnel restrictions on its faculties.

[18] Consolidated University of North Carolina, Faculty Committee on University Relations, *Final Report,* 1958 (mimeographed), p. 15.

## The Zone of Controversy

A vast number of college and university employees are today engaged in advancing the cause of higher education outside the classroom. It has become customary to speak of these employees as the "nonacademic" personnel of the university. This is not an altogether happy choice of terminology.[19] Research technicians, staff members engaged in counselling activity, and others are at work in areas that are central to the life of the modern institution of higher learning. And their contribution is not easily distinguished nor separated from the work of faculty members themselves.

Nonetheless, the status of these so-called nonacademic employees has been the source of sharp conflict in recent years between campus and capitol. Most personnel technicians admit that the faculty member is a rare type of species not easily discovered or classified under normal personnel procedures. But few personnel officers would admit that any such status should be accorded to nonteaching employees, especially those engaged primarily in such housekeeping tasks as business office and buildings-and-grounds personnel. State personnel officers are quick to point out that secretaries and janitors perform the same duties no matter where they are employed in state government.

Personnel agencies have thus come to concentrate nearly all their energies on the nonteaching staffs of colleges, and it is here that real trouble has flared. For administrators, researchers, and auxiliary staff people can no more be pressed into the convenient molds of ordinary personnel systems

---

19 The College and University Personnel Association, a national organization dealing with employer-employee relations on the campus, has officially adopted the term "staff" to designate the non-faculty members of the academic community.

than college faculties. The very definition of a nonacademic employee is elusive, and the work that he performs is novel.

Efforts to regulate the nonteaching staff generally evoke three different kinds of complaint from the responsible head of a college. First, the personnel controls are too rigid to adapt to an academic environment. Second, the state personnel agencies have not given service, only control. And last, the consumption of time and money in working through state personnel offices is staggering.

## THE UNBENDING RULE

College officials are wholly in accord with employment policies where selection is on the basis of merit. But they do question whether a centralized state agency following the rigid rules and procedures can meet the peculiarities of college personnel requirements as well as the educational institution itself.

Certainly one primary goal of a merit system is to establish procedures that allow highly qualified persons to accept specialized jobs, or conversely, to prevent inadequate persons from filling difficult jobs. Presumably civil service examinations are designed to select the right person for the right job, and there is substantial evidence to suggest that state civil service agencies have made progress in refining their examinations and procedures to measure the fitness of applicants for specific posts. Nonetheless, the strict application of formulas for selecting college personnel has sometimes stopped universities from choosing the best person for a particular position. Instead of matching the qualified person to the job, a civil service rule may exclude the very person who is most capable of performing a unique activity. In New York, a medical technician in the state university was conducting research on infant mortality. Because of the background and training he acquired in the course of his work, he was regarded by college officials as one of the best informed men in the state on New York's system of vital statistics. But when the state civil service commission actually placed this job in a classification, it was designated as suitable to a statistician. To retain his job, the medical technician was then required to take the general test given under the civil service classification system to all statisticians seeking state employment. Since his profession was medical and not statistical, he failed the test and had to be relieved of his duties.

Again reversing the intended goal of the merit principle, inflexible procedures may put an unqualified person in an important position. At the University of Massachusetts, a chairmanship in the School of Home Economics became vacant. Despite the fact that the previous incumbent had been a full professor, the Division of Personnel and Standardization (which at that time had jurisdiction over academic as well as other state employees) informed the university it could hire only an assistant professor to fill this vacancy. The university protested that it could not very well hire an assistant professor to preside over persons of higher rank already in the department. But only after nine months of negotiation and after personal intervention by certain members of the Board of Trustees did the personnel agency relent and accede to the university's request for appointment of a chairman at the rank of professor. Even then the agency did not give in on the principle involved, but insisted instead that it had yielded only because of political pressure brought by the Board of Trustees.

Frequently state personnel agencies are unable to service educational institutions with the precise kind of examination needed for particular assignments. The New York civil service agency gives only one test for the position of technician physiologist. But the various medical centers within the university system have distinctly different needs for technicians in this area, some requiring muscle physiologists, heart physiologists, brain physiologists, or still other specialties. However, the civil service register in this area is set up only to provide the university with general physiologists. As a result, these institutions are often unable to fill key vacancies with what they regard as qualified personnel. Although this situation has long been known to the state personnel agency, its attitude has been that it is several years behind in the construction of tests and cannot provide the medical centers with any early help in meeting their problem.

Another (and often overlooked) consequence of rigid personnel rules is their effect on the university's utilization of its own resources. One prominent educator, speaking of his experiences as president of a midwestern university, put it this way:

> My main objection to the state civil service was that their standards were all right but we got most of our unskilled library workers, stenographers, and other workers, from either students or the wives of the graduate students, or the wives of the young instructors. And when we came under civil service two things happened. We had to let most of them go because for one reason or another they might not be on the top of the list from which we had to select. Second, we had to pay higher rates. Then the state civil service commission, without consultation with anyone, would from time to time raise their salaries and we did not have the money to pay them without taking it away from the educational department. In other words, it was a penetration by a state agency into the institution—a penetration by a state agency that knew nothing about our problem and did not even consult with us.

As a result of these encounters with rigid rules, many college officials have been reinforced in their belief that state personnel officers have failed to appreciate the novel requirements of personnel at an academic institution. More serious, however, is the way failure to adapt inflexible rules to the special demands of the educational process can do violence to research and teaching programs that do not fit an orthodox pattern. Certainly the experiences of New York and Massachusetts testify to the injury that can be done to an educational staff by procedures designed primarily to recruit personnel for state insurance departments or prison systems.

Outside of the purely academic vein, of course, there are activities on the college campus that bear some resemblance to work in conventional agencies of state government, and it is here that personnel controls have made their largest inroads. What needs to be understood, is that university employees who are not professors are frequently called upon to perform jobs that differ from the routine and often require special competence. A secretary in a biological laboratory of one college serves also as a laboratory technician, because only through her scientific understanding of experiments is she able to record the data on her typewriter. A secretary to a chairman of a department of psychiatry not only performs *pro forma* secretarial duties, but also handles confidential records on psychiatric patients. Surely for the biologist in charge of a major research project or the professor of psychiatry, the freedom to select assistants with unquestionable qualifications is of the greatest importance.

Elsewhere—at another level of employment—a janitor at many institutions serves in a multiple capacity of cleaning man, gardener, and traffic director at football games. One state personnel office refused to allow janitors to direct traffic because this would mean they were placed in two separate employment classifications. Closer to the academic scene, the custodial staff of colleges frequently work around experiments using fragile research equipment, the disturbance of which could destroy months of scientific labors or even result in serious injuries. At one institution with a particularly low salaried classification for janitors, officials reported that "our laboratories cannot be kept as clean as is essential for scientific work because we are unable to secure proper personnel for this type of work."

## SUPERVISION WITHOUT SERVICE

In a few states, at least, the procedures of state personnel systems do not actually serve higher education, but only impose controls without lightening the load of college personnel offices at all. This is quickly illustrated in the case of recruitment. Although college officials are often required to adhere to every jot and tittle of personnel regulations, the civil service eligibility lists are frequently empty and the college has to do its own recruiting. College officials do not object to locating their own employees. But the irony of their position is that civil service rules compel rigid conformity without giving the colleges the main service that a personnel agency should perform: selecting and making available competent candidates for vacant positions.

A New England university is frequently compelled to use its own officials for recruiting possible candidates and also to administer the examinations prepared by the state personnel office. And at least 75 per cent of the clerical employees in a Kansas college have been recruited by the college and encouraged to take the civil service examination. In another Kansas college the state personnel division supplied only two employees to the entire physical plant maintenance staff over a period of fifteen years. In effect this leaves the personnel agency with the work of filing data, approving procedures, and certifying the employment of the new clerk. Under such circumstances, as one official remarked, state personnel requirements do not relieve the colleges of any burdens, but merely add on more paper work and controls.

Inability of personnel agencies to step up recruitment sufficiently for college personnel demands has left educational institutions short-handed in many areas. A teachers college in Maryland has been unable to hire senior stenographers and practical nurses for this reason, and the same school had a prolonged vacancy in the important position of registrar because the lists for this classified position had no qualified candidate.

TIME AND MONEY

When college administrators treat the subject of state personnel systems as applied to higher education, few words lead to more acrid discussion than "delay" and "expense." This reaction, of course, is not unique among educators.

In 1953 the *Public Personnel Review* asked personnel officers: "If you were asked to justify in dollars and cents the benefits of your personnel program, what would you say?" While several defended their operation as being a money-saver for government, some denied that personnel programs could be evaluated properly in terms of cost.[20] Certainly it would be difficult to measure the effectiveness of personnel controls on a cost-per-employee basis, for variations from state to state are radical. In Illinois, the personnel agency spends $7.34 per employee; in Wisconsin, $12.39; and in California, the cost soars to $27.22 for each employee who is placed on the state payroll.[21] Services, of course, vary correspondingly. But whatever the cost, there is no doubt that the personnel system places a burden of expense upon the

20 "Symposium," *Public Personnel Review,* XIV (1953), pp. 129–31.
21 *A Report: Survey for Examination and Recruitment Procedures of the New York City Civil Service Commission,* 1951, p. 18.

state treasury that must be justified in terms of its accomplishments.

Time is another element that must be factored into any careful judgment on the applicability of a statewide personnel system to the campus. For a painful amount of time can be consumed in processing forms, administering examinations and interviews, and placing the employee on the payroll. Naturally, central personnel agencies cannot service the colleges and universities at the same speed that the institutions themselves could do the job. What might require twelve separate steps when two separate offices are involved could be reduced to six if the college had authority to hire. But the amount of time spent in hiring a person or promoting him, as the state personnel officer sits in judgment, is not the most important factor. Other elements loom larger —equitable treatment for applicants, consideration of the state's overall needs instead of the singular needs of one institution, and a steady flow of qualified employees for all units of government.

Nonetheless, after taking into account the difficulties brought about by delay and increased expense on college campuses when a statewide personnel system prevails, there is much to be said for giving educational institutions their own authority to deal with personnel.

Some colleges report consistent delays of four months in clearing appointments with the state personnel office. Often the college or university has permission to hire a provisional employee as long as he is hired in accordance with personnel regulations, but such an employee has no guarantee that he will be retained until formal clearance is received from the state capitol. In some instances this clearance has been stopped on technical grounds.

One institution complains that provisional appointments have drifted "for such long, unsettled periods that employee morale has been damaged and several valuable employees have resigned." A case in point is a laboratory technician who was kept in a provisional status for two years and three months, then resigned.

Colorado requires state college staff appointments to be reviewed not only by the personnel agency, but also by the governor's office, and both offices must give their approval for any additions to the college staffs. In some instances one of the offices has approved the creation of a position but the other has disapproved it, catching the college in a political crossfire. This practice, coupled with procedures that cause delays up to three months, only compounds the personnel troubles of the educational institutions. As one official remarked, "people are hired and go to work in the hope and with the prayer that they will ultimately be appointed to the job they hold."

At an eastern university located in a rural community, the requirement that its nonacademic personnel be hired from an eligibility list based on statewide examinations proved thoroughly exasperating. This involves bringing people on the eligibility list to the campus for employment interviews. But most of the applicants on the list are from cities, and express little interest in accepting work in a rural community. On one occasion the university had to contact twenty-six people on the eligibility list to fill one clerical position. The task took three months, and each of the twenty-six contacts involved a complicated procedure of applications and reports concerning the individuals on the list. By the time the clerk finally was hired, the university business office had spent an inordinate amount of time—all at the expense of neglecting other duties.

## THE STATE'S PERSPECTIVE

For state officials who disapprove of institutional autonomy in personnel, of course, the stringency of controls is necessary to accomplish the goals of personnel control. They reject the belief that the unyielding rules of personnel systems have hampered the operation of academic institutions. On the contrary, they submit that statewide extension of personnel administration has solved the problems of uneven salaries, excessive discretion in hiring and firing, and overloading of payrolls that provoke frequent complaints in states without merit systems.

In states with taut personnel classifications, some colleges have by-passed regulations in order to remove employees from the state classification system. Colleges in one midwestern state designated extension representatives, cafeteria managers, and bookstore operators as professors, and a college bursar was given the title of dean, all presumably to give the institutions a needed flexibility in employing and paying administrative personnel. Confronted with such practices, legislators and personnel officers have reacted by sterner measures than ever to induce conformity regardless of the motives that impelled the college or university to adopt these tactics.

Many state personnel agencies, however, do understand the diversity and complexity of higher education and stretch their regulations to allow colleges some elbow room in dealing with personnel matters. Oregon has given the state colleges under personnel regulations a maximum of operating freedom in personnel, and state officials follow the lead of the educational institutions in the design and execution of personnel programs.

Nonetheless the threat of arbitrary control over personnel policy, even where state personnel agencies have given colleges considerable authority over employment matters, does undermine campus confidence. And on occasion, some state personnel officers have spoken out against such practices. One former personnel officer, speaking to his fellow professionals, criticized personnel rules that rob state agencies of initiative with the comment that these regulations are ". . . mostly for the advantage of the civil service office. They permit pulling the rug from under an operating official whenever it best serves the purpose of the civil service commission or a pressure group." [22] Elsewhere a distinguished student of administration puts it this way:

> At a time when the urgency, difficulty, and complexity of governmental performance are daily increasing, at a time when industrial personnel administration is moving toward a recognition of the values of experimental and thorough inquiry into human behavior, tempered in application by informality and flexibility in the human relations of organized effort, the public service becomes steadily more dependent upon a cold, impersonal, rigid quantification of human ability and worth in public employment. Nor is even this the full measure of the inadequacy. The methods relied upon lack the objectivity which is their sole claim to usefulness; they provide merely the appearance, not the substance, of the relevant measurement of ability and merit.[23]

Full exemption of the campus from personnel regulations continues to be stoutly defended by college officials. But lacking full exemption, educational administrators insist that the colleges and universities need a maximum of flexibility for conducting their novel work of teaching, research, and administration.

[22] W. L. Johnson, "Let's Untie Operating Officials," *Public Personnel Review*, XI (1950), p. 60.

[23] Wallace S. Sayre, "The Triumph of Techniques Over Purpose," *Public Administration Review*, VIII (1948), p. 137.

## Experiments in Compromise

Where a strong personnel system exists, many colleges and universities have sought ways of co-operating with the state program without subjecting themselves entirely to state control. Although achievement has been uneven, novel and creative ideas have brought improvements in several states that have pleased educators as well as state officials.

In the states that have exempted the state colleges and universities from statewide personnel systems, there is no evidence that these exemptions have created tensions between educational institutions and conventional state agencies. Nor are there strong misgivings among state personnel officers in these areas.

The most common objection to outright exemption is that the colleges depart from orthodox personnel practices when they operate their own programs. Some secretaries are paid more than others; recruiting and hiring may not be done systematically; or faculty salaries are not based on a fixed pay scale. The academician's reply to these objections is, first, that many colleges do in fact have systematic and modern personnel programs; and second, that the departures from orthodox procedures are deliberate actions to take care of the exceptional requirements of higher education.

Some discontent arises among state officials where colleges and universities without personnel restrictions occasionally pay higher salaries than the prevailing salaries in classified employment. But here again, the exempted institutions can point to colleges under state personnel controls where submarginal salary scales have weakened research programs or a clerical staff in competition with private business. A midwestern medical school felt this kind of pinch acutely because classification of personnel was required for the nursing service—a field of high demand. Since the medical institution's teaching hospital treats unusually complicated cases requiring specially qualified personnel, what administrators term "insurmountable difficulties" had been encountered in staffing the hospital with competent nurses.

State officials are also restive in some states about the high salaries paid to top academic officials—salaries frequently above those of governors and invariably higher than personnel directors. The impulse here is to press the institution into a uniform salary pattern for the state, but the control of these top salaries more often falls to the state budget office than to the personnel agency. There is general agreement that administrators do not belong under standard personnel classification.

As discussed previously, one group of states exempts the colleges and universities from any restrictions on the faculty while retaining personnel authority over staff employees. Here the disputes usually flare over the inclusion of borderline cases in one category or the other. Some state officials object to including nonteaching deans, business officers, or research personnel in the academic classification, while college administrators insist that the academic body cannot be restricted to classroom teachers.

One state university, censured by the state personnel division for classifying several members of the research and business staff in the academic category, is attempting to negotiate with state officials for a buffer category of personnel. Under such an agreement the state would permit employees in a twilight zone to remain under college control.

Another compromise advanced by the same university would have the state deputize the university's own personnel officer to handle all staff personnel affairs on the campus. Since the college maintains an office for the handling of academic personnel, the proposal would allow the state to decentralize its responsibility for the selection of nonacademic personnel to the university. As the university sees it, the savings to the state in the central personnel office would more than offset any added expenses of the school. At the same time, the personnel office would retain general supervision and be able to enforce the standard procedures laid down by the state personnel system.

Other state universities such as Rutgers have voluntarily accepted state salary scales even though not legally compelled to follow them. Elsewhere, the University of Maryland has recently taken important strides in developing its own salary scale for faculty personnel to meet state demands for an objective salary program.

Illinois schools are meeting the challenge of state personnel controls by designing their own administrative techniques to ward off legislative and executive directives from the state capitol. And present indications suggest that these institutions have forestalled state controls with a unique and highly workable civil service system that applies to nonacademic personnel in the six state colleges and universities of Illinois.

The story of the Illinois university and college administered system goes back to 1941, when the University of Illinois, previously covered under the general state civil service system, was able to obtain legislative approval to set up its own civil service administration for nonacademic personnel. Prior to 1941, the university had suffered under personnel restrictions and interference, but under the new plan university officials refined and expanded the program to the satisfaction of state officers, heads of the university, and perhaps most importantly, to the people who worked under the classified plan.

Meanwhile, nonacademic personnel in the state's five

smaller colleges remained under the direction of a state personnel system that occasionally was subject to political pressure from governors and legislators. In some instances, a new state administration meant new staffs for the schools, including business managers along with clerical and custodial personnel changes. Moreover, other tensions also mounted because the smaller colleges did not enjoy the same degree of independence as the University of Illinois.

Faced with continued unsettlement in personnel matters, the universities and colleges of Illinois joined forces in 1951 to ask the legislature for a completely new law establishing a central university and college personnel system to be operated by the six institutions. Thereafter a new law was adopted that provided for an over-all merit board, made up of representatives of the several governing boards of higher education in the state, to make broad policies, but guaranteed maximum local autonomy for each member institution.[24] Incorporating many of the tested practices of sound personnel systems, the statute established open and continuous competitive examinations and a flexible classification and compensation plan that took into account the peculiar problems of each school.

Today the institutionally operated personnel system encompasses over seven thousand nonacademic positions, including many on the top management level, on the six state campuses. Administrators are well satisfied that the system has eliminated most of the malpractices found under the old state personnel system and has not curtailed the freedom of action that individual institutions need to meet the unique demands of their programs. Actually, several observers hold that the college system has quickly developed into a more

[24] Illinois, 67th General Assembly, House Bill 381. The basic personnel statute was modified somewhat by the adoption of a general state personnel code in 1955.

efficient and effective system than the central state program which had been in operation for a number of years.

The Illinois college-wide personnel program also incorporates a set of procedures for the conduct of collective bargaining, an innovation that has particular pertinence for the employment policies of state colleges and universities in the years ahead. For certainly the unionization of government employees has injected a new and formidable element into the relationship between state government and state institutions of higher education. Many institutions may, in fact, find that employees will resort to unionization or appeal to the legislature where the institution does not furnish any other method of relieving employee grievances.

Some suggestion of the growing power of public employees' unions comes from California, where the State Employees' Association has had a substantial influence on civil service policies in the state. On its rolls are a number of employees from the University of California, although the university is not under the jurisdiction of the state personnel agency. Over the years the university followed the policy of giving its own nonacademic employees raises equal to those received by other state employees. But on one occasion when the state employees received a five per cent raise, the university, for reasons of its own, was unwilling to go along with the increase. This decision contributed to the efforts of one group which succeeded in having an amendment to the constitution introduced at the 1957 session of the legislature that would have taken away from the Board of Regents all control over nonacademic employees and transferred these employees to the jurisdiction of the State Personnel Board. The amendment failed, but the attempt suggests that unionization may play a part in altering the legal status of the university insofar as its control over staff personnel is concerned.

## Summary

Today, twenty-eight states have comprehensive personnel control programs, while the remainder have diverse forms of merit systems that comply with federal grant-in-aid requirements. Originally negative in character, the rules and regulations of civil service were designed to prevent nepotism and squalid political practices. In short, they were aimed essentially at the political agencies of government.

Long before the appearance of statewide personnel systems, however, institutions of higher education were entrusted with full authority over their faculties and nonacademic personnel. Eventually as the statewide system edged onto the campus and part or all of the nonacademic staff were placed under personnel controls, the ability of colleges to meet their goals was often disrupted. Both principles—the merit system for civil service and institutional freedom in personnel management—have great worth, but the two have been unable to occupy the same space without conflict and tension.

Twenty-seven states still leave educational personnel in the hands of the colleges, but the remaining twenty-one states now apply personnel regulations to higher education. Customarily these controls are moderate and apply only to nonacademic personnel. But occasionally, as in Massachusetts, New York, and New Jersey, controls have been exceptionally rigid and have left deep marks on the educational program. Yet with rare exceptions, state and academic officials are in complete agreement that faculties themselves should never be exposed to state personnel controls.

The principal shortcomings of state personnel control over nonacademic employees—secretaries, technicians, and custodial personnel—stem from the inability of personnel rules to adapt to the novel requirements of higher education in teaching, research, and related activities. Time and again experimental and creative work on the college campus demands flexible and especially qualified personnel, and evidence that unbending personnel regulations have severely hindered this type of work in a number of states is well documented.

Aside from adverse effects personnel controls may have on the actual program of state colleges and universities, the bureaucratic bloom of personnel procedures has harried the staffs of many educational institutions. Delays of several months, empty employment registers, and mountains of paper work have snarled the business offices of many colleges.

Few challenge the lofty aim of a state personnel system, and many look for substantial easements in its inflexibility and improvement in its procedures and rules. College officials themselves share the outlook of an important segment of the personnel profession that has been working for several years to liberalize the more confining tendencies of personnel controls. Highlighting most criticism is the theme that personnel responsibilities should devolve upon the line agencies whenever possible (as the federal government has started doing in recent years). Thus while the personnel profession has no intention of doing away with the merit system as an instrument of government, as some have seriously or facetiously contended, there is nevertheless a movement to restudy the whole philosophy of the civil service movement to determine its adequacy for modern government. But so far, state governments have simply not kept up with the major trends in personnel administration—trends that assigned greater responsibility to the operating agencies themselves in order that they may better achieve their own purposes.

With uneven results, some states with personnel controls over higher education have sought to accommodate the special needs of higher education. Nonetheless, outright exemption of higher education has brought the greatest reduction in tension and improvement in the personnel programs of colleges and universities. Delegation of authority to the college administrators has given greater flexibility in states that have personnel systems. And in some states, notably Illinois, academic institutions themselves have developed their own personnel system that embraces the best features of civil service without jeopardizing the essential flexibility of an educational program.

CHAPTER VIII

# The case of the small college

A REVOLUTION in the size and purpose of the smaller state colleges has raised three major problems affecting state control of higher education: (1) the problem of defining the proper administrative controls for the burgeoning colleges; (2) defining the legal status of the state colleges as compared with that of the state universities; (3) defining the proper scope of the job to be done by the smaller institutions.

One issue stands out: as the small colleges skyrocket to new levels of responsibility, the legal and administrative apparatus initially created for them is placed under stress. What happens is that states often apply one rigid set of rules to state colleges and another less rigid set to the state university. The result is a double standard that poses knotty problems for the schools as well as the states. Yet the present imbalances in the case of the state college cannot be resolved by the simple erasure of all distinctions between the college and the

182

university, for the heritage of the state college is distinctly
unlike that of the state university.

## The State College Revolution

Fifty years ago the state college was a rarity; it existed
mainly in embryonic form as the state normal school for the
education of elementary- or secondary-school teachers.[1] The
normal school of that era was not actually regarded as an
institution of higher education. Its students came to school
with little more than an elementary education themselves;
the reward for graduation was not an academic degree but
only a teaching certificate. The normal school, to all intents
and purposes, was a state-operated auxiliary of the public
school system and was administered as an ordinary state
agency.

Then, by rapid stages, the normal school underwent a
metamorphosis; it stiffened its admission requirements; it
granted bachelor's degrees and took on the title of teachers
college. By 1938, according to one survey, nine-tenths of the

[1] This discussion does not suggest that the history of state-supported higher
education is perfectly divided between the normal schools and the state universities. Actually, the history is considerably more complicated. The state-
university movement began in the eighteenth century and was given impetus
by the provisions of the Northwest Ordinance of 1787, which set aside tracts
of land for higher education in the new western states. A second major wave
in the development of universities came with the passage of the Morrill Act
in 1862, when in many states a land-grant institution was set up alongside the
existing state university. In other cases the Morrill grants supplemented the
funds of the university already in existence.

Within the state-college group there are several mining and engineering
schools such as the Michigan College of Mining and Technology and the
Montana School of Mines. While most of these schools offered bachelor's degrees from their inception, and a number have become leaders in professional
education, they share with other state colleges many of the problems discussed
in this chapter.

old normal schools (public and private) had become teachers colleges or institutions bearing a similar name.[2] Bit by bit the schools added courses in the humanities and social sciences, offered degrees in subjects other than education, and blossomed out as liberal arts colleges. Many sought permission from their legislatures to become universities. So pronounced was the change that by 1956 nearly two-thirds of the institutions had become institutions of general higher education, and the old normal school was only a memory.

But wherever the new institutions turned, they found that their normal-school inheritance tagged behind. Despite the new responsibilities of the colleges, state officials and the general public in several states continued to regard them, administratively at least, as overgrown normal schools. Some states willingly approved the legal transformation from normal schools into state colleges but did not provide the administrative independence usually granted institutions of higher learning.

In Illinois, for example, it was not until 1951 that the five smaller schools attained full legislative recognition of their status as colleges. Established as normal schools in the last half of the nineteenth century, these Illinois institutions in 1917 were stuck haphazardly under the jurisdiction of an agency known as the Code Department of Education and Registration, a state agency that handled licensing of nurses, plumbers, and pharmacists as well as the supervision of the colleges.

Under this system the normal schools were treated as ordinary line agencies of government. President Felmley of Illinois State Normal University reacted vigorously to this offhand manner of handling the teacher-training institutions.

2 Karl W. Bigelow, *Moving Forward in Teacher Education,* mimeographed, 1956. The author bases his figures on the membership list of the American Association of Colleges of Teachers Education.

"It seems to me," he wrote, "that all the hardships that this new system is bringing us are due to non-recognition of differences. . . . The normal schools have been tacked on to an administrative machine that fits charitable and penal institutions of the state." [3] For a simple normal school, such administrative treatment might have been acceptable, but for institutions on their way to becoming full-grown colleges the arrangement was regarded as a straitjacket.

All purchases, requisitions, warrants, and other business items were routed through departmental channels and became part of the mass of State House paper work. Non-academic employees became subject to State Civil Service regulations. Salaries became limited by classification maxima and an enormous variety of administrative decisions were made by "Springfield" rather than by the board or the local school authorities. [4]

Finally, in 1951, as conditions grew unbearable for the schools, a joint alumni council of four of the colleges prepared legislation that would grant autonomy to the colleges. [5] College officials pointed out to the legislature that they were no longer the knee-pants normal schools of a half century ago and their development was being seriously stunted. Legislators promptly gave the colleges an autonomous board and removed many of the petty administrative controls that had been imposed in earlier years. Subsequent legislation took away other restrictions in the area of architectural work and pre-auditing. In every instance the schools have been able to improve their own staffs and services for taking over the new responsibilities that accompany their operating freedom.

[3] Quoted in Richard G. Browne, "Let's Have an Autonomous Teachers College Board," *The Alumni Quarterly,* Illinois State Normal University (November 1949), p. 5.

[4] *Ibid.*

[5] The fifth, Southern Illinois University, had escaped from the Code Department on its own.

Other states made the transition from normal school to college easily and undramatically. The small colleges of Indiana and Kansas, for example, have matured without special notice, and the problems that they confront in state-campus relations are not the unique result of their normal-school origins.

There are a few states in which the issue of proper administrative controls over the teachers colleges has not yet come to a head. The teachers colleges of New Hampshire, Vermont, or Maine are administered as units of the state boards of education and are subject to exceptionally detailed controls. But the schools are still so small, and their academic programs so underdeveloped, that the question of their legal and administrative status has not been seriously raised.

One generalization arises from these diverse administrative experiences: as long as the colleges more closely resemble normal schools than institutions of higher education, the necessity for greater freedom of operation is less apparent. The smallest institutions with the most restricted curriculum are not in as good a position to claim independence as the larger state colleges or the state university. But as the colleges grow and increase their instruction and research, the pressure for relaxing technical controls becomes greater.

State officials know, however, that a simple change in the name of an institution is not a valid argument for a change in administrative controls. As David Riesman recently remarked, "There are certainly colleges in this country . . . which cheapen the very idea of college." Part of the cheapening of the college name comes from instances of indiscriminate name-changing among the smaller institutions in some states. A few normal schools have shifted nomenclatures from teachers college to state college, and to state university, almost as fast as they could convince the state legislature to change their names. Overnight, teachers colleges have been transformed into universities, even though they offered no evidence of expanded degree programs or research activity. Even more disturbing, some of these universities in-name-only have constructed makeshift graduate programs and new departments without adequate planning and personnel. The quest for dignity in higher education has led many a school to fabricate an educational program that it cannot effectively sustain.

Fortunately, most of the institutions that have progressed from normal school to state college are fully deserving of the name, and in many instances recognition is long overdue. The state colleges of Michigan or California are outstanding in the quality of their programs as well as the size of their enrollments. Seven of California's eleven state colleges enroll over 6,000 students, while three of the institutions exceed the 10,000 mark. Iowa State Teachers College, still clinging proudly to its old title, has a well-developed general academic program. But without doubt the flurry of name changes has added materially to the confusion surrounding the relationship between state government and the swiftly changing institutions of higher education in the states.[6]

6 An indication of the wholesale name-changing presently going on is found in U. S. Department of Health, Education, and Welfare *Education Directory, Part 3* (Washington: U. S. Government Printing Office, 1958). In 1957–58: four teachers colleges in Alabama changed their names to state colleges; Colorado A & M College became Colorado State University; and Colorado State College of Education dropped the "Education" part of its title. Three state colleges in Illinois changed their names to universities, as did one in Michigan. Oklahoma A & M College became Oklahoma State University of Agriculture and Applied Science. Two colleges of education in Oregon became state colleges. Memphis State College, Tennessee, changed to Memphis State University. East Texas State Teachers College became East Texas State College, and Texas State College for Women became Texas Woman's University. (One legislator, during the debate on the name change of the women's college, facetiously proposed that the name should be Texas Ladies University because the term "Woman" was not sufficiently flattering to the fairer sex. The galleries of the legislature,

## The Double Standard

A natural outgrowth of the normal-school origins of the state colleges is the fact that most states maintain what are in effect two separate systems of higher education—the state college system and the university system. With the exception of ten states,[7] the laws establishing and governing the state colleges are separate from those pertaining to the major state university. In most of the states, however, this legal separation does not signify that the college system is necessarily inferior. States like Delaware, Washington, and Indiana govern their colleges with separate laws but give these schools all the rights and privileges of the major university.

Yet a third of the states follow a double standard whereby the smaller colleges must conform to closer state control than the major university. In eight states—Alabama, California, Colorado, Idaho, Michigan, Minnesota, Missouri, and Wisconsin—the smaller colleges are created and governed by rigid statutes while the major university enjoys a wide degree of independence based on the constitution itself.[8] As the president of a small college in Minnesota remarked, "The state university was created by charter and is provided for in the constitution of the state, whereas the state colleges were cre-

packed with students from the women's college, cheered with delight.) Finally, Utah State Agricultural College became a State University.

[7] Arizona, Florida, Georgia, Iowa, Kansas, Mississippi, Montana, North Dakota, Oregon, Rhode Island. All of these have a single board of regents and one law covering all institutions; Montana places its six institutions under the holding company title of "The University of Montana." Others, of course, have unified systems of higher education, but the initial laws establishing the state colleges and the university are distinct.

[8] Oklahoma and North Carolina provide for their universities in the constitution and their small colleges in statutes, but there are no significant differences in treatment since the schools have recently been brought under the jurisdiction of master boards.

ated by the legislature and are controlled completely, directly, and eternally by the legislature." In other cases where both the university and the small colleges are created by legislation, the university is ordinarily granted exemption from certain fiscal and administrative controls that are imposed upon the smaller schools. And in a few states, administrators of small colleges feel that despite an apparent legal and administrative equality, the natural political advantages of the major university cause the smaller institutions to be shortchanged in appropriations.

A fairly typical case of the double standard in operation comes from Colorado. The constitution of Colorado created the Board of Regents of the University of Colorado, granting corporate status to the board and assigning it substantial freedom in the management of its own affairs. The constitution further established the terms of the board members and prescribed the method of their selection. Given this constitutional status, the university has been free to recruit and maintain its own academic and nonacademic personnel. It does its own purchasing of supplies and equipment and enjoys considerable flexibility in the handling of funds.

In marked contrast to the University of Colorado and its Board of Regents, the three other boards that govern state colleges were created by statute and lay claim to few of the prerogatives of the university. The Board of Trustees of State Colleges, for instance, exists entirely on the basis of statutory law. The three state colleges under its supervision must channel all purchases through the office of the state purchasing agent, who standardizes major purchases and maintains supervision over all bids. A pre-audit of expenditures is applied to a large number of the operating funds of the colleges. The Colorado Civil Service Commission has authority to recruit, classify, and dismiss all nonacademic personnel of the state colleges, although in practice the colleges do much of their own recruiting.

The existence of these two standards of operation is not a subject of open controversy in Colorado, but it is apparent from interviews that the administrators of the smaller colleges have considerable cause for envy of the constitutional status of the University of Colorado.

## VARIATIONS ON THE STANDARD

The double standard of laws applying to the state colleges and the major university manifests itself in diverse ways. Several eastern and New England states (unlike Colorado with its constitutional university) govern both the university and the smaller colleges by statute. But in Massachusetts, Vermont, or New Jersey, for example, the statutes affecting the state colleges are considerably more rigid than those applying to the state university.

Once in a while the double standard provides ammunition for legislators who want to establish tighter controls over the university and can point to the smaller colleges as evidence of the fact that institutions of higher education do not require special treatment. The autonomy of the University of New Hampshire is currently under some legislative attacks. This university does not have constitutional immunity from supervision, but statutory provisions grant it exemptions from most of the controls that apply to the teachers colleges of New Hampshire. State officials contend that while there may be some case for relaxing controls over the teachers colleges, the university itself should definitely be brought under closer supervision. A comparable attitude is found among state officials in Nebraska, where the state university has long enjoyed a separate constitutional status.

Occasionally a destructive form of competition is nurtured

by this double standard. With the smaller colleges getting a smaller portion of the educational appropriation, they are under some temptation to attack the superior legal position of the university in their struggle for increased appropriations. Conversely, the university may feel itself threatened by competition from the smaller colleges, especially in the area of graduate study. Many of the tensions between the large and small schools are largely a product of differences in size, but the difference in legal treatment can reinforce contention. In Alabama conflict between the state colleges and the state university stems in part from the inferior legal status of the state colleges.

There are still other states where legal provisions do not reveal any official discrimination against the small colleges, but where the administrators of the smaller schools feel that their position is not as favorable as it should be. One college president in North Carolina has reluctantly concluded that his small institution is the stepchild of the system of higher education, not because of any legal distinctions but because of legislative and administrative neglect of his institution. Another president of a Texas college deplored the tendency of the state to give "third rate treatment" to the state colleges.

Not in every double-standard state, however, has inferior legal status been a millstone for the state colleges. The smaller schools of Michigan have made common cause with the universities and have used the example of the large institutions to elevate their own positions and win new freedom. As one Michigan president observed, "The universities should continue to have [their] freedom. The state colleges, however, should be granted the same freedom of operation. There is a growing feeling in our state that legislation should be enacted that would give the small colleges this freedom of action." Recently the Michigan legislature, in connection with an "austerity budget," departed from the traditional line-item appropriation for the state colleges and gave each of them a lump-sum appropriation along with the major universities.

Nor can it be said that the lack of protection always places state colleges at a disadvantage. According to an authoritative source, the state colleges of California have even discovered a silver lining to their statutory basis.[9] Closely tied both to the legislature and the executive departments, the state colleges admittedly lack the financial and administrative autonomy of the University of California with its status as a constitutional corporation. But in partial compensation for the colleges' lack of operating freedom, the legislature has taken a paternal pride in the colleges that it has created. Legislators have suggested that they like to do things for the colleges because they have had a good deal more to do with their development.

In addition, the scattered locations of the California state colleges enable them to appeal to the regional interests of a large number of individual legislators and encourage them to promote the special interests of the colleges (regional pride would, of course, support these institutions if they had constitutional autonomy). Each of the eleven colleges is thereby in a position to rally legislative support for the entire system of state colleges. Meanwhile, the University of California, although vigorously supported by alumni groups and others in the legislature, suffers to some extent from its constitu-

9 The California state colleges (except for several new ones opened in recent years) began as two year normal schools, and "for a long period they served the single purpose of training elementary teachers, mostly young women. Today they have become multipurpose institutions. Ten [now eleven] in number (with more being built), they range in location from the extreme northern end to the southern tip of the State. Their curricular offerings cover a wide range of subject fields and they grant the first graduate degree in educational service." T. R. McConnell and staff, *A Restudy of the Needs of California in Higher Education* (Sacramento: California State Department of Education, 1955), p. 63.

tional remoteness and lack of political support in the grass roots. Yet most of the California state college administrators are convinced that all parties—the colleges, the university, and the legislature—would benefit if the state colleges had constitutional autonomy.

## THE ARGUMENT FOR STRICT CONTROL

Although the existence of the double standard is more the result of historical accident than any deliberate plan, some state officials, university officials, and even state college officials have expressed the view that the colleges require firmer guidance from the state capitol than does the state university.

The foremost reason advanced by the advocates of stricter control is that the colleges do not need the flexibility demanded by a large university. For one thing, the university is practically a government in itself, operating a network of programs in research and instruction that is too complex for the statehouse to regulate in detail. But the college, it is pointed out, concentrates on one primary activity—classroom instruction—that does not entitle it to the same claim of complexity made by the university. A related contention is that the research carried on at a university deserves a special exemption from state control. College and university administrators tend to agree, at least, that free research is the most sensitive facet of academic life and the one most susceptible to maltreatment in the state capitol. According to this line of reasoning, the more research that an institution performs, the more freedom it needs from state control. Accepting this premise, one college president in Maryland holds the view that "Since the functions and purposes of a large university differ from the functions and purposes of the smaller colleges, [he has] no objection to a state university having constitutional and statutory autonomy."

Other educational officials refute the idea that a state college needs more control than a university. They argue that higher education virtually by definition requires freedom from restrictions, whether research or classroom teaching is involved. The friction that results from controls, they contend, simply does not show up as readily in the small college as it does in the more dramatic programs of the state university. It is easy, for example, to document the harm caused by petty purchasing controls over a medical research project; to obstruct the purchase of classroom instructional materials is fully as harmful, although its consequences are more difficult to measure.

A persuasive argument for stiff technical controls over the small colleges is that the small colleges do not have large enough staffs to handle purchasing, accounting, architecture, and similar tasks. Some colleges actually welcome state assistance even when accompanied by controls. "The civil service controls, building requirements, and auditors' controls I welcome," said one eastern state college president. "The small colleges," said a state purchasing officer, "are grateful for whatever help we give them in centralized purchasing while the university resists our services." But most of the small college administrators—especially in colleges exceeding enrollments of two or three thousand students—would vastly prefer to handle their institutional needs, using the services and facilities of the state agencies whenever the state could do a better, faster, or more economical job than the college.

Finally, one of the most frequent reasons advanced for the retention of strict controls over the state colleges is that the state colleges appear to be satisfied or at least habituated to controls, and there is no compelling reason for changing the status quo. In the words of a college president in Nebraska: "I am sure that our state university enjoys prestige by virtue of its size and the many major functions which it performs, which our state teachers colleges do not enjoy. It seems to me that this is perfectly natural. . . ." Other college presidents profess their satisfaction not only with the favored position of the university but with the greater measure of state controls exercised over the smaller institutions. On the other hand, a preponderance of state college presidents are restless in the face of state controls and the advantages enjoyed by the university. Yet they are forced to recognize that the state college has certain disadvantages that give it a secondary position in higher education in the states.

## BUILT-IN HANDICAPS
## FOR THE SMALL COLLEGE

"The big problems of the small schools in this state," said a college president in New Mexico, "are extra-legal and have nothing to do with state controls." In New Mexico as in other states, the small colleges often are located in small towns in sparsely populated areas. Cut off from the cultural and political life of the state, and often hard pressed for adequate housing, recreation, and municipal facilities, the smaller colleges face a difficult task in attracting and keeping faculty members. What is more, smaller classes and certain fixed costs tend to increase the per capita costs of higher education at the smaller colleges. Publicity, too, is a problem for the isolated small colleges; metropolitan newspapers frequently cover the state university regularly but rarely visit the small colleges. Hence, as one educator in Colorado noted, there is less likelihood that problems of academic freedom or state interference in the small college will reach the headlines.

Another built-in disadvantage for the small colleges is a political one. State legislatures, often loaded heavily with lawyers and college educated businessmen, frequently have a strong representation of alumni from the state university.

The presence of old college ties between the institution and legislature has worked to the advantage of the university in many states—the University of Illinois, the University of Mississippi, and Texas A & M are cases in point. The small college can rarely hope to exercise any measure of influence through its graduates in the legislature. At the same time, as in California, the colleges can organize their influence in other ways to put across their plans in the legislature.

A comparable disadvantage for the small colleges is found in several of the states with central governing boards for all institutions. Although board members normally seek to act in the broad interests of all institutions, the opportunity for the major institutions to dominate the board with former students is a subject of concern for the small college administrator. One state with a central governing board of twelve members has six board members who are graduates of the principal state university and four who are graduates of the second state university. Small college spokesmen feel that the board members, given a difficult choice, will be inclined to decide in favor of *alma mater*.

Over and above the accidents of geography and politics, however, the fact remains that the state university is a unique institution whose special responsibilities may entitle it to a different kind of attention from the state. More than any other educational institution, the state university is the great center of service, research, and learning for the state. It is the leader in new ideas, not only in esoteric fields, but in the immediate and tangible problems of agriculture, industry, and business. The services rendered by Michigan State University to the farmers of the state have been of immense value to agriculture. Conversely, the farm bloc in the Michigan legislature has been influential in winning support for the spectacular growth of Michigan State University. No *quid pro quo* is involved, but the service that the university is able to render to the state makes it a natural recipient of financial support.

Confronted with the facts of their handicap, some small colleges have considered the prospect of becoming a branch of the state university in order to share in the advantages of university operation. The faculty of one teachers college in New Hampshire debated this possibility at some length. Yet other college presidents welcome the difference in treatment as a challenge to build and expand their own programs. They prefer to take their chances in a competitive atmosphere.

## *The State Board of Education and the Small College*

It is indicative of the normal-school origins of the state colleges that seventeen states assign the responsibility for the government of state colleges to the state board of education, the agency which oversees the elementary- and secondary-school systems of the state. Eighty-five small colleges are governed directly by state boards of education.[10] State colleges

[10] Within these seventeen states, several small colleges are exempted from control by the state board of education and are given their own governing board. Elsewhere, following the tradition of higher education developed in the great universities, small colleges in twenty-seven states are governed by individual boards of trustees (120 small institutions have individual boards). Six other boards govern several small colleges but not the university.

"Major state university," as used here, applies to those institutions which historically have been known as universities, and not to the many state colleges which have recently acquired, often quite properly, the title of university. "The land grant institutions, although many originated as colleges, have generally shared the major university tradition." The comprehensive state university, in the words of President Morrill of the University of Minnesota, "is the institution which offers more than liberal arts and teacher-training, that conducts high level graduate training and research, that trains for some, at least, of the traditional professions or the newer specialties. It is an institution that clearly transcends the state or regional outlook, comprehending in its service the national and nowadays the international needs." From

governed directly by independent boards of trustees ordinarily profess a thorough satisfaction with the methods by which the schools are run, but the schools under the supervision of state boards of education sometimes tell a less encouraging story.

## THE GOVERNMENT IN MINIATURE

The complaints of state colleges against state boards of education generally fall into two categories. First, the work of the state board of education is so divided among elementary, secondary, and higher educational problems that the colleges run the risk of being forgotten or treated as subcollegiate institutions. Some presidents decry the fact that the board is unable to give sufficient attention to the unique problems of higher education and tends to think along lines geared more properly to elementary or secondary education. Other presidents, of course, welcome the opportunity to be left alone as much as possible. Nearly all would agree, however, that there is a difference between being left alone in the interests of freedom and being totally neglected. One president, criticizing the neglect of his institution, blamed the laws of his state rather than the board of education. "There is no question," he said, "that the board has been given by law more rseponsibilities than a single lay board can properly handle."

The second disturbing feature involves the professional staff working for the state board of education. "I think," said a college president, "the general feeling is that the State Board of Education has been more or less a rubber stamp of

---

"The Place and Primacy of the State University in Public Higher Education," an address to the annual meeting of the National Association of State Universities, May 5, 1958. This distinction is made in order to show the differences in the traditions of the state college and the state university.

the State Department of Education." Another president observed, "the Board of Education [functions] as a government in miniature with which the schools must negotiate all matters. Such matters include far too many purely administrative activities."

The state college presidents to a remarkable degree support their governing boards, whether they are boards of education or regular boards of regents, but they do fear the development of a bureaucracy above the administration of the college. Some presidents, in fact, view the professional staffs of the departments of education with as much trepidation as they view the executive control agencies, and several have found that their work is compounded by having to settle all matters first with the bureaucracy in the department of education and then again with the regular state agencies. One, for example, was disturbed about the requirement that all personnel changes must be approved by the state department of education. "Here again," he said, "we see a state agency making professional judgments relative to the filling of vacancies and the establishment of new positions. Instead of having the help of the department, it represents a preliminary hurdle."

Yet the fact remains that a questionnaire sent to small college presidents reveals that approximately 70 per cent express a general satisfaction with the system under which they are governed, and a few are even lyrical in their praise.[11] "In our state," said a New Jersey president, "the State Board of Education is ideal in its conception of its task and in its actions. We like its operation in every respect."

---

11 Some state college administrators are skeptical about this professed satisfaction. "Evidently," observed one president in a letter to the Committee, "they do not wish to accept responsibility for leadership under greater autonomy. An administrator simply cannot move his institution forward to improved standards under department of education controls."

Even where colleges have their own governing boards, of course, state boards of education influence the academic curriculum through their power to set teacher certification standards. But except for a few chords of dissatisfaction with arbitrary decisions by state boards, college administrators accept the certification power of the state boards as proper and necessary means of setting minimum standards for public school teachers in the state.

*Summary*

Beset by growing pains as a result of their phenomenal expansion in recent years, the smaller state colleges today face certain issues in state control that complicate their development. The issues, and the pains they produce, are grounded in the historical background, legal status, and educational role of the smaller schools.

Historically, the typical state college began as a normal school for the training of elementary teachers. Since no one thought of the schools as institutions of higher education, many states treated them as regular agencies of government. But when the normal schools began their climb to collegiate ranks, their old administrative status seemed less and less appropriate in their new role. Some of the growing colleges found this administrative obsolescence a serious handicap, while others even turned it to advantage.

Legally, however, the state colleges encountered another obstacle to their development in the form of the double standard which prevails in public higher education. The laws governing the colleges permit considerably less independence than laws relating to the state university, and in a third of the states these laws remain unchanged. Several universities rest on the state constitution while their sister colleges stand only on statutory law. Minnesota's Commissioner of Administration, characterizes the situation in his state in this manner.

> The university, once it receives its appropriation, is beyond the reach of the central government. . . . We could badger them a bit but we don't. . . . But in the case of the state colleges, they are subject to full and complete central control. . . . We control every expenditure.[12]

The consequences of this double standard vary: it stimulates creative competition between institutions in some states; in others it gives the colleges a mark to shoot at. But in many instances the double standard has bred restlessness. Some state officials have used it as a pretext for bringing the university under the same firm control as the college. Some colleges have grown jealous of the university's favored position, and in their scramble for full privileges have precipitated new controls from the capitol.

Finally, the normal-school ancestry of contemporary colleges is reflected in the fact that state boards of education govern all or some of the colleges in seventeen states. This system touches off conflict because of the assumption on which it rests—the belief that the colleges are nothing more than an extension of the elementary and secondary school system. Some college administrators also question the usefulness of this dual system of control whereby all transactions are routed first through a professional staff in the state department of education and then through state agencies of centralized control. Yet there are not a few administrators who are entirely content with their governing bodies.

Taken together, these problems can be viewed as part of

---

[12] A statement prepared for the Committee on Government and Higher Education, September 27, 1957. Dr. Naftalin's own philosophy of higher education, however, leads him to give the colleges all the latitude permitted by law.

the incomplete process of adjusting academic machinery to new responsibilities. But in another sense they point to a more serious issue. Until the colleges enlarged to their present scope, few states were forced to judge whether state colleges should undertake the same work as the state university or whether they should be granted similar autonomy. Now a feeling of urgency accompanies the examination of the problem, and professional survey teams in many states are tackling the question. The revolution in the state college is only background to the larger issue.

CHAPTER IX

# The quest for co-ordination

INCREASINGLY OVER THE last half-century, co-ordination has been offered as an omnibus solution to the ills of wasteful competition and unregulated growth in public higher education. Faced with a perennial scarcity of tax revenue, state officials have turned to co-ordinating devices as the solution to unrestrained growth of state colleges and universities, proliferation of new degree programs, and unnecessary duplication of courses. As junior colleges and community colleges have now appeared in greater number, statewide co-ordination has been urged as a necessary step to integrate the new schools into the state system. Some advocates of co-ordination also suggest that the programs of private and public institutions should be synchronized.

Yet there is a sharp division of opinion on the merits of co-ordination. Many studies of higher education have presented convincing evidence that steps are needed to curb empire-building on some college and university campuses.[1] But other students of higher education stoutly oppose the notion that co-ordination is a panacea.[2] Some educators and state officials are asking critical questions on the basis of their experience with co-ordinating agencies: do co-ordinating agencies really improve higher education, or do they merely add another layer in the already confused network of state controls? Who is really responsible for the success of higher education in a co-ordinated system? Has indiscriminate co-ordination hampered the effectiveness of the traditionally independent public institution, whether it is a large university or a small college? The answers have varied greatly from state to state.

In some cases statewide co-ordination has unified the educational institutions without sacrificing distinctive characteristics of individual institutions and has improved the relationship between state government and higher education.

[1] See discussions of the need for co-ordination in: Massachusetts, Special Commission on Audit of State Needs, *Needs in Massachusetts Higher Education,* Special Report, Boston, March 1958, Part III, pp. 31–33; South Carolina, Fiscal Survey Commission, *State Institutions of Higher Learning,* Report No. 3 to the General Assembly of the State of South Carolina, Charleston, S. C., 1956, pp. 4–6, 18–23; Tennessee, Legislative Council Committee, *Public Higher Education in Tennessee,* Report to the Education Survey Subcommittee, Nashville, Tenn., 1957, pp. 280–305; Joint Legislative Committee on Higher Education, *Special Report,* Baton Rouge, La., 1958, pp. 7–8; North Carolina, Commission on Higher Education, *State-Supported Higher Education in North Carolina,* Raleigh, N. C., 1955, pp. 18–97; and Michigan, Survey of Higher Education, Staff Study No. 12, *Control and Coordination of Higher Education in Michigan, The Survey of Higher Education in Michigan,* Lansing, Mich., 1958, pp. 5–26.

[2] E. g., ". . . the State ought to have a central agency in Springfield to control all State-supported higher education. This idea appears repeatedly in the Report. It is offered as a preconceived solution. It so dominates the authors of the Report that they fail to evaluate certain basic issues." George D. Stoddard, President, University of Illinois, *The Russell Report: Memorandum to the Board of Trustees of the University of Illinois,* Urbana, Illinois, March, 1951, p. 4.

For several institutions co-ordination has brought new freedom and vigor as old state controls have dropped away. But elsewhere, co-ordinating agencies have not been so successful: state government has attacked them for inaction, while educational institutions have been disturbed by their arbitrary policies.

## The Trend to Co-ordination

Moves for the co-ordination and unification of higher education are not entirely recent phenomena. New York created a State Board of Regents in 1784, even though New York was the most recent state to establish a state university. The charter of the University of Georgia as amended in 1785 also contained the germ of a centralized system that was not to be realized until modern times in the state of Georgia.[3]

The trend toward centralization in this century began in South Dakota in 1896 with the establishment of a unitary board of control over higher educational institutions. By 1932 eleven other states had adopted this system of unified supervision. Of these, Georgia, Montana, and Oregon appointed chancellors to serve as executive officers under the unitary boards. In North Carolina, three state institutions were consolidated under a single board with a president as executive officer.[4]

Basic co-ordinating mechanisms have been refined and multiplied into many different forms distinguished by certain minor variations.[5] But while terminology and details

3 Edward C. Elliott, "The Board of Control," in Raymond A. Kent (ed.), *Higher Education in America* (New York: Ginn & Co., 1930), pp. 600–32.

4 For a discussion, see David S. Hill, *Control of Tax-Supported Higher Education in the United States* (New York: Carnegie Foundation for the Advancement of Teaching, 1934), pp. 43, 628, 629.

5 See, for example, North Carolina, Commission on Higher Education, *op.*

may differ, there are essentially five major means of co-or-dination: (1) directly by legislatures or executive agencies; (2) voluntary co-operation; (3) consolidation; (4) central governing boards with direct authority over day-to-day operations; and (5) master boards with supervisory powers over regular governing boards.

## Legislative or Executive Co-ordination

A number of states, of course, do not regard the lack of an overall co-ordinating system as a disadvantage. A study commission in Tennessee made these observations about the benefits of educational diversity:

> This pattern tends to maximize institutional initiative and to encourage broad local participation in planning and program development. It encourages competition for students, staff personnel, and financial resources; and it appears to foster a tendency for an institution to become multipurpose in character.[6]

But others feel that particularism and excessive competition have been the besetting sins of higher education in America.

Actually there is no such thing as a completely unco-ordinated system of higher education. In those states where there is no central co-ordinating board for higher education, the legislature, and to some extent the governor, serve as the centers of co-ordination; they do this mainly through budgetary procedures. In some places there is partial co-ordination whereby the state colleges are governed by a

---

cit., pp. 98–100; Tennessee, Legislative Council Committee, op. cit., pp. 277–313. The most concise yet thorough treatment of the various types of co-ordinating units appears in Michigan Survey of Higher Education, op. cit., pp. 27–60.

6 Tennessee, Legislative Council Committee, op. cit., p. 278.

central board (often the state board of education), while the state university and land-grant college have separate and independent governing bodies. This system is found in such states as Alabama, California, Maine, Maryland, Massachusetts, Michigan, Minnesota, Nebraska, and New Hampshire. But in the eyes of administrative reformers these arrangements do not constitute a genuine system of co-ordination. Co-ordination today is thought of primarily in terms of an all-inclusive statewide system.

## Voluntary Co-operation

Although the majority of states are without any formal device for co-ordinating the activities of institutions of higher education, many of these states maintain some arrangement for achieving a measure of co-operation among the schools.[7] These informal arrangements may be rather inactive. But in some states—among them California, Colorado, Illinois, Indiana, and Ohio—the voluntary technique has been employed with visible results.

The voluntary approach has long had support in Indiana and Ohio and appears likely to gain strength in Colorado. In Indiana and Colorado, several staff members from the state colleges and universities devote much of their time to assembling and analyzing cost and enrollment data for the voluntary councils. Indiana has a highly informal arrangement that enables the four state institutions to work together in preparing budgets, but leaves each governing board free to handle its own funds when appropriations have been made. With regard to space, teaching loads, research and

7 For a discussion, see T. C. Holy and H. H. Semans, "Co-ordination of Public Higher Education in California," *Journal of Higher Education*, XXVI, No. 3 (March, 1955), pp. 141–42.

service programs, the four state institutions of Indiana join the twenty-six private colleges of the state in a truly state-wide system of self-appraisal.

Although the Ohio voluntary organization is not as highly developed as the Indiana system, the Ohio Inter-University Council has long provided an opportunity for voluntary co-ordination of the requests of the six state universities. Observers say that this informal system has eliminated much of the destructive in-fighting among colleges that in other states has led to the imposition of state controls.

The Illinois Joint Council of Higher Education has been somewhat less consistent in sustaining co-operative action, and there has been some criticism of the lack of unity among the Illinois institutions. Governor Stratton, for example, recently told a press conference that all of Illinois' state universities should eventually be placed under a single board of trustees, although he believed that immediate action would provoke continued unsettlement. Part of the turbulence comes from the emergence of Southern Illinois University as a major factor in the politics of higher education in the state. But whatever the causes, the prevailing dissatisfaction with present co-ordinating mechanisms is reflected in the fact that Illinois has conducted five studies of higher education since 1945.

California has a unique arrangement between the state colleges and the University of California. A Liaison Committee of the Regents of the University of California and the California State Board of Education conducts studies of higher education in California designed to provide information for co-ordinated planning. It does not, however, attempt a unification of the budget requests of the two boards, nor does it have any jurisdiction over the final decisions of the governing boards. The membership of the liaison group is made up of representatives from the two governing boards.

The emergence of this co-ordinating device reflects the rapid growth of the state college system and the need to arrive at some efficient division of labor between the colleges on the one hand, and the university system on the other.

While the voluntary system has functioned well in a few states, a number of state officials and some educators challenge the effectiveness of the voluntary approach. Some feel that voluntary councils are a façade designed to give the appearance of co-ordination without disturbing vested educational interests. In the words of a state official, "our voluntary system is a back-scratching outfit," whereby the schools support each other's special interests. While such criticism may be overstated, it is true that most voluntary councils, with such exceptions as discussed above, have had little impact on educational practice.

More telling, perhaps, is the criticism that voluntary arrangements lack legal sanctions to enforce the hard decisions that must be made in a period of rapid growth in higher education. It is here, in the eyes of some critics, that the voluntary system is weakest. Yet it is undeniable that some states have managed to develop a satisfactory program of higher education without resort to coercion. In these cases the success of a voluntary approach appears to depend on an absence of strongly conflicting interests among the educational institutions of a state.

## Consolidation

One of the least employed but potentially most drastic means of co-ordination is the outright consolidation of several institutions into one university. Perhaps the best-known case of consolidation is the University of North Carolina, which since 1931 has encompassed the North Carolina State

College, at Raleigh; the Woman's College, at Greensboro; and the Chapel Hill campus of the University of North Carolina. Each institution is headed by a chancellor, while the consolidated system is directed by the president and the board of trustees. The other institutions of higher education in North Carolina have separate boards of trustees and are not integrally connected to the consolidated university.

Another example of a consolidated arrangement is the Texas Agricultural and Mechanical College System, which includes Texas A & M and three smaller colleges, each with a president. Several other states approximate consolidation. It has been suggested that the University of California is virtually a consolidated system, although the units of the system are technically considered as branches of the university and not as separate institutions.

With these exceptions, the idea of consolidation has lain fallow throughout the history of American higher education. There are, however, indications that it is being revived under the pressures of growth in several states. Minnesota is currently debating the merits of various forms of co-ordination, including a plan to consolidate all of Minnesota's state colleges into the University of Minnesota. Similar suggestions have been made in New Hampshire, but no action has been taken.

A principal deterrent to consolidation as a means of statewide co-ordination is the physical decentralization of higher education in every state. The incorporation of several institutions under a single name—as the University of North Carolina—does not change the fact that separate campuses still exist and are administered by resident executive officers. Some observers feel that if consolidation were extended to all institutions in a state it would cause a loss of initiative and responsiveness in the individual institutions. But advocates of this system feel that efficiency and prestige will be gained if all the schools are joined under one administrative roof. The evidence as yet is too sparse to permit firm conclusions.

## The Central Governing Board

Eleven states have unified all institutions of higher education under the direction of a single board of regents exercising direct authority over each school.[8] No intermediary governing boards stand between the central board and the campus administrators. High praise for the central governing board comes from states which have employed the system for a number of years. But in states where central boards have been proposed as a reform of the existing decentralized systems, there has been considerable resistance to this change.

Among the states claiming noteworthy success for the central board, Georgia, Iowa, Oregon, and Kansas are the most prominent examples. In each case, both state and academic officials assert that the central board has solved several critical issues. By presenting an integrated budgetary request to the legislature, the central board substantially diminishes harmful fighting among the competing institutions. It is claimed that the single board system permits a more rational allocation of resources among the institutions without sacrificing the distinctive features of each institution. Finally, proponents of the unified board believe that the arrangement is highly efficient since it permits the smaller institutions to take advantage of the administrative services of a central office at a lower cost than they would be able to perform these services for themselves.

But opponents of the central governing board contend

[8] Arizona, Florida, Georgia, Iowa, Kansas, Mississippi, Montana, North Dakota, Oregon, Rhode Island, and South Dakota.

that a single board for several institutions is incapable of giving proper attention to each institution. They point out further that such boards may easily suffer from the same problem of bureaucratic centralization that is bothersome elsewhere in state government—the central office loses its responsiveness to the special needs of each institution, and inclines to think more of control than it does of higher learning. It is also felt that the large institutions may dominate a central board at the expense of the smaller schools. It does appear that in centralized systems without a strong chief executive, where the central office serves more as a clearing house than an executive agency, the institutional presidents are the actual leaders in the formation of policy; indeed, this may be the merit of the system.

Yet, on balance, there is little evidence that the central governing systems have harmed the individuality of educational institutions, or that they have played favorites with certain colleges. Nor do their administrative procedures appear to be much more cumbersome than those of individual governing boards. Some of the central boards, in fact, are careful to decentralize many administrative functions to the separate institutions in order to give them latitude. It is true, however, that central boards are unable to give the same amount of attention to each institution that individual governing boards are capable of giving.

There remains the question of whether the presence of a central governing board reduces the controls that are exercised by state government. In some states, a central board has definitely worked for a reduction of state controls, but in others it has had little if any effect on the increasingly close supervision of state agencies over higher education.

In Rhode Island, whose institutions came under a central board in 1939, there was a notable release from state controls when the central board took over. This resulted largely from the strong wording of the statute setting up the board, which proclaimed the independence of the new board in unequivocal terms.

Georgia also gives its central governing board system virtually free rein in the affairs of higher education, but the reasons are not quite the same as in Rhode Island. While the constitutional amendment establishing the Georgia Board was firmly worded to guarantee the independence of higher education, it is also true that the state of Georgia has not developed many of the advanced agencies of administrative control that have fastened on to higher education in other states. It remains to be seen whether Georgia's schools will keep their administrative independence as the state evolves new control agencies.

On the other hand, in Kansas, Florida, and Iowa, states with central governing boards where the legal basis of the board gives more room for state encroachments, the state agencies have superimposed a number of controls despite the presence of a centralized co-ordinating board. While Iowa schools appear to have been released from several controls in the last few years, the picture in Kansas is one of rapidly growing state control, despite the presence of a well-established central board.

What this suggests, of course, is that states which employ central governing boards for higher education do not always succeed in centering authority and responsibility for the government of higher education in the board itself. State control over the workings of a central board and its constituent institutions may be as close as it is where each institution is governed by a separate governing body.

*The Master Board*

Many educators and state officials feel that the most promising device that has emerged for the co-ordination of higher education is the so-called "master board." The master board differs from the central governing board in one essential respect: it does not replace the regular institutional governing boards, but is established and given separate identity as a co-ordinating body to deal with areas of policy which require a statewide approach, such as finance. The governing boards themselves retain control over the internal policies of institutions of higher education. Master boards have now been set up in seven states,[9] and surveys of higher education in several other areas have called for their establishment.[10]

While the seven master boards now in existence face the common task of co-ordinating higher learning, they vary a great deal in the amount of power they are assigned to achieve this objective. One of the strongest of these co-ordinating groups is the State Board of Regents in Oklahoma, established in 1941 as the first master board in this country.[11] The Oklahoma board fixes the standards or formulae upon which each institution's budget request is based, ties these requests together in a unified budget which it submits to the legislature, and then allocates whatever funds the legislature appropriates for higher education among the separate schools. The Oklahoma board also has extensive authority

[9] New Mexico, New York, North Carolina, Oklahoma, Texas, Virginia, Wisconsin.

[10] Michigan, 1958; Louisiana, 1958; Illinois, 1950; South Carolina, 1956; and West Virginia, 1956.

[11] Oklahoma, *Constitution,* Art. VIII–A, Sec. 2. For earlier efforts at co-ordination in Oklahoma, see Schiller Scroggs and H. G. Bennett, *The Beginnings of Co-ordination in Oklahoma,* Office of State Co-ordination Board for Higher Education, State Capitol, Oklahoma City, 1934.

over other matters of educational policy, including the question of whether or not a new degree-granting program should be established at any school.

In the case of Oklahoma, the arrival of a co-ordinating board under a skillful chancellor cut down substantially on the control exercised over higher education by other state agencies. Before the adoption of the constitutional amendment which created the Oklahoma board of regents, the colleges in the state underwent a long history of disastrous political interference in their internal affairs. College presidents rose and fell as state administrations changed, and appropriations for higher education were commonly parcelled out in response to political pressures rather than demonstrated need. Today competition and conflict among the schools has been markedly reduced, and the co-ordinating board has come to stand as a buffer between the schools and outside interference.

The New York board, which was set up in 1948, does not altogether fit within the category of master boards, since, like a central unitary board, it directly governs many of the institutions under its jurisdiction. However, the New York board usually is classified as a co-ordinating body, perhaps because several of the New York institutions retain governing boards of their own with authority to make recommendations on the annual budget and to submit nominations for the school's presidency. As noted in previous chapters, New York is a state in which agencies of fiscal control exercise a great deal of supervision over the operations of public colleges and universities.

New Mexico provides an illustration of one of the most successful experiments at co-ordination through a master board. Upon its establishment in 1951, New Mexico's Board of Educational Finance was explicitly restricted to the task of fiscal co-ordination. And its first executive officer was

wedded to the belief that a co-ordinating board should scrupulously refrain from interference with the operating authority of institutions under its jurisdiction. Added to these
favorable auspices has been the fact that the board has received consistent support from each of the state's institutions
of higher education before the legislature. As a result the
New Mexico co-ordinating board has come to play a prominent and accepted role in the state system of higher education. Witness, for example, this description of its influence
over recent financial policy:

> In the 1955 Legislature. . . . The advice of the Chan-
> cellor and Executive Secretary of the Board of Educational
> Finance was sought on every aspect of the appropriation
> bill that pertained to the State educational institutions.
> The appropriation Act, as finally passed and signed by
> the Governor, gave each college-level institution 98 per
> cent of the amount recommended by the Board of Edu-
> cational Finance for 1955–1956, and 99 per cent of the
> total amount recommended for 1956–1957. The 1955 Leg-
> islature also passed a special Act providing funds for capi-
> tal outlay purposes in the college-level institutions, the
> first such Act in many years. The amount appropriated
> to each institution in this Act followed a pattern recom-
> mended by the Chancellor and Executive Secretary of the
> Board of Educational Finance.
> The 1957 Legislature followed the same procedure as
> the two previous Legislatures, and followed exactly the
> recommendations for distribution among the institutions
> of the amount available for appropriation.[12]

In appraising the results of the New Mexico experiment,
it should be noted that both the personality of the first
chancellor and the co-operation of the schools have been
indispensable to its success.

In the future the New Mexico board may well have diffi-

12 John Dale Russell, "The Board of Educational Finance of the State of
New Mexico," August, 1957, (mimeographed).

culty avoiding the pitfall of all master boards, that of becoming loaded down with operating as well as co-ordinating responsibilities. Under its enabling act, the board is directed to center its attention upon the financing of the state's institutions of higher education. "The Board shall be concerned with the adequate financing of each of said institutions and with the equitable distribution of available funds among them." [13] There has, however, been a tendency to vest day-to-day authority in the hands of the board, even when the board does not itself seek such power. The governor, for example, has now authorized the board to approve all out-of-state travel requests for educational personnel, and the legislature has given it the power to pass on the establishment of all new graduate programs by the schools. If this trend continues, relations between the board and the schools may be considerably less harmonious in the future than they have been in the past.

In 1955 three more states, Wisconsin, Texas, and North Carolina, moved to adopt the master board device, and in 1956 Virginia became the seventh state to inaugurate this system. The Wisconsin Board differs from its counterpart institutions in Oklahoma and New Mexico in that the Co-ordinating Committee for Higher Education draws some of its membership from the two institutional boards in the state, the board of trustees at the university as well as the state college board.[14] This arrangement assures adequate recognition of the institutional point of view in the decisions of the co-ordinating group, but it may blunt the edge of the co-ordinating function in cases of conflict with the interests of one or more of the separate schools.

[13] New Mexico, *Laws of 1951,* Ch. 190.

[14] Additional information on the history of co-ordination in Wisconsin is in Donald E. Boles', "The Administration of Higher Education in Wisconsin," *Journal of Higher Education,* XXVII, (Nov., 1956), pp. 427–39.

The establishment of new master boards is often attended by skepticism on the part of college officials, and the success of a master board may hang in the balance for several years as it feels its way into the area of co-ordination. A contrast between the experiences of Virginia and Texas is indicative of the sensitive conditions under which master boards must make their start.

The Virginia board was created under the watchful eye of the educational institutions of the state, and the enabling statute clearly reflects the views of these institutions. The new board has the authority to "limit curriculum" in the colleges, but it has no apparent sanctions for the enforcement of its decisions. Its budget powers are purely advisory, and the statute clearly perserves the right of each institution to plead its case directly with the legislature if it should disagree with the recommendations of the Virginia Council of Public Higher Education.

It is true that the statute creating the Virginia master board can be interpreted broadly so as to serve as a potent co-ordinating device. But the actual operation of the board in the first two years of its life has produced very little in the way of effective co-ordination. After an initial period during which the board failed to set forth definite policies for the educational program of the state, the legislature reacted by cutting forty thousand dollars from the master board budget. With a tiny staff, the board was unable to do substantive research into the problems of higher education (the 1958 budget for Virginia's thirteen institutions was reviewed by one man in six weeks). And as yet there has been no clear distinction between the authority of the master board and the authority of the regular institutional governing boards. Thus both the legislature and the individual schools are watching with some dissatisfaction as the new board attempts to establish itself.

In contrast to the Virginia situation, the Texas Commission on Higher Education has moved cautiously but effectively into a prominent co-ordinating role. The Texas board was created with the full support of the major educational institutions, which foresaw the need for statewide co-ordination. Yet the strong wording of the master board statute was grounds for considerable apprehension among college administrators. There was even talk that a move would be made to abolish the board if it assumed too much authority.

Within two years after its creation, however, the Texas Commission on Higher Education could list several major accomplishments. It had compiled usable information on nearly every phase of higher education in Texas. It had developed budgeting formulas for general administration, teaching salaries, libraries, and building and custodial services—and the eighteen state-supported institutions generally supported the use of the formulas. The Commission has also promulgated a statement of the role and scope of each state institution—again with the acceptance of the institutions—which was to serve as a flexible guide in the evaluation of program requests and budgeting. And the Commission has been actively engaged in the consideration of requests for new degree programs, changes in the status of colleges, and other major educational policies.

While there is still some concern among college officials that the Texas master board could bring interference with the internal policies of individual schools, the measure of acceptance has been notable. One official of the University of Texas, writing in the university's alumni magazine, stated:

> To be completely realistic, the University of Texas has its best chance to achieve real distinction by being a part of a co-ordinated system of higher education. . . . Texas cannot afford an unco-ordinated, unregulated development

of eighteen, or more separate institutions of higher education.[15]

But elsewhere, the prospect of a master board's being established causes widespread apprehension. In the words of the president of the University of Minnesota:

> It is the newer super-fiscal co-ordinating board, created in the supposed interest of "efficiency and economy," with the single idea of holding down state appropriations, usurping the authority of long-experienced institutional state university boards of trustees and regents long-accustomed to know their own institutions and live with their responsibilities day by day and year after year, that I fear. I can foresee in their operations the leveling down of the strong to level up the weaker in response to political pressures. I can foresee the invasion of institutional autonomy by governors and budget officers, the downgrading of the primacy of the state university whose preeminency has been built and whose productivity has been proved by enlightened and resourceful leadership and the devotion of high-level scholars and scientists over the years.[16]

While executives at the larger state universities are thus in a position to speak out frankly against the danger of supervision under the guise of co-ordination,[17] the smaller schools have perhaps even more to fear from the activities of a powerful master board. For the co-ordinating board can present a powerful obstacle to the development of a growing state college or teachers college. Unless a co-ordinating board is alert, it is likely to perpetuate institutional arrange-

15 F. Lanier Cox, "Texas Commission on Higher Education," *Alcalde*, the alumni magazine of the University of Texas, June, 1958, p. 30. See also his earlier article in the May, 1958 issue of the same publication, pp. 8–9, 27–28.

16 J. L. Morrill, "The Place and Primacy of the State University in Public Higher Education," an address to the National Association of State Universities, New York City, May 5, 1958.

17 See also LSU Alumni Federation, *The Superboard and the Freedom of LSU*, (Baton Rouge, 1958) pp. 4–7.

ments that are no longer in accord with changing demands for higher education within a state.

## Co-ordination in Conflict

Perhaps the most serious difficulties encountered by a master board have appeared in North Carolina. After four years of intensive dispute between the master board and the University of North Carolina, it appeared early in 1959 that a settlement had been reached which would substantially reduce many of the original powers of the master board.

North Carolina established its co-ordinating board in 1955 upon the recommendation of a Commission on Higher Education, which was set up as a result of widespread concern over the growing duplication of functions among the state's twelve institutions of higher education. Like the Oklahoma master board, the North Carolina Board of Higher Education was assigned extensive authority, including the power to "prescribe uniform practices and policies to be followed by . . . institutions," to "determine the major functions and activities of each [institution]," and "to make decisions concerning requests from each of such institutions for transfers and changes . . . in the budget. . . ." [18]

Acting under this authority, the board made several decisions that caused college officials to suspect that the board intended to assume wide authority over the internal affairs of the state colleges and university system. A short time ago the board cut down a decision by the University of North Carolina Board of Trustees to build five-hundred units of housing for married students. The board not only lowered the number of projected units from five-hundred to three-hundred but also went on to prescribe exactly how the units

[18] North Carolina, *Acts of the 1957 General Assembly*, Ch. 1131.

were to be distributed among graduate, veteran, and professional students. While deploring this cut-back (which involved federal rather than state funds), university officials were especially disturbed by the board's action in establishing its own rental priority system. This action was regarded as a clear infringement into the area of internal university management

Here as elsewhere, the heart of the difficulty lay in establishing a proper sphere of authority for a co-ordinating body without undercutting the traditional legal responsibilities of institutional governing bodies. Members of the university's board of trustees had long taken legitimate pride in their ability to exercise proper judgment in matters of educational policy at an outstanding educational institution. Moreover, there was concern over the apparent duplication and even triplication of effort that was caused by the insertion of the master board into the administrative hierarchy of the state.

To correct the existing tensions and to clarify the proper sphere of authority of the State Board of Higher Education, a joint committee of representatives of the master board and the trustees of the University of North Carolina began to hammer out changes in the law establishing the master board. In January, 1959, the committee turned in its report to the governor for submission to the legislature.

The plan was a compromise which took away several of the powers of the master board that had caused difficulty in the past. Under the proposed revision, the master board would no longer have authority to require institutions to abolish programs without the approval of the legislature. Its budget powers would be reduced from a mandatory to an advisory status. And the traditional responsibilities of institutional governing boards would be reaffirmed. At this writing, the legislature had not yet made its decision on these changes.

The state colleges and universities in North Carolina are already subject to a formidable array of controls imposed by the fiscal and management agencies of state government. It remains to be seen whether North Carolina's master board will succeed in liberating higher education from some of the control exercised by other state agencies. To the extent that it does succeed, it may become an instrument of deliverance as well as surveillance. Except in the case of Oklahoma, the presence of master boards has not as yet significantly reduced the extent of state administrative controls over higher education.

### Co-ordination Across State Boundaries

The movement for co-ordination in higher education has also developed at the regional level in this country. At the present time three regional boards are at work forging bonds of interstate co-operation. The oldest of the boards, the Southern Regional Education Board, was created in 1949 through the efforts of the Southern Governors' Conference. Though the southern program is more fully developed than those of its counterparts, the Western Interstate Commission for Higher Education and the New England Board of Higher Education, the pattern of operation and authority is essentially the same for all three interstate programs.

The regional boards have a twofold function: first, to study and evaluate higher educational problems for the region as a whole; and second, to provide a mechanism for sharing limited facilities and programs among the public educational institutions of the states involved in the compacts.

The operation of the regional boards does not infringe on the independence of participating members. In the New England compact, for example, the University of Maine offers a well developed pulp and paper training program. Rather than have other states offer duplicating programs in this field, the regional board has arranged for interested students from other states to apply to the University of Maine for their training. The university retains full controls over applications, but under the terms of the contract gives special consideration to regional applicants. The arrangement lifts a burden from other New England universities and allows the University of Maine to use its facilities to the fullest. Adequate financial compensations are arranged.

The studies and surveys made by the interstate agencies (frequently financed by foundation grants) are prepared solely for the information and guidance of member states. The regional boards have no authority to compel acceptance of their findings. Nevertheless, the studies have undoubtedly been influential in shaping educational policies in the member states.

In addition to these formal interstate compacts, colleges and universities are developing many new techniques of interstate co-operation and co-ordination. Many public institutions participate in interlibrary loan services that cross state boundaries. Arrangements also exist for sharing expensive equipment, such as electronic computers, which single institutions cannot afford. In purchasing, many state educational institutions are members of a national co-operative educational purchasing service through which they can obtain, on many items, a more favorable price than state purchasing agencies.

At both the regional and national levels, colleges and universities are also active in associations and conferences which contribute to further co-operation and voluntary co-ordination of activities. The Office of Education of the United States Department of Health, Education, and Welfare serves as a center for advice and information for institutions of higher education. Viewed in this light, the public institutions of higher education are frequently ahead of conventional state activities in developing and using working patterns of national co-operation and co-ordination.


*Summary*

Both state and college officials agree that the pressure for a co-ordinated statewide approach to higher education will take on increased force in years to come. Rising enrollments, mounting costs, and institutional rivalries combine to accentuate the need in every state for a system of higher education stripped of unnecessary proliferation and duplication of program. But there is far less agreement on the means by which the goal of co-ordination is to be achieved.

In those states where a central governing board exercises direct control over each of the state colleges and universities, the pressure for co-ordination usually takes the form of proposals for strengthening the power of the board's executive staff. In Florida, for example, there has been a move to elevate the head of the board's staff to the position of chancellor. There is no compelling evidence that central governing boards have hindered the effective educational work of individual institutions. Co-ordination is not, however, as much of a problem in these states as it is where institutions of higher education are governed by separate boards of trustees. It is in these states that charges of wasteful competition are more frequently heard.

In the absence of a central governing board, attempts at co-ordination have usually taken two chief forms. In a number of states attempts have been made to achieve a satisfactory division of labor among colleges and universities by voluntary agreement. Indiana and Ohio stand out as examples of this approach. While the voluntary system has achieved some results, it has been subjected to criticism on the ground that it lacks the toughness necessary for effective co-ordination.

The master board is the newest and perhaps the most controversial path to co-ordination that has yet appeared. Here an overhead co-ordinating body is superimposed over the separate institutional governing bodies, which (in law at least) retain operational control over the state's institutions of higher education. The master board has worked better in some areas than in others. It presents a delicate problem of balance, since the co-ordinating board must be granted sufficient authority to achieve its mission without opening the door to capricious interference with policy questions that lie properly within the jurisdiction of an institutional governing body.

At its best, an effective system of co-ordination can do much to relieve pressure for greater state control over higher education. For there can be little doubt that much of this pressure comes from the particularism and intensive competition that have long plagued higher education in some areas. But at its worst a tightly co-ordinated system of higher education can leach quality and originality out of state colleges and universities. It needs always to be borne in mind that some of the finest public institutions of higher education have sprouted in a highly unco-ordinated administrative environment.

# CHAPTER X

# The statehouse and the campus

"NO STATE COLLEGE or university," observed Georgia's former Governor Ellis Arnall, "can be completely free from political control." A school may have constitutional or statutory immunity; it may be independent of administrative restraints; but ultimately, as a public institution, it must share in the problems and benefits of a democratic community. What is more, educators and state officials agree that it would be disastrous to remove public higher education entirely from the wellsprings of governmental influence.

Examples of unsavory political activity affecting education are not hard to find. In Governor Arnall's own state of Georgia, the experience of public higher education has been marked by several unhappy political episodes. Mr. Arnall tried during his administration to give the University System of Georgia almost complete immunity from political interference. His constitutional reform granting autonomy was expressly drawn to cure the troubles suffered by higher education at the hands of a former governor. The provision was adopted, but even Georgia's rigorous constitutional protection has not formed a perfect seal against political waters. In Georgia, as elsewhere, an occasional governor, legislator, or private citizen still agitates for the removal of a professor or the elimination of a controversial course.

Carried to extremes, political manipulation can doom a fine university. But politics is much more than the sum of interference, harassment, and manipulation—it is the avenue through which a democratic society reaches peaceful decisions. The politician himself often performs valiant service for higher education. Governors have actively campaigned for improved higher educational facilities, and by making higher education a constructive political issue have brought substantial gains to their colleges. Legislators often champion higher education, even at possible expense to their own political fortunes. And the people of the states, by means of articulate demands, pressure groups, and personal contacts with state officials, have had much to do with the increased appropriations for higher education in recent years. All of these activities are just as political as the attempt of a governor to oust a professor from his job. Any discussion of political influence upon higher education must balance the proper with the improper.

## The Politics of Control

Sometimes higher education provides useful grist for the political mill. In a midwestern state, a superintendent of education with responsibility for several colleges complained that the governor "borrowed" the superintendent's ideas and achievements and claimed them as his own. The superintendent, himself an elected official, needed political credit for his accomplishments. The governor, perhaps needing the political capital even more, deftly nailed a number of the superintendent's policies to his own platform. But both the superintendent and the governor were in full accord on the most essential point: higher education should be radically improved in quality and quantity. Thus while politics whirled above the heads of the colleges, the result turned out happily.

In New York, Governor Dewey won public acclaim for his leadership in the creation of the State University of New York in 1948. Here was the political issue: New York needed badly to organize its system of public higher education, a hodge-podge collection of small colleges and professional schools. But any governor who was to lead the reform movement had to reckon with powerful forces that would resist any aggrandizement of public institutions. The political solution—as it must be called—was to create a central administrative office for the scattered state institutions without establishing a new university with a central campus. For advocates of a single administration for public higher education, this move was a step in the right direction. At the same time this solution avoided establishing a large new university that could have cut into the enrollments of existing colleges within the state. On both counts the governor gathered political rewards, and it is generally agreed that the state's system of higher education was improved by the administrative reform.

On the darker side, enemies of the Chandler administration in Kentucky are resentful of the "dictatorial" and "ruthless" manner in which higher education has been handled. Actually the treatment of higher education under Governor Chandler may well have been less autocratic than in several earlier administrations. Whatever the merits of the case, however, public colleges in Kentucky have found themselves the center of an unpleasant gubernatorial brawl.

Customarily most of the politics of higher education is confined to the triangle formed by the governor, the legislature, and the public college, and the political issue nearly always turns on the appropriation of educational funds. The appropriations process is discussed elsewhere, but here should be noted some of the peculiarly political sides of the fiscal triangle. For there may be circumstances in which the college is the victim of a fight between the governor and the legislature that actually has nothing to do with higher education. It is then that the political character of higher education strikes home painfully—when funds are cut off or reduced because of some broader and often unrelated controversy. This happened in Iowa.

A Democratic Governor, Herschel C. Loveless, proposed in 1957 an expanded capital outlay program for the colleges in addition to a 20 per cent increase in operating costs. Later the Republican legislature gave the Governor less than he asked for operating expenses but increased the amount for capital outlay. But then the legislature refused to follow the Governor's lead in the manner of financing an adequate capital outlay program (among other disagreements, the legislature insisted on retaining a high sales tax, while the Governor wanted to retain the level of corporation taxes). In consequence, the Governor felt that he had no choice but to veto the entire capital outlay bill, leaving higher education with no new building program for the entire year.

Iowa was a case in which politics reached down to injure an innocent victim. Such cases are more apt to occur when a governor of one party faces a legislature controlled by the opposing party.[1] In these circumstances almost any proposal

[1] Iowa, Minnesota, and Michigan have been recent cases in point.

by the governor, no matter how meritorious, stands a chance of being criticized, revised, or killed out of partisan considerations. But in a number of states, political leaders lay aside their party labels when they come to appropriations and laws for higher education. For one thing, the treatment of public colleges and universities is an extremely sensitive issue, and few public officials are willing to become known as obstructionists of higher education.

During Governor Adlai Stevenson's term in Illinois (1949–53), the strongly Republican legislature and a Democratic governor worked harmoniously together on matters of higher education even though partisan strife was much in evidence elsewhere. Legislative leaders particularly in the pivotal Senate Appropriations Committee, were careful to see that assaults upon the Governor's program did not injure the academic program of the state's educational institutions.

College officials are well aware of the dangers inherent in the factionalism of state government, and they are relieved when legislative-executive relations are sufficiently amiable to avoid trouble for the colleges. But educators also recognize that the only way they could be removed completely from political influences would be to remove them from the workings of state government. As long as higher education is an official member of the state system, it retains the benefits of access to the key officials of government—the governor and the members of the legislature.

When executive agencies begin to shut off the college from contact with these officials, the educator's voice becomes weaker. The possibility of being forgotten by political leaders, of being swept into a corner, is as disconcerting to academic officials as the prospect of occasional minor political disturbances. Completely objective, nonpartisan treatment is eminently desirable but rarely achieved, and college presidents are careful to see that their lines of communication to high political office are kept open so that no minor state employee can countermand policy decisions.

## POLITICS IS A TWO WAY STREET

Further evidence of the political climate in which higher education must operate is frequently observed in the activities of state college officials at budget and appropriation time. In states where influence and friendship count heavily in the allocation of funds, presidents must stay in close contact with the governor and the legislature to explain their case for increased appropriations. They have been forced to keep in touch with political officialdom because to do otherwise would cost them the tenuous hold they already have on their institutional income. Conventional agencies of government are notoriously aggressive in their representation of needs, and the college that refuses to make itself heard above the clamor stands a good chance of being passed over either in the governor's budget or in the appropriation bill.

The practice of college presidents depends largely on the traditions of a particular state. In Oregon, where all colleges are governed by a single board, there is little contact between the institutional heads and the state officials. Nearly all business is transacted formally through the offices of the State Board of Higher Education. By way of contrast, the highly personal political traditions in Texas and Tennessee make it imperative for college presidents to state their case frequently and personally before legislators and administrative officials. In most of the states where politics is rampant in budgeting and appropriation, college presidents are virtually forced to adopt the tactics pursued by state highway departments, mental health agencies, and agricultural commissions.

Much of the work of the college administrator in contacting government officials cannot properly be called political. It consists of little more than providing objective information to policy makers. Yet there are several states where the "academic lobbyists," as one governor called them, carry their activities into the corridors of the legislature to state the case for higher education. A few major universities have regular staff members whose primary responsibility is to maintain contact with executive and legislative officials. Other universities use their alumni offices to do a similar job. While most college presidents would insist that these representations are a normal way of keeping state officials in touch with the needs of higher education, some would welcome a change of pace that would permit college administrators to devote more time to internal affairs and less time to mending fences. Their politicking is little more than a matter of survival.

A few states have experimented with the formula system of appropriations and report that adoption of a formula reduces political scrapping. Yet as long as political officials retain the ultimate power of allocating the state's money—and clearly no mathematical formula can eliminate that responsibility— higher education will be required to participate in the political maneuvers surrounding budgeting and appropriations.

In one other way the long arm of politics extends to the college campus: the faculty, staff, and even the student body of a state college are an important source of a state's political leadership. In 1957, the presidents of several state universities were mentioned seriously as candidates for governor. President Donald Russell of the University of South Carolina resigned his post to run, without success, for the Democratic gubernatorial nomination in 1958. And in Maryland, Maine, Kansas, Michigan, and Connecticut, college presidents have been sought as candidates for the governorship in recent years. Below the presidential ranks, professors at the Iowa

State College and at Michigan State University were chosen as Republican candidates for governor in 1958.

Most college presidents adopt a policy of aloofness from party politics and are careful to see that they do not become too closely identified in public with a particular faction in the legislature or the administration. They are also careful to maintain good relations with both political parties. It must be said, however, that the evolution of the college presidency as a job for top quality executives has enhanced the president's appeal as a candidate for high political office. This development has its perils for higher education, since other candidates may attack the college as a means of cutting down a potential rival before he gathers strength.

## State Governors and Higher Education

The state governor today is the most prominent single official in a college's relation to state government. Not only does the governor lead the way in shaping the general fiscal policies that influence higher education, but also his power to appoint college governing board members, his role in many states as an ex-officio board member, and the resources of his personal staff all combine to place him in a commanding position to affect the activities of state colleges and universities.

Many changes have occurred in the governor's office since the day when legislatures kept their governors in a position of almost total debility. Observers speak of the "emergence of the modern governor" in this century as one of the most important developments in American administrative history. Under the steady demands of reformers, more and more states have moved to assign to their chief executive new and far-reaching powers that make him head of the state in fact as well as in name.[2]

One writer lists the elements behind the governor's new-found power as (1) the development of the four-year term; (2) executive reorganization; (3) the executive budget, with an accompanying restriction upon legislative power over fiscal policies; (4) creation of administrative management agencies in the governors' offices; and (5) the "centralization of publicity in the Governor's office." [3] Each of these developments has figured in the governor's dealings with higher education.

## THE GOVERNOR'S PURSESTRINGS

In general governors have been highly restrained in the exercise of their stronger fiscal authority. Actual practice, of course, depends upon the special conditions in each state, but higher education has occasionally suffered because of the personal fiscal activities of a state governor. In addition, subordinate financial officers may prove even more of a problem, as the discussion in previous chapters has indicated. The aim of

[2] In early days few governors were elected by the people, but rather were chosen by the legislature. Virginia's constitution of 1776 provided for a governor to be elected annually by the legislature. He could have no more than three successive terms, and his executive powers were subject to the "advice and consent" of a council elected by the legislature. He could not recommend measures to the legislature or veto their acts. See F. N. Thorpe, (ed.), *Federal and State Constitutions*, 59th Congress, 2nd Session (7 vols.; Washington: U. S. Government Printing Office, 1909), VII, pp. 3816–17. The best survey of the growth of gubernatorial power is Leslie Lipson, *The American Governor from Figurehead to Leader* (Chicago: University of Chicago Press, 1939). See also Coleman B. Ransone, *The Office of Governor in the United States* (University, Alabama: University of Alabama Press, 1956) and *The Office of Governor in the South* (University of Alabama: Bureau of Public Administration, 1951).

[3] William H. Young, "The Development of the Governorship," *State Government*, XXXI (Summer, 1958), p. 181.

this section, however, is to illustrate the manner by which governors have been able to use their financial power to influence educational policies.

First, a word about the forms of this fiscal power: in the arsenal of new controls assigned to the governor, the modern executive budget has been the principal instrument of administrative control. Even in states without the complete executive budget, however, the governors have usually managed to acquire other forms of budgetary influence. In forty-one states the governor is the official budget-making authority. Six other states make him chairman of a budget board or commission. Only in Arkansas does he stand aside while the legislature makes the decisions on budgeting and appropriations.[4] To be sure, while the executive budget gives the governor the initiative in fiscal matters, it does not assure his triumph in the event of conflict with the legislature on tax or expenditure policy.

In the larger states—New York, California, or Pennsylvania, for example—the governors are not often concerned with the detailed finances of state colleges and universities but rather with the total figures that fit into the over-all state budget.[5] The governor of California rarely concerns himself with the inner workings of educational finance. His fiscal office handles virtually all details of budget preparation and analysis, including the interviews and hearings with college officials. A deputy to the principal budget officer is responsible for the budget of the state colleges and the University of California, a job, incidentally, that involves more public ex-

[4] Council of State Governments, *The Book of the States, 1954–55* (Chicago: Council of State Governments, 1954), p. 183. For a more complete discussion of the budgeting process, see Chapter IV.

[5] It should be noted, however, that the governors of these and thirty-three other states have the power of item veto over legislation, including appropriations bills, which gives them a great deal of potential control over detailed finances.

penditure ($265,925,000 in 1957) than the total state expenditures of Vermont, Wyoming, and Delaware combined.[6] Because of the magnitude of the governor's responsibility in California, it is not surprising that the direct controls over higher education emanating from the governor's office are few.

Turning to the smaller states and those without the full-dress executive budget, it is not unusual to find governors who are more closely involved in the detailed financial operations of higher education. But even in the smaller states the governor usually confines his interest to the total amount that can be given to higher education out of the available revenues of the state. Sometimes the process is quite informal. Georgia's governor, for example, is his own budget officer. He serves with the state auditor on a two-man budget committee that makes up the general budget for state agencies. Instead of engaging an army of budget analysts to cover every item in the requests of higher education and other state functions, the governor has personal talks with the responsible officials, and, in the words of the state auditor, "figures out what the market will bear." The governor does not deal personally with the presidents of the Georgia colleges but with the chancellor of the University System of Georgia, who prepares a general request for all institutions of higher education. Nor does the governor look in detail at the request of the regents. Like his counterparts in the larger states, his concern as chief executive is naturally directed toward the totals at the bottom of the budget page.

Most governors nevertheless have the reserve power to bear down upon the minor details of higher education if they choose. Governors in Kentucky in recent years have been particularly interested in the building programs of the state

6 U. S., Bureau of the Census, *Compendium of State Government Finances in 1957* (Washington: U. S. Government Printing Office, 1958).

colleges and have used their formal powers of the budget to shape the building programs on several campuses. Illinois' Governor William Stratton (1953–), regarded by educators and state officials alike as an expert on state finance, has followed a policy of direct personal negotiation with college and university officials. In Illinois this negotiation does not entail direct interference. Governor Stratton believes that educational institutions—or for that matter any institution of the state—deserve the personal attention but not the personal direction of the chief executive. He makes certain that college officials are able to present their case directly to him before he makes the necessary political decisions about the state's financial resources, and he familiarizes himself with college finances in great detail. Illinois college presidents, viewing warily the states in which budget analysts handle all financial matters for the governor, are glad of this opportunity to deal openly with a governor whose fiscal judgment they respect.

Across the nation most governors clearly have the official budgetary power or the persuasive ability to exert a profound influence over the finances of higher education. But few governors have the time or the inclination to dictate detailed fiscal policies to the state colleges. As practical men of politics, they recognize that excessive concern for internal educational policies could easily be construed by the public—and sometimes rightly—as unwholesome meddling in higher education. Most governors, in fact, show a genuine respect for the institutions and the leaders of higher education and see little reason for substituting their own judgment for the judgment of educators.

## APPOINTING THE REGENTS

Seldom does a single governor appoint the entire membership of an academic governing board, since governors' terms

are short and regents' terms are ordinarily long and staggered. Even more important, governors have been unusually
careful to appoint qualified members to academic governing
boards. Still, the power of appointment is the subject of occasional abuse by governors who choose to play politics with
higher education.

Only recently one state governor set out to pack the board
of regents of the university for the express purpose of undercutting the constitutional independence of the university.
He was anxious to block the access of the university to the
legislature and to hold it under strict control. In addition
the governor may have intended to use the university as a
scapegoat in his frequent forays against radicalism (even
though the university is noted for its staid conservatism).
Failing to achieve success by direct assault, the governor had
another opportunity to carry out his plans when several vacancies appeared on the board of regents. The governor
picked his appointees with the clear aim of bringing the
board into his own camp. Interestingly enough, once the new
regents assumed their duties they cast off their obligations to
the governor and identified themselves with the university.

This switch in loyalties is a fairly common one. Witness
the way in which many court appointees of American presidents fail to go along with presidential policies after they
assume office. From an executive point of view, the uncertain
loyalty of board appointees may be a barrier to effective government. But in the unique business of academic governing
boards, the tendency of board members to become defenders
of the institution rather than agents of the governor is—and
here most governors would agree—often the means of academic salvation.

The chance that a governor will use his appointive power
to pry into educational affairs is never entirely absent. There
are governors who hand-pick board members to bring the

college campus under partisan control. There are also governors who prefer to appoint political cronies of dubious qualification rather than eminently qualified citizens. But on balance, gubernatorial appointments show that governors normally choose competent and uninstructed members.

The truth of the matter is that governors have come to regard the selection of a high quality governing board as smart politics as well as sound administration. Regardless of how a university may be set apart legally from the direct administrative control of the governor, the successes and failures of the higher educational system invariably brighten or darken the public image of the governor. In a society that frowns at political favoritism, the appointment of unqualified persons as regents could scarcely improve the political standing of the governor.

The fact that a governor selects board members who share his own political or economic views, of course, does not necessarily imply that a governor is packing a board for some ulterior purpose. This practice is rarely questioned unless it flares into a blatant attempt to undermine educational operations. Outside of higher education, "board packing" is an old and familiar device. Tied down by a Lilliputian system of government in which innumerable boards and commissions escape his administrative discretion, the governor customarily tries to place men of his own views on the boards that he cannot control directly. Once the governor has attained a majority of appointments on the boards, he stands a much better chance of commanding the policies of the independent agencies. In fact, many a governor has succeeded through his powers of appointment in running various non-educational boards and commissions almost as if they were directly under his executive authority.

But there can be no question that the governor's power of appointment gives him a direct route into the internal affairs of higher education. For if there is a close identity of interests between a governor and his appointees the net result is policy control from the governor's office. Governor Philip LaFollette (1935–39) of Wisconsin placed members on the Board of Regents of the University of Wisconsin who shared his belief that the president of the university should be removed—and the president was ousted in short order. In Washington, Governor R. H. Hartley (1925–33) summarily removed two members of the Board of Regents of the University of Washington to make room for two new appointees. His ultimate aim was the removal of the university president, Henry Suzzallo.[7] In Texas, Governor Allan Shivers (1951–57) appointed board members of strong and constant sympathy to his conservative views. After three terms in office he had appointed all the members of each educational governing board, and observers agreed that his influence would be felt for a number of years after his retirement from office.

Limitations on the governor's appointing powers are often written into the laws of the state. Eleven states stipulate that membership on governing boards must be apportioned among the leading political parties of the state. In practice this provision is not oversignificant, since a single governor will not have an opportunity to appoint a majority from his own party during his tenure in office. The provisions primarily affect the actions of a succession of governors from one party.

Another restriction on the governor's appointing power permits the governor of a few states to name only a fraction of the entire membership of the governing board. The Board of Trustees of Pennsylvania State University, which has a unique legal status, is composed of thirty-two members, five of whom are ex officio; nine are elected by the alumni asso-

[7] *State ex rel. Davis* v. *Johns*, 139 Wash. 525, 248 Pac. 423 (1926); *State ex rel. Rupp* v. *Jordan*, 139 Wash. 706, 248 Pac. 432 (1926).

ciation; twelve are elected by a statewide bodies of delegates, and only six are appointed by the governor. The state senate confirms the governor's appointments, repeating a practice followed in thirty-three states. Indiana University uses a split system in which a minority of the board is elected by alumni and a majority is elected by the state board of education.

Other state laws define the qualifications and character of board members to be appointed by the governor. South Dakota limits the selection to the "best known citizens of the state" chosen from different geographical areas of the state. Trustees of the University of Tennessee must include in their ranks two members from Knoxville, two from Memphis, and one from each congressional district. The hand of the governor is thereby restrained on several counts, and his appointive power is hardly as formidable as might otherwise be the case.

## THE GOVERNOR AS EX-OFFICIO REGENT

"By virtue of office or official position," the governor in twenty-one states is assigned to "ex-officio" membership on the boards of one or more colleges or universities, and several are ex-officio chairmen of the governing boards.[8] This

---

[8] *Alabama*, U. of Alabama and three smaller institutions, chairman of all; *Arizona*, Board of Regents, University and State Colleges; *California*, U. of California; *Colorado*, Colorado State U.; *Connecticut*, U. of Connecticut, chairman; *Delaware*, U. of Delaware; *Florida*, State Board of Education, chairman; *Illinois*, U. of Illinois; *Kentucky*, U. of Kentucky, chairman; *Louisiana*, Louisiana State U., chairman; *Massachusetts*, U. of Massachusetts; *Montana*, State Board of Education, chairman; *New Hampshire*, U. of New Hampshire; *New Jersey*, Rutgers, the State U.; *New Mexico*, U. of New Mexico and several smaller institutions (an amendment to the constitution in 1949 did not, however, mention ex-officio membership, leaving the governor's exact status unsettled at this writing); *North Carolina*, Consolidated U. of North Carolina, three smaller institutions, chairman; *Pennsylvania*, Pennsylvania State U.; *South Carolina*, U. of South Carolina and two smaller institutions, chairman,

contact with the workings of higher education has had both favorable and unfavorable results. Ex-officio membership has been denounced as a dangerous interference. It has been praised as a boon to the prestige and effectivness of the governing board. And it has been damned as a useless vestige of nineteenth-century governmental organization.

Ex-officio membership today is on the wane, and often as the result of a public reaction against the highhandedness of governors who were ex-officio members on university boards. Before World War II, twenty-four governors held ex-officio memberships on boards of higher education. Most were on only one board (as in Connecticut, Louisiana, or Arizona), but a few harried governors served on four, five, or even ten separate governing boards.[9] Then, in quick succession four states dropped their governors from all ex-officio memberships on educational governing boards.

Rhode Island started the movement in 1939 after a series of damaging encounters between the governor and the regular members of the Board of Regents of the (then) Rhode Island State College. A complete reorganization of the governing board removed the governor and four other state officials. This was done, as one college official said, "with the specific intent of taking the board out of politics."[10]

---

also member of two more small boards; *Tennessee,* U. of Tennessee, State Board of Education; *Vermont,* U. of Vermont; *Wyoming,* U. of Wyoming.

[9] John H. McNeely, "Governor as Member of Boards," *School Life,* XXV (1939), pp. 56, 64. The author wrote at the zenith of the period of ex-officio memberships. It was natural, then, that he should detect a "trend . . . recently developed among the States toward the centralization of authority over the various State governmental agencies in the governor as the State's supreme executive officer." He said that the governor, "because of enhanced authority and prestige is frequently enabled to exercise a strong influence over the board in the internal management and administration of the institutions. This is especially the case where the governor has been legally designated to serve ex-officio on the governing boards" (p. 56).

[10] Rhode Island, General Assembly, *Acts of 1939,* Ch. 688. For additional discussion of the situation in Rhode Island see pp. 39-40.

Arkansas followed in 1941 with a legislative act that fixed the number of board members and sharply rebuffed the governor in the actual wording of the bill. "It is hereby found and declared," stated the act, "that the Board of Trustees of the University of Arkansas should be free of political influence to the greatest extent possible, and to that end the Governor and the Superintendent of Public Instruction should not be members of said Board, ex officio or otherwise. . . ." [11] Behind the brusque language of the bill was a chronicle of gubernatorial hostility toward the university and a disruption of board proceedings by the ex-officio governors.[12] President John Clinton Futrall fought off several moves by the governor to have him fired. President (later United States Senator) J. W. Fulbright was less fortunate in his efforts, and he served only two years in the presidency before being fired by a board that was dominated by the governor. Then came the new law passed by an indignant legislature, and the next president, Dr. Arthur M. Harding, was spared the fate of his predecessors.

Mississippi in 1944 and then Georgia in 1945 amended their constitutions and excluded the governors from membership.[13] The Georgia constitutional amendment was the aftermath of the attempt of Governor Eugene Talmadge to remove Dean Walter Cocking from the faculty of the Univer-

[11] Arkansas, General Assembly, *Act 302*, Section 3, 1941.

[12] One year after the Arkansas legislature removed the governor from ex-officio membership, a constitutional amendment was proposed by petition and adopted by the voters. It wrote into the constitution the provisions of the law of 1941—a fixed number of ten trustees appointed by the governor and confirmed by the senate except where a member is appointed to fill an unexpired term. In the latter case the board members themselves confirm or reject the governor's appointee. The governor cannot remove a board member except for cause, and then only after a proper hearing on the charge and with the written approval of the remaining board members. Arkansas, *Constitution*, Amendment 33, 1942.

[13] Georgia, *Constitution*, Art. VIII, Sec. 4, par. 1.

sity of Georgia. The amendment's language was plainly pointed at Talmadge when it said, "The governor shall not be a member of said board."

While these four states were stripping their governors of ex-officio membership in higher education, one state, New Jersey, placed its governor on the board of trustees of Rutgers when the institution changed over fully from private to public status, leaving the balance in 1958 at twenty-one states with governors as ex-officio members.

As a practical matter, governors are not exceptionally active in board meetings in most of the states. Their crushing work load in other areas keeps them away from board meetings unless there is urgent business.[14] A few, however, take an aggressive and sometimes paternal interest in the affairs of the college or university, and an official in one state contended that "the governor completely dominates the board meetings."

Each governor who participates in governing board meetings has his own manner of operation, but the odds are that his role will be that of mediator and persuader. His political stature often helps him solve the dilemmas of divided governing boards. The board of Delaware State College, the predominantly Negro institution of the state, was locked in a controversy that threatened to undermine the already precarious position of the school. The head of the college's English Department, Dr. George Kent, had made statements

[14] Students of public administration have little affection for ex-officio memberships in any area of government. In the words of Leslie Lipson, "Such requirements that the governor himself directly participate in administrative minutiae are of manifest futility. They defeat their own ends. The governor has so much to do that he cannot give time to all the boards. If, however, he does attend, either he is frittering away his energy on henhouses and piggeries or he has to secure a majority vote on important matters by 'trading' with the other members. In neither case can there be effective over-all supervision of general administrative policy." *Op. cit.*, p. 37.

that convinced some members of the board that he should be fired from his post. Other members disagreed, and a four-to-four tie threw the board into stalemate. The president threatened to resign if the professor was not reinstated, and it was at this point that Governor Caleb Boggs moved into the picture to persuade the board members to reappoint the professor. The Governor was successful in his efforts, although two of the board members resigned in protest over the proceedings.[15]

How do educators and regular board members feel about the activities of governors as ex-officio members? The reaction is varied. It is by no means, however, entirely adverse to ex-officio membership. The president of one board saw lasting advantages:

> The advantage, as I see it, would be that some partici-
> pation in the activities of the board gives him an under-
> standing of the problems and plans of the body. Not the
> least of these is finance. While the legislature has the final
> say regarding money assigned to us, the governor presents
> our requests as a part of his total legislative budget re-
> quests. His approval or disapproval of our legislative ap-
> propriation request carries some weight, especially if he
> has any degree of control over the legislature. His influ-
> ence can be used also with regard to legislation affecting
> the colleges.[16]

Another board member has pointed out that a governor's ex-officio membership acquaints him with the kind of person he should appoint to the board. Board members also concede that the governor can help the board to see their problems within the context of the state's whole social and

[15] An extensive discussion of the Delaware State College upheaval is found in *Southern School News*, June, 1958.

[16] This quotation and the comments in the next paragraph are based on a committee survey of 300 governing board members.

economic condition, thereby averting a charge of narrow-mindedness on the part of the board.

Criticisms of the governor as an ex-officio member are equally pointed. A college official observed that the governor "often introduces purely political attitudes." The presence of governors is, to some board members, a constant source of intimidation; the prospect of voting on controversial issues in the presence of the man who appoints the membership is distasteful to some. And one educator who generally approves of ex-officio membership made this qualification:

> First, the governor is under terrific pressures and really has too little time to serve effectively. Secondly, governors are usually controversial figures. Some of them, naturally, until they become better informed, are apt to consider the institution as a place where political obligations can be paid.

But while there are governors who use ex-officio membership to their own advantage, a few governors have found such membership to be a political embarrassment. As Governor of California (1943–53), Earl Warren was an ex-officio member of the Board of Regents of the University of California when the regents were plunged into a controversy over a loyalty oath for faculty and employees of the university. Since Governor Warren had been present at board meetings when the fate of the faculty members was discussed, it was natural that newspapermen should question him vigorously about his own position on the delicate matter. And Governor Lane Dwinell of New Hampshire (1955–58), an ex-officio trustee of the university, was drawn into an acrimonious situation after a meeting of the trustees, at which he was present, voted to accept the AAUP Academic Freedom Award. This action of the university was highly unpopular with some conservative elements in the state. In both cases the governors were reluctantly pulled into controversies that involved internal policies of the institutions. But the newsworthy position of the governor on the board magnified the significance of the disputes and forced the governors to take stands on the issues involved.

ATTACK AND INTERFERENCE

Colleges seldom forget that the governor can, if he chooses, make life miserable for higher education by means of outright political attack. A number of reputable universities attest to the sting of the governor's whip, and in several instances, as in Utah, Iowa, or Kansas, the marks have taken long to heal. To some extent these political attacks are the price that public higher education must pay for state support, but in another sense the attacks are a tragic commentary on the destructive strength of irresponsible governors.

The motives are diverse in the instances of attack or interference. A governor may be anti-intellectual or may decide to remake higher education to his own liking. Huey Long (1928–31) certainly qualified on both these counts when he "took over" the state university in Louisiana. A governor may conscientiously feel that the only way to produce needed changes in educational policy is through open warfare. But there is evidence that many of the attacks can be traced back to the need for exciting political issues in listless gubernatorial races. One observer in Colorado has suggested that the two-year governor's term is especially responsible for the cases of interference in higher education. Governors barely enter office before they must start a new search for issues to carry them through the next campaign. Lacking material in other fields, the governors can usually find something to debate in higher education.

Perhaps more than any other state activity, higher education is especially vulnerable to ill-advised broadsides from the state capitol. One governor, seeking to impress constituents about his concern for economy, publicly ridiculed the expenditure of university funds for a rare book. An attempt at reasoned explanation by the university president could not offset the harm brought by this ridicule. The scars left by the incident have greatly embittered college officials.

One governor of a midwestern state has cast himself as the enemy of the existing order in higher education. There is, to be sure, disagreement about his motives. The injured parties regard his actions as a desperate attempt to find political issues for future campaigns. The governor contends that the only way to change the policies of the board of trustees and the administration is to attack them dramatically in the press. The result has been a precipitous decline in good relations between the statehouse and the campus. Ironically enough the governor has launched his war against the colleges in the name of "getting the colleges out of politics." Casting college officials as villains, the governor has insisted that he is "battling off a bunch of politicians" who are trying to build vast educational empires for their own glory. He has publicly scoffed at their building programs, the competence of their professors, and the integrity of the college presidents and leading administrators. He regards it as foolish that the educational institutions should carry on any research. "Why," he asked an interviewer, "should research be tied to sorority rushing and all that goes with it? A university's main job is to teach, and I am in favor of restricting their work to nothing but teaching."

Governor Bracken Lee of Utah (1949–57) became well known in the state for his vitriolic attacks on the University of Utah. He was matched by the late Governor William Beardsley of Iowa (1949–54), who frequently assaulted institutions of higher education during his term of office. In these cases the governors were convinced that they had legitimate complaints against higher education, but chose to stage a public, political fight rather than to work quietly behind the scenes. And in each instance the colleges involved in the controversy were implacably convinced that the governor had no constructive motive whatever, only political gain or vengeance.

Another category of gubernatorial action concerns not so much outright attack on the university, but simply interference in the internal policies of the institutions. Again, it is a happy fact that most governors tend to stay out of the internal affairs of higher education. There are, however, examples such as a Georgia governor's telegram to the university regents "requesting" that the regents refuse to allow racially mixed football contests, with obvious reference to a pending contest between the University of Georgia and the University of Pittsburgh in the Sugar Bowl.

There is yet another problem in the annals of interference, one that by its nature eludes documentation. For the instances of direct interference that are known to the public are only the fraction that appears above the surface. Beneath is a considerably larger portion of undetected but nevertheless real involvement of the governor in higher education. This is the subtle side of control, the covert activity of governors (and most certainly other officials of state government, including legislators) in shaping the policies of higher education. The problem of verification here is almost insurmountable, since telephone calls, casual conversation, or destroyed letters leave few benchmarks for the person who seeks to document the rumors about interference that circulate around every campus.

Some of these stories concern faculty members who have been denied raises or promotions because they have antagonized governors who control or strongly influence the board of trustees. A midwestern governor reportedly named his political favorites to administrative jobs on the state college campuses. An official of a state university reported that a governor had baldly offered to construct two and one-half million dollars worth of new buildings on the university campus if the official would appoint the governor's choice to a deanship. The president rejected the request, and lost the dormitories, though it is said that smaller schools in the state accepted such offers with alacrity.

The list of off-the-record pressures is a long one. Among the stories there are doubtlessly falsifications or gross exaggerations. There are also valid accounts of intrusion. But these stories have a way of influencing the minds of leaders, regardless of the truth or falsity of the statements. Staff interviewers visited several states in which both state and educational officials were extremely jittery about unseen pressures and hidden controls. In almost every instance there was reference to a story, admittedly not subject to proof, about a serious interference in higher education. The apprehension of future disturbances is enough to color the attitudes of college administrators, and a long time is required to rebuild the mutual trust that can easily be shattered by undercover political maneuvers.

## GUBERNATORIAL LEADERSHIP AND CONCERN

It would be a distortion to close any review of the personal relation between governors and higher education without emphasizing once again the amicable and creative work of most governors in improving higher education in their states. No better index of the genuine concern of governors can be found than in the record of the Governors' Conference of 1956. There, in a round-table discussion, governors from all parts of the country pooled their ideas and their problems in the field of higher education.

Governor Boggs of Delaware (1953–), for example, stressed the crucial importance of higher education. "I am proud," he said, "that our state has been making considerable progress in meeting these very important responsibilities. I believe our people recognize that expenditures for education are, in fact, a sound investment for the people and the state, as well as the future of our nation." And New Jersey's Governor Meyner 1954–), expressing great concern for the future of higher education, exhorted his colleagues to be leaders in carrying to the people the urgent need for an expanded program of higher education.[17]

Governors are divided on the issue of proper controls over higher education just as they are diverse in their political views. Some, for example governors Simpson of Wyoming (1955–58) and O'Neill of Ohio (1957–58), strongly favor maintaining a high degree of independence for all areas of higher education. Others—and here could be named governors Docking of Kansas (1957–), Anderson of Nebraska (1957–58), and Russell of Nevada (1951–58)—are convinced that the future must bring tighter fiscal controls over the public colleges and universities.

Time and again in personal interviews with the staff, governors throughout the nation repeated their devotion to the improvement of higher education. While they might in certain instances disagree with college administrators about the controls that should be placed over funds and personnel, most governors are aware of the pressing needs of higher education and are determined to fulfill those needs. Good sense conspires with good politics to put most governors on record as friends of the schools.

[17] *Proceedings of the Governors' Conference,* 1956 (Chicago: The Governors' Conference, 1956), pp. 44-80.

## THE GOVERNOR'S STAFF

The executive office is never a one-man show. Whether he is assisted by a single professional aide and a couple of secretaries (as he is in several of the western states) or by a company of over forty assistants (as in New York and California), the governor's personal staff makes decisions and enforces policies that touch—sometimes heavily—upon higher education. The governor's office in Wisconsin, standing midway between the largest and the one-man secretariats, typifies a staff in operation.

One component of the Wisconsin governor's staff is a Research Bureau, outwardly a group that studies various state problems and makes recommendations to the governor. But the Wisconsin Research Bureau has played a more imposing part in the affairs of government than its name implies. One governor who was at odds with the state purchasing department turned the Research Bureau into an extra-legal purchasing office that approved requisitions and did most of the work in making the state's purchases. As the personal agent of the governor, the Research Bureau has conducted investigations of state fiscal activities, including an investigation of purchasing procedures at the University of Wisconsin. Up to the present time, however, the Research Bureau has never attempted to use its close ties to the governor or its investigatory power to harass academic officials.[18]

18 In an increasing number of states the college campus is becoming a manpower pool for governors and other top executive officials. The administrative assistants to several governors were associated with state universities before they moved to the statehouse. The states are especially inclined to borrow professors of economics, political science, and business to conduct studies of state problems. Professors at the University of Kansas, for example, have made studies of most of the governmental functions of Kansas, and many of their recommendations have been adopted. The growing emphasis on professional assistance in state affairs may serve to draw the university and the government closer together as they consider mutual problems.

Wisconsin is one of several states that require the governor to approve out-of-state travel by state employees. This familiar requirement, one of the perennial headaches of college presidents, has been a nuisance to the governors, and most are glad to delegate the job to one of their personal staff. Consider the incongruous position of a governor of New Mexico being required to pass on the application of a professor to present a paper in St. Louis on the "Homing Habits of Ants in the Sandia Mountains"! The governor's administrative assistant takes this responsibility in Wisconsin, although his decisions are always subject to reversal by the governor. To the relief of college officials, a professor's request for travel is rarely denied by gubernatorial decision.

In nearly every state, the governor's professional assistants have much more to do with higher education than their formal responsibilities indicate. The administrative assistant serves as a contact and idea man for the governor. When college presidents need to discuss educational matters with the governor, they ordinarily take up the matter first with the administrative assistant, who relays the information to the governor or else arranges an appointment. The administrative assistant often drafts the governor's budget message, and it is likely that the assistant's own views of the needs of higher education will influence the governor's final decisions on the educational budget. And in a score of other ways—advising on regent's appointments, keeping the governor briefed on educational activities, or making decisions on fiscal policies— the administrative assistant and other members of the governor's staff serve as *alter ego* for the governor in his association with the colleges and universities of the state.

One potentially sinister activity of the governor's staff is dramatized by a recent incident in a southern state. A member of the governor's personal staff paid a clandestine visit to a college campus to investigate a professor whose political views were under suspicion of the governor. The aide was known to be on the campus for two days, checking anonymously with students about the professional competence of the professor. Faculty members and college officials were puzzled if not deeply disturbed by the stealthy movements of the governor's assistant, but no protest was made. The practice of using a personal aide as an uninvited detective on the college campus has not been duplicated in other states, but it does suggest that a governor's staff may be used far beyond the bounds of ordinary administrative assistance.

*Summary*

The association between a governor and higher education in large measure is dictated by law. Most governors are officially responsible for the higher education budget and the appointment of regents. Some governors serve ex officio on governing boards. But beyond and above the law, the high political position of the governor enables him to wedge himself deeply into the affairs of higher education.

Although the states assign dissimilar fiscal and appointive powers to their chief executives, most governors are in a position to make crucial decisions affecting the budgets of higher education. Yet despite their authority in fiscal regulation, governors generally use great discretion in evaluating the judgments of competent educators. Not only does a governor's administrative burden require him to leave detailed decisions to college heads (there are exceptions), but most governors regard it as political wisdom to avoid an excessive concern with the minor fiscal details of higher education.

The governor's authority to appoint regents, while seldom abused, has led a few governors to attempt to take over governing boards by packing them with loyal partisans. A certain

identity of interests between a governor and his appointees
normally leads to a measure of influence by the governor.
However, board appointees often tend to identify more
closely with the institution than with the governor who appointed them to office.

As ex-officio board members in twenty-one states, governors
are in a position to exercise close personal influence over
the affairs of governing boards. In scattered states and at different times, governors have taken their ex-officio membership as a signal to dominate the work of governing boards.
The results have nearly always been regrettable, both for
the governor and the institution. In the process of reorganizing higher education since 1939, four states have deliberately
removed the governor from ex-officio membership. Yet while
the presence of a governor on a board may tend to intimidate
or disturb other regents, a number of governing board members see definite advantages in having a governor on their
board—the added prestige, the chance for a governor to fa-
miliarize himself with the school's needs, and the prospect
of more favorable treatment in the legislature.

The governor is a political figure—inevitably so—and his
job brings him into daily contact with the political affairs of
higher education. It may be a hurried conference to settle a
personal fight between a college president and a state budget
officer. A constituent may seek the governor's influence for
a campus appointment. And few governors can escape the
pressures of alumni, legislators, and loyal fans to get something done about the coach of state U's slumping football
team.

In a more serious vein, the governor is in a position to
alter profoundly the academic destiny of public colleges and
universities. There are records of violent public attacks by
governors that have harmed higher education greatly. Other
pressures from the governor are covert and undocumented—

an unwritten instruction to a governing board, an informal veto on the choice of a new college president—and they serve to create an atmosphere of distrust and even fear among college administrators.

But with exceptions, most governors in recent decades have fought to improve higher education, and at the same time have refrained from becoming too involved in the internal affairs of the schools. Dozens of forward-looking governors have made it a cardinal rule to let colleges operate without political pressure, although they may permit their executive agencies to exercise firm administrative controls over the colleges. Many governors have allied themselves with higher education to win larger appropriations, even in the face of public resistance to increased expenditures.

Finally, the governor's personal staff serves as a link between a governor and higher education. Empowered to conduct investigations and research, staff assistants can visibly influence educational policies. A governor's aides often are given responsibilities that officially belong to the governor, as in several states that require the governor to approve out-of-state travel. And the administrative assistant to the governor, with his authority to schedule talks with the governor, to prepare policy statements, and even to recommend appointees to governing boards, may make vital decisions for the governor in his dealings with the colleges.

CHAPTER XI

# Legislators and
# legislative committees

FOR MORE THAN three-hundred years American legislatures
have been vitally concerned with the promotion of higher
learning. As far back as 1636, the General Court of Massachusetts Bay Colony established Harvard College and granted
funds, including the proceeds of public lotteries, for the support of the college.[1] Since that time the ebb and flow of
legislative interest in higher education has varied, but over
the years legislatures have consistently demonstrated an abiding awareness of the importance of colleges and universities
to the life of the community.

The rising tide of college enrollments that overtook the
colleges during the 1947–50 veterans boom intensified leg-

[1] Elmer Ellsworth Brown, *The Origins of American State Universities*
(Berkeley: University of California Press, 1903), p. 31.

islative interest, and the current upsurge in enrollments, reflecting the accelerated birth rate of the war years, promises to accentuate this interest still further.[2]

Today not only are more young people reaching college age but also a substantially larger proportion of them are demanding admittance to our colleges and universities. Under these circumstances, along with the fact that in the past twenty-five years the size of funds given by states to higher education has increased by more than 800 per cent— $1,958,000,000 [3]—the reasons behind a sharpening legislative interest in higher learning are evident. Moreover, legislators who are according higher learning a leading position are encouraged in this by the weight of public opinion. For the public today is insistent upon extending opportunities at the collegiate level for the youth of the nation.

While the interest of legislators in the problem of higher education is applauded by college officials, it must be said that educators are apprehensive where this concern has spread into internal policy areas traditionally regarded as the responsibility of the university. There is, of course, virtually unanimous agreement that politics has no place in educational policy. But the definition of internal educational policy is often a subject of disagreement between educators and legislators. In addition, there is dispute over the extent to which an institution of higher education should be responsive to the immediate will of the public as expressed through the legislature. A state educational institution is publicly supported, but as an instrument of innovation the university

2 Howard A. Boozer, "A Limited Review of Institutional Planning for the Future" (unpublished staff study, American Council on Education, 1955).

3 It should be noted, however, that current operation cost per student in state institutions, when expressed in constant 1947 dollars, dropped 13.1 per cent between 1952 and 1957. Council of State Governments, *Statistics on Expenditure, Enrollment, and Capital Outlay in State Supported Institutions of Higher Education* (Chicago: Council of State Governments, 1958).

FIGURE 3

# U.S. college age population and public
# and private enrollment: 1900–1958

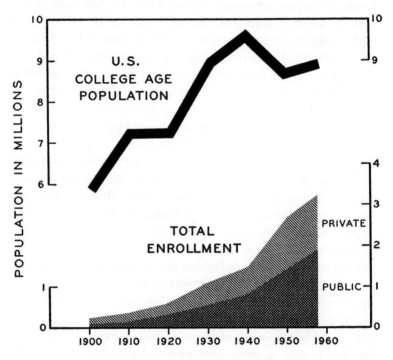

*Sources:* U. S. Office of Education, *Statistics of Higher Education, Faculty, Students, and Degrees,* 1953-54; U. S. Bureau of the Census, *Current Population Reports,* Series P-20, No. 89, Series P-25, No. 193 (Washington: U. S. Government Printing Office). Percentage of public and private enrollments for 1958 based on opening fall enrollments, 1957.

must be something more than a mirror for the prevailing interests of society.

It is within the limitations of public resources and public policy, then, that the university and the legislature must seek agreement on the division of their responsibilities. No easy guidelines can be suggested for the division, but a discussion of specific cases will show some of the major points of friction that have appeared in recent years.

In 1955, the legislature of Mississippi adopted this concurrent resolution:

> . . . it is the consensus of the Legislature of the State of Mississippi that individuals who are members, or endorse the theories, of organizations dedicated to the overthrow of our way of life and the spirit and intent of the laws of the State of Mississippi should not be invited to address audiences at any State Supported Institution in Mississippi; and
>
> BE IT FURTHER RESOLVED, That the governing authorities of our State Supported Institutions are urged to carefully investigate and consider the background and character of persons proposed as speakers to audiences at such Institutions, and to use caution and discretion in extending invitations to speakers and to refrain from extending such invitations when the investigation discloses the probability of the proposed speaker's endorsing such alien theories. . . .[4]

In reality, the governing board of the Mississippi colleges had established a "screening rule" of its own only a few days before the adoption of the legislative resolution. Both actions were sparked by a visiting speaker on one campus who had expounded pacifistic views. There was widespread agitation in the legislature, and the governing board, perhaps hoping to avert more drastic legislative interference, stipulated that:

> All speakers invited to the campus of the State Institutions of Higher Learning must first be investigated and

[4] Mississippi, *Laws of 1955*, Chap. 155, Senate Concurrent Resolution, No. 6.

approved by the head of the institution involved and when invited the names of such speakers must be filed with the Executive Secretary of the Board of Trustees.[5]

With this language, the board of trustees assigned responsibility for speakers to the heads of each educational institution. In practice, the screening of speakers in Mississippi has been a relatively calm procedure, with only a handful of rejections—usually on grounds that the speakers were "too controversial" and would "cause more harm than good." The fact of the matter is that most interested parties, including the faculty and administration of the colleges, are at least in passive accord with the idea behind the screening process, which is to "avoid controversy" on subjects such as integration, pacifism, unions, and socialism. The Mississippi legislature, in fact, publicly commended two of the leading institutions for their "actions in safeguarding our culture and traditions from vicious attacks and influences contrary to the beliefs of the people of Mississippi and the South." [6]

Yet the very ease with which the Mississippi "censorship" resolution has been handled is a commentary on the integral connection between political power and internal academic affairs. What the Mississippi case suggests is that the pressures from legislatures are by no means limited to the formal language of the law. Despite the legal independence of Mississippi's colleges and universities, they have had to conform, at least superficially, to the political forces of the state, particularly as expressed through the legislature.

Many legislators take the view that higher education should not enter areas disapproved by the legislature. In many areas of the South, this would mean that no one should

5 Mississippi Board of Trustees of Institutions of Higher Learning, Resolution adopted February 17, 1955.

6 Mississippi, *Laws of 1956*, Chap. 441, House Concurrent Resolution No. 21.

advocate integration or perhaps even teach its implications on a public college campus. There is little doubt that repercussions would follow any such attempt, and many conscientious and fair-minded educators have chosen to compromise on the integration issue in order to make the most of academic freedom in other intellectual areas.

The academic point of view, of course, is strongly in opposition to the idea that legislatures should approve topics of education. The great lesson of the free academic tradition is that higher education must be free to roam the avenues of knowledge without the guidance of preconceived political dogma. And yet the fact remains that public higher education cannot easily defy the power represented in a state legislature. As long as legislators feel that they should dictate, by law or by innuendo, the form and substance of higher education, colleges and universities will have the shadow of political interference over their campuses. The question is whether a free system of higher education can exist under such circumstances. The answer depends largely on the spirit and dedication of educators who work within the political system.

It should be noted that the case of the Mississippi legislature indicates the farthest extent of contemporary legislative involvement in educational affairs, and in this sense is atypical. Seldom do state legislatures ferret into policies that are generally conceded to be internal responsibilities of the universities—selection of faculty members, choice of texts, and content of courses. Nor are recent cases of legislative interference confined to the Southern states where integration is a major issue. On the contrary, as later pages will show, other areas of the country have their full share of legislative problems.

THE POLITICS OF APPROPRIATIONS

The primacy of politics in legislative-campus relationships is most convincingly illustrated through the appropriation process. Basically, of course, appropriating funds is a matter of resource allocation, and the distribution of these funds by the legislature is a necessary part of the democratic process. In theory at least, the legislative allocation of funds is to be decided upon some rational calculation of need. But here lurks one of the most persistent difficulties in educational-legislative relations.

For the legislator the merit of a proposal on higher education tends to rest upon the kind of education people of a community demand. For the university administrator, educational policy must be tested by the technical feasibility of a program and its relation to the over-all educational pattern the institution is seeking to develop. While educators are sensitive to community demand, they are required to look beyond immediate necessities to the broader demands of science and the humanities.

Certainly this distinction between what might be called the realm of public policy and the sphere of professional competence is one of the vaguest and most ill-defined lines of demarcation existing in government. Making this distinction in university-legislative relations has been a problem in curriculum requirements, tuition and admissions policy, research programs, and other matters of educational policy. It was with this conflict in mind that the *Shreveport Times* recently called upon the Louisiana legislature to refrain from dictating curriculum, which it said was the proper function of university personnel.[7]

[7] February 16, 1958.

## CURRICULA

Curriculum requirements comprise one of the oldest forms of legislative influence in educational policy, with common examples being statutory requirements for courses in American government, American history, or courses reflecting regional influence (such as Scandinavian). Typical of this legislative practice is the following provision of Florida law:

> The board of control and the president of the university of Florida, and the president of the Florida state university, are authorized and directed to provide for a chair of Americanism and southern history at the university of Florida, and at the Florida state university; and to establish and maintain a professorship in each of said colleges for courses of lectures on American ideals, American government, American institutions, and American citizenship.[8]

Except where efforts are made to prevent duplication of courses, provisions of this kind are ordinarily positive rather than negative, that is to say they enjoin upon the university the duty of teaching a designated course, rather than prohibiting it from giving instruction in any particular area. One authority in the field of civil liberties, Robert E. Cushman, has pointed out that "these are positive requirements rather than restraints. There can be no objection to them except as they require some special indoctrination."[9]

Of course some tinkering with the curriculum is to be expected in a democratic community. But it is also worth noting that, carried too far in response to pressures from organized groups, this legislative practice of specifying the course to be taught can easily lead to imbalance in the educational curriculum. The chairman of the political science

8 Florida, *Statutes* (1957), Chap. 239, sec. 6.
9 Robert E. Cushman, *Civil Liberties in the United States* (Ithaca, New York: Cornell University Press, 1956), p. 75.

department at one state university complained that a student seeking admission to his department had, as a result of his travels, taken three required courses in the local government of individual states but had never been asked to take a general course in American national government. New York legislators were put under heavy pressure in 1958 to establish a course on "The Therapy of Bereavement." And in California a bill was finally defeated that would require each state college to give a course in embalming.

It should be added, however, that universities themselves are far from faultless in the matter of compulsory curriculum requirements. Actually a large share of the statutes affecting curriculum have come about as a result of pressure on the legislature from various departmental officials within universities.

## RESEARCH

As far as research is concerned, legislators themselves acknowledge the existence of an enclave of independence for educational administration where the legislature should not encroach. Chairmen of ways and means committees, members of budget and finance committees, as well as speakers of the house, have spoken out repeatedly in favor of as much discretion as possible for the schools in handling of research funds. Yet in spite of such disclaimers, legislatures frequently affect the direction of research by running special independent projects through the appropriation process.

The earmarking of funds for the support of a particular kind of inquiry provides an almost irresistible inducement for universities to channel research in specified directions. Illustrations of this practice abound. The Illinois legislature at a recent session appropriated $5,000 to the university to carry out research on horse-radishes, an act of generosity that stemmed in good part from a plague of horse-radish disease in the southern part of Illinois. And top administrative officials at the University of Michigan were surprised to discover after a recent session of their legislature that they had been awarded a grant of $12,500 for research in cystic fibrosis at the medical school.

Earmarking appropriations for special university research projects is extensively practiced in California. Prominent examples are appropriations for smog control, eradication of fruit flies, and distillation of sea water. That each of these subjects is a matter of compelling public interest is commonly acknowledged. But educators note nonetheless that loading a cargo of responsibilities upon a university without prior inquiry into its ability to move into such specialized areas, or without attempting to see if some projects are more suitable for commercial laboratories, is apt to distort the over-all educational program.

Heavy research obligations assumed by some universities have already stirred up professional concern for educational programs. And occasionally legislative directives that strike without warning produce something of a crisis in legislative-campus relations. This happened in California after World War II when the president of the university received a call from Sacramento that the legislature had appropriated funds for the immediate establishment of a School of Engineering at UCLA. This project had not been requested by the Board of Regents and university officials; the university maintained it was not prepared to assume such an obligation; and the trustees refused to accept the appropriation. (It will be recalled that California is one of six states in which universities have been granted constitutional autonomy.)

Legislators contend—quite properly—that many of these directives for specialized research or even the establishment of entire schools for teaching and research, have come about in response to prodding by constituents. And as is the case with curriculum requirements, some individuals and groups perched within the ivory tower are not at all loath to seek legislative help in fulfilling their own ambitions for jurisdiction over a research program. This can pose an acute problem in a state in which there are two or more large universities jockeying for academic preeminence. Legislative help may even be sought to give one university a monopoly on research in a particular area. The legislature may thus be forced into mediating between rival claims, in much the same way as Pope Alexander VI was once drawn into the position of dividing the pagan world between the Spanish and the Portuguese. The world of atomic energy today seems ripe for similar partition, for legislation recently enacted in Florida states that "the intent of the legislature is to concentrate applied research at the University of Florida and basic research at Florida State University, except as the Board of Control may permit non-duplicating applied research at Florida State University." [10]

Yet the issue is not one easily resolved. Should the pressure of constituent demands be the sole criterion for determining the university program? Is legislative prescription of special schools, required courses, or specific research projects, an intrusion upon professional educational judgment—judgment that should be made by the governing board of trustees? Among educators the preponderant answer would be a loud "yes."

Admittedly, say the educators, large-scale operations calling for a long-range commitment of state support should be subject to approval by the representative assembly. But the initiation of these projects, they insist, should reside with

[10] See U. S. Office of Education, *Survey of State Legislation Relating to Higher Education*, July 1, 1956 to June 30, 1957 (Washington: U. S. Government Printing Office, 1957), p. 28.

those responsible for the educational program. The alternative is an erratic research program shaped by political pressure rather than a disinterested calculation as to where research is most needed.

TUITION AND ADMISSIONS

Less overt in operation but formidable nonetheless in appropriation matters is the implied threat of legislators to reduce funds unless there is university compliance with particular conditions. Recently this has been increasingly noticeable in setting tuition rates.

In addition to explicit statutory instructions in New Hampshire, the legislatures in Colorado, Connecticut, Iowa, Indiana, Michigan, and Nebraska all served notice on their state universities that unless tuition rates were voluntarily stepped up by the institutions themselves, these rates would either be raised by law or else appropriations would subsequently be reduced.

The Colorado General Assembly in its 1957 general session deducted $175,000 from the university's budget request as the amount which it estimated could "be raised by an increase of $10.00 per year in resident tuition and $25.00 per year in nonresident tuition at the Boulder Campus, plus a small increase in fees for the summer schools." [11]

Some tuition fees, of course, have not kept pace with the inflation of the dollar, and universities have been slow to

11 See Colorado, General Assembly, Joint Sub-Committee on Appropriations, *Report on the General Appropriation Act, House Bill No. 455,* March 1957. The University is not, of course, legally bound to follow legislative instructions in this regard, especially since they are embodied in a committee report rather than ordinary statute. But they are delivered with telling political impact, in view of the leverage the legislature can muster in matters of appropriations. At its last regular session, the Michigan legislature also brought pressure to bear upon the two major state universities to raise tuition fees by 25 per cent.

revise their charges. It was only after a long battle that the Texas legislature raised tuition in Texas colleges from $25.00 —a depression figure—to $50.00 a semester.

The portion of the educational budget derived from tuition is a subject of legitimate legislative interest. At the same time, educators point out that setting tuition rates solely on a financial basis may undercut the distinctive responsibility of public higher education to make available low-cost education to all citizens of the state. Clearly the maintenance of opportunity for the poor but gifted student is an important staple for the success of public higher education. Thus, legislators must constantly balance the need to put higher education on a financially sound basis with the need to keep open channels of educational opportunity in our society.

In some states the policies and practices followed by the schools with regard to admissions has also been subject to legislative regulation. A statute enacted at the 1957 session of the Arkansas legislature "provides for the selection of 90 freshmen medical students annually, or 120 annually by 1959, by competitive procedures, allocated proportionally by Congressional districts, with priority within each district being given to applicants from counties of low population who intend to practice medicine in communities of 2,000 people or less. [It] also provides that the stipulations regarding the future admission of students in excess of 90 may be disregarded if the accreditation of the School of Medicine would be endangered." [12] While admitting the right of the legislature to concern itself with such matters as the availability of medical care in rural areas within the state, college officials at the University of Arkansas object to this provision on the grounds that it tends to lower standards by basing the admission of students on factors other than academic ability.

[12] U. S. Office of Education, *op. cit.*, p. 9.

## APPROPRIATIONS ACTS

Formal appropriation acts may themselves represent varying degrees of fiscal oversight. In some states such as Maine, the single-line, lump-sum grant is used in appropriating funds for support of the state university. In this way, the Maine legislature restricts itself to providing what in its judgment is an equitable allocation of public resources for the university's maintenance, and through the size of the grant sets the general limits for the higher education program.

More extensive controls follow, of course, where appropriations are broken down into general classes of expenditure, as personal services, supplies, and equipment. This method, now practiced in Connecticut, Delaware, West Virginia, and Wisconsin, not only allows legislators to set the general limits of the educational program, but also to designate limits on the methods to be employed in achieving the over-all program. It is at this stage of appropriation control that the line between public policy and educational administration again becomes blurred.

Elsewhere, at the other extreme of appropriation control, lie the detailed line-item accounts. Southern Illinois University has received an appropriation that specified an item for stationery and office supplies; while in New Jersey the legislature made specific appropriations to its institutions of higher education for travel, telephone and telegraph, and postage.

## THE HIDDEN PERSUADER

Some of the more stringent detailed controls exercised by the legislature over the colleges are unknown to the public, one reason being that the degree of control does not always appear on public budget documents or in appropriation acts.

Sometimes fiscal controls are exercised through itemized schedules on file with appropriations committees or budget staffs.

Detailed schedules on file with the Ways and Means Committee of the Massachusetts General Court are considered binding by the State Budget Director, even though this degree of itemization does not appear in the formal appropriations act. And until recently subcommittees of the Oregon Joint Ways and Means Committee sent memoranda to the full Committee covering their understanding of the way in which funds would be spent, with copies going to the fiscal control agencies of the executive branch and to the operating institutions. While these memos had no legal force, of course, they were regarded as formidable instruments of control by the agencies concerned.

Recently the Oregon attorney-general invalidated the off-the-record attempt of the Joint Ways and Means Committee to set an arbitrary limit of one-thousand students at Oregon Technical Institute. *The* (Portland) *Oregonian,* in an editorial approving the attorney-general's action, welcomed "some desirable light on an undesirable legislative practice."

> It is a general—and objectionable—practice of legislative bodies . . . to seek to extend their influence into executive departments by committee edict. The committee charged with studying appropriation measures—the joint Ways and Means Committee in the specific instance of the Oregon Legislature—often gives its approval to bills with invisible strings attached. These halters take the form of admonitions to executive agencies to follow committee desires in applying the appropriation—or else. Such injunctions have no force in law . . . but they are normally effective.[13]

13 *The* (Portland) *Oregonian,* September 5, 1958.

LEGISLATIVE RIDERS

Whether appropriations are made in lump sum or by line item, vexing problems still arise for institutions of higher education from the use of legislative riders. One relatively trivial example occurred recently in Texas. Here a legislative rider forbade college presidents from traveling to the state capitol (Austin) at state expense during sessions of the legislature. The ostensible purpose of this rider was to prevent presidents from doing a little in-fighting for their colleges in the legislative corridors. Unhappily, however, this restriction declaring the capitol out of bounds failed to recognize that college presidents might have real need to be in Austin for educational conferences or equally important non-legislative work. Also troublesome in the same state was a rider so vaguely worded in defining travel allowances that a great deal of uncertainty and disallowance of expenses resulted.

Riders frequently regulate admission policy, as for example an Oklahoma statute of 1955 stipulating that one-hundred students per year be the minimum admitted to the entering class in the University of Oklahoma Medical School. Legislative riders are also used in some cases to declare certain subjects out of bounds for university research. This intent is well illustrated by the Florida legislative rider to a general university appropriation act which provided that no part of the appropriation could be used by the Marine Laboratory to study Red Tide, the marine organism that has been killing large numbers of fish off the Florida coasts in recent years. Presumably one of the motives behind this rider was to prevent some duplication in this field of research by another school, but it has also been suggested by one long-time member of the Florida senate that an important factor underlying this rider was the lobbying activity of certain firms which were pumping industrial wastes into the sea.

Like ordinary legislative restrictions, the legislative rider can harry administrative policy at several points, and it is often the source of complaints. A rider to the general appropriation act of Texas in 1957 prevented all agencies for which appropriations are made from accepting the donation of real property or from spending any appropriated moneys for the purchase of real property without specific authorization from the legislature. This restriction presented a serious problem to the University of Texas Institute of Marine Science, located on the Gulf coast. The institute, badly in need of a new dock, was blocked from accepting a gift of land for this purpose by the legislative rider. Moreover, it was stopped from buying the land (by this time the owner, still undaunted, offered to sell it or lease it for a dollar) and the institute was finally compelled to spend $1,500 to rebuild the old dock. Since the cost had to be amortized in rental payments, this also raised the cost from $30 to $75 per month.

To restrain what legislators consider to be educational expansionist tendencies, the rider is frequently invoked. In New Mexico the legislature attached a rider to an appropriation act that forbade the installation of any new graduate program without express consent from the central Board of Educational Finance. Here the intent was to discourage unnecessary duplication of high cost-per-student graduate projects.

## THE CONSEQUENCES OF DETAILED CONTROL

College administrators cannot, of course, question the right of a representative body to make basic policy decisions in higher education as in other areas of state activity. Nor do they dispute the fact that legislatures are acting within their proper authority in exercising general oversight over the administration of colleges and universities. And yet it is felt that a legislature defeats its own purposes when it constantly makes detailed judgments on matters of curriculum and research, freezes into statutes admissions policy and other matters requiring flexibility, or sets up a multiplicity of watchdog agencies to insure the honesty and legality of all administrative transactions.

There are several snares to the practice of having the legislature single out small portions of an institutional program for special attention. Whether it comes about by reason of widespread public demand or special group pressures, the special listing always involves some hazards to the quality of educational standards. It may distort the balance and breadth of approach needed for careful programming in higher education or it may perpetuate certain activities far beyond the period of efficient academic usefulness. And it may involve institutions of higher education in functions which are essentially commercial rather than educational.

Highly doubtful also, is the wisdom of compelling administrators, operating in the changing environment that confronts higher education today, to be bound by itemized details forecast two to four years in advance of events. Most budget systems, of course, do allow transfers for contingency spending. But the involved cycle of winning approval, plus the tendency of fiscal officers to interpret appropriations literally, are trying impediments to educational administration. Only the most evangelical believer in planning would commit himself to details in appropriations for several years in advance, yet rigidly enforced details of appropriations to public universities are based, essentially, upon just such expectations.

This all-embracing kind of supervision is regarded as a perfect recipe for institutional mediocrity in the field of

276 THE CAMPUS AND THE STATE

higher education, or indeed in any other area of state administration. It is the view of college officials that competent and
imaginative personnel will never be attracted to serve in an
institution run by remote control from a state bureaucracy,
and that the prevailing climate of administrative caution and
academic inertia which excessive surveillance breeds is almost certain to provide the state with second-rate institutions
of higher education.

Colleges themselves are not faultless, however—far from it.
Colleges and universities have on some occasions been slow
or reluctant to enter a field where there is a legitimate demand for their services (social work is an example), or they
have embarked upon programs where there are conflicting
interests with commercial groups. What this suggests is that
educators must continually reassess their policies and programs in the light of shifting public requirements and educational objectives. As M. M. Chambers observed in a letter
to the Committee, "A university should not be dictated by
considerations of immediacy; but neither should it be blind
and deaf to emergencies."

At the moment, however, there seems little danger of extended delinquency in the matter of being sufficiently responsive to public needs. In general, the public universities
are more likely to be criticized for being overzealous in
catering to community fads.[14] Not only have they been censured for undertaking programs that strike some as subvert-
ing the true mission of higher learning—basketweaving, ball-
room dancing, or courses in social adjustment—but they have
also been criticized for competing with each other in this

[14] For criticism by educators, themselves, see Abraham Flexner, *Universities:
American, English, German* (New York: Oxford University Press, 1930); Nor-
man Foerester, *The American State University, Its Relation to Democracy,*
(Chapel Hill: The University of North Carolina Press, 1937); Robert Hutchins,
*The Higher Learning in America* (New Haven: Yale University Press, 1936).

type of empire building. Typical of this complaint is the admission Michigan legislators drew from university authorities during appropriations committee hearings in the spring of 1958 that there is duplication of extension work and that the University of Michigan and Michigan State University have "side by side services in some communities." [15]

## LEGISLATIVE ORGANIZATION

Certainly one factor among the disruptive elements that mar legislative-campus relations is the ponderously inefficient patchwork of legislative organization. For some time the excessive increase in legislative committees has disturbed students of state government.[16]

State senates average 25 and lower houses average 32 standing committees. And these figures do not, of course, include special or interim units. California, for example, between 1937 and 1947 set up 326 interim committees; and in 1947, alone, it set up 93.[17] The 46 legislatures in session in 1955 created a total of 454 interim committees, or an increase of nearly 100 over the 1953 record. Leading the parade, California established 102, New York 44, and Massachusetts 34.

Beyond the multiplication of committees functioning with markedly different degrees of effectiveness, legislators have also sought aid through other auxiliary agencies. The resulting legislative assistance services include bill-drafting services, reference bureaus, legislative councils, research committees,

15 *Detroit Free Press*, March 26, 1958. Although two or more schools were offering courses in the same town, their courses did not duplicate each other.

16 E.g., Belle Zeller, ed., *American State Legislatures* (New York: Cromwell, 1954); Council of State Governments, *Our State Legislatures* (rev. ed., Chicago: Council of State Governments, 1948).

17 Of the 326 interim committees only 194 produced reports of public record. Lawrence W. O'Rourke, *Legislative Assistance* (Los Angeles: University of California, Bureau of Governmental Research, 1951), pp. 22–25.

278 THE CAMPUS AND THE STATE

statutory revision committees, budget analysts, and legislative auditors.[18]

"Legislative service agencies," writes a student of these units, "have developed far beyond their original conception, evolving from giving technical and informational aid to providing assistance on basic policies and continuous review of government programs." [19]

The Nevada Legislative Counsel Bureau, primarily a research arm, also is empowered to determine how laws are being observed. Under this authority the counsel challenged as illegal the practices in a number of state agencies and particularly attacked the University of Nevada as an alleged violator of state law. Admittedly the university administration had behaved in a high-handed fashion,[20] and in some cases concerning the acquisition of property apparently acted *ultra vires*. But observers of the state scene—many of whom agreed that the university had failed to conform properly to state regulations—were disturbed by the manner in which the counsel assumed judicial as well as legislative authority. An observer in one prominent state newspaper asserted that the counsel's office had begun to overshadow the legislature itself because the counsel had "managed to hoodwink successive legislators into believing that his word is law. . . ." "The legislative counsel," continued the writer, "in addition to telling the lawmakers what they should or shouldn't do, has also set himself up as the legal adviser to all state departments.

18 See Edward F. Staniford, *Legislative Assistance* (Los Angeles: University of California, Bureau of Governmental Research, 1957); Mary B. Parsons, *The Legislative Branch and Assisting Services* (Office of the Research Analyst, New Hampshire Legislative Council, 1956).

19 Staniford, *op. cit.*, p. v.

20 Nevada Legislative Counsel Bureau, *The University of Nevada: An Appraisal; Report of the University Survey* (Carson City: State Printing Office, 1957). This is the survey conducted by Dean E. McHenry and a staff of consultants. See the summary of major findings and recommendations, pp. 184 ff.

In certain instances, at least, the University of Nevada was on firm legal

. . ." [21] While the counsel's militant techniques do not alter the facts about the conduct of the state university, they clearly contribute to the present state of tension and ill will in campus-legislative relations in Nevada.

The rise of agencies of fiscal oversight has been impressively swift. California established the first permanent legislative budget staff as recently as 1941, and today over 21 states have similar staffs. Ten are located within a legislative council, and more than eleven exist as separate agencies.[22] Occasionally, legislative budget analysts duplicate the functions of executive budget officers. This is true in Texas where college budgets go to both executive and legislative budget staffs and each agency prepares separate budget documents from the same data. Somewhat bewildering in view of the bustling concern administrators show for raking away duplication among state agencies is the scant attention that has been given to this growing duplication between the two branches of government. Already, institutions of higher education as well as other state agencies have found themselves caught in a crossfire between rival centers of power as legislative and executive budget staffs struggle for supremacy.

Legislative auditors, first established in Maine in 1932, now number twenty-three.[23] In theory, at least, the auditor verifies accounts as to accuracy and financial integrity. "At no time," comments the Council of State Governments, "should the judgment of auditors regarding the desirability of an expenditure for educational purposes be substituted for

---

ground. University resistance to a legislatively created advisory board of regents was sustained by the State Supreme Court, and the university's refusal to operate under the State Planning Board for construction programs was upheld by the state attorney-general.

21 Denver Dickerson, *Las Vegas Review Journal,* January 20, 1957.

22 Staniford, *op. cit.,* p. 17.

23 Council of State Governments, *Book of the States, 1958–1959* (Chicago: Council of State Governments, 1958), pp. 61–63.

the judgment of school officials. Such a procedure would tend
to give auditors control of educational policies." [24]

Where the auditor confines himself to post-auditing there
is little disagreement with university authorities. But there
is a perennial debate between them over appropriate accounting and reporting methods. Auditors favor standardization
and tend to prefer standard systems throughout the state.
Universities, however, prefer the educational accounting and
reporting system developed under the sponsorship of the
American Council on Education, which they feel is far more
compatible with their actual needs.

Occasionally difficult or awkward situations develop. In
New Hampshire, the Legislative Budget Assistant (who pos-
sesses post-audit as well as budget functions) reported "mismanagement" of university accounts. Actually this charge
was largely a difference of professional opinion over what
accounts were necessary for the institution, and an independent contract audit subsequently found no impropriety as
might have been implied by the assistant auditor's report.
Technical changes were recommended, however, to bring
the system into line with current practices.

Educational administrators ask if these legislative agencies are the first step toward creation of a legislative watch-
dog over universities. They report an earnest desire to render
proper accountability, but they are increasingly perplexed as
to whom they should be accountable. Traditionally, university administrators have discharged their accountability to
the institutional board of trustees and through them to the
legislature. But they are now concerned with the consequences that may flow from trying to satisfy too many masters while still carrying out their prime responsibility
effectively.

24 Council of State Governments, *The Forty-Eight State School Systems*
(Chicago: Council of State Governments, 1949), p. 17.

Thus legislative committees and technical service agencies —the legislative counsel staffs and legislative budget offices —have on occasion proven disconcerting to administrators in higher education. Yet it is undeniable that these committees and agencies have appeared in response to urgent needs in the state legislatures and in most instances have rendered distinguished service to the states. In part the legislative bureaucracy has grown because legislators lack sufficient time to accomplish their myriad duties as a collective body. Special legislative survey commissions on higher education have laid the foundations in many states for a systematic expansion of the educational program. Careful planning by legislative agencies has avoided many of the disasters that customarily befall important educational programs in the rush and roar of closing business.[25]

## The Art of Communication

Above and beyond these technical issues, legislators and educators agree that both sides have been remiss in open and helpful communication. It is significant that most of the disturbances in legislative-campus relations, including many of those chronicled in the foregoing sections, were either caused or aggravated by broken lines of communica-

[25] Despite scheduling of legislation, however, sound plans are often lost or else hastily drawn projects rush through the legislative mill with little consideration. In 1955 the Ohio legislature passed, at midnight on the evening of adjournment, an act establishing a State Planning and Improvement Board with powers that would have deprived the colleges of their autonomy in the construction of self-liquidating projects. Not until 1957 was the legislature able to remedy this situation by exempting such projects.

Kansas has passed more than half of its acts on the final day; Rhode Island nearly half; and Nevada over a third. Council of State Governments, *The American Legislature: Structure and Procedures* (Chicago: Council of State Governments, 1954), pp. 54–56.

tion. But improving the flow of information in both directions involves more than a simple recognition of need, for there is often disagreement between the campus and the legislature about the nature of the information that should be exchanged.

How, for example, should a legislature make its desires known to a college? A group of legislators in Minnesota chose the frontal assault by calling upon the university to select a new head of their department of agricultural economics whose philosophy of agriculture would coincide with the legislators' views. Also in the field of agriculture, one midwestern state senate gave *sub rosa* instructions to its university to reject a candidate for a job as dean of agriculture. The blunt reason: the candidate's background in tobacco agriculture was not acceptable to the midwestern hog and corn legislators. The Texas House of Representatives conducted an open investigation—at appropriation time—of the well-known institutional economist Clarence Ayres, on the grounds that he taught socialist theories. These gestures served notice that university policies were subject to constant political surveillance. It is this variety of outside influence that educators think improper.

In a more personal vein, artless legislators may keep university offices busy with requests for special favors or complaints about specific policies. A state senator calls the university to inquire about dormitory space for the daughter of a friend, and mentions in ominous tones that the shortage of dormitory space is caused by the university policy of admitting out-of-state students. A state representative suggests to the medical school that a youth in his home district is eminently qualified to enter medical school—despite the absence of any visible qualifications. A senator phones the president of a university—"Doctor, this is your favorite senator." "Hello, Buck," comes a skilled reply from the president, "what game is it and how many tickets do you want?" Educators have learned to live with these daily communiques from the capitols, but they are always apprehensive that an insignificant request may pave the way for a genuine disruption of academic policy.

What higher education welcomes from the legislature is a steady supply of information about the available resources of the state, thereby enabling the schools to plan ahead in the light of the economic realities of the state. In Oklahoma, for example, college officials are given advance word about the prospects of tax revenue for the coming fiscal year, and they have found it to be of great value in the preparation of realistic budgets. College officials also need information about particular needs of the state that may be served by the facilities of the colleges. They do not solicit legislative approval for every minor decision on the campus.

But if communications have faltered between the legislatures and the colleges, higher education must assume a major share of the responsibility. One of the common reasons for legislative intrusion on educational administration has been the lack—or the suspicion of lack—of full information from universities regarding campus operations and plans. Some of the mightiest state universities in the country have suffered severe appropriation cuts in recent sessions, partly if not entirely because of their unwillingness to make a complete disclosure of information requested by the legislature. Although college officials may have had good reason for their reluctance to impart certain information to the legislature, their explanations did nothing to change the shrinking appropriations.

Some universities have balked at disclosing their method of computing student enrollment, leaving themselves wide open to the charge that they are padding enrollment figures in order to get higher appropriations. This reluctance has given impetus to the movement to establish statewide formulas for computing enrollments. Other schools have refused to disclose information on costs at the same time as they have asked for large increases in appropriations. The legislative reaction is to assume that chaos governs fiscal policies on the campus.

Still other colleges have confronted legislatures with accomplished facts in the form of newly constructed buildings or new programs that were not included in the previous appropriation. While many of these developments are a natural part of the growth of an institution, in states where such quick switches are practiced, the legislature is likely to feel hoodwinked by the colleges. In the words of the Minnesota Commissioner of Administration:

> In their concern to protect their financial position, some college and university administrators have given the public the impression that what happens within the college or the university is not necessarily the concern of the larger public. They appear to operate on the premise that they have a higher obligation to the institution itself than they do to the state. This is a point that ought not to be lost sight of: some of the trouble, some of what we call difficulty over fiscal independence, is of the college's making, because it sometimes happens that the college or university will view the state's executive agencies, or even the state legislature, as an adversary. As a result, the public is sometimes not fully informed about management practices and policies. This tends not only to weaken public support for higher education, it also deprives the institution of invaluable internal assistance in the management of its complex organization.[26]

The legislatures in some states are also inclined to feel that college officials look down upon the representatives of

[26] Statement prepared for the Committee on Government and Higher Education, September 27, 1957.

the people. "I am only a lawyer," said one Missouri senator, "but I think I can understand enough about education to realize the problems without these educators talking down to me." Another legislator deplored the unwillingness of college administrators to talk hard facts. "When we come to the campus for an inspection trip," he complained, "the college people assume that the only thing we want to do is go to a football game and eat fancy food. There is a desperate need for campus officials to give us information. In fact, such a presentation would virtually insure the success of a program on any college campus." And this comment comes from a Florida senator: "Legislators are not well versed in the field of education. They can have the wool pulled over their eyes—and they do. But when they find out things are not right, they become suspicious."

Legislators are baffled by inequities in fees and costs among institutions of similar character. They are disturbed by evidence of back-biting competition among colleges for students and new programs. They often do not approve of teaching loads and space utilization on the college campus. In many or most of these instances, the practices are part of the normal educational pattern, but to a legislator hard pressed by competing demands, higher education easily looms as an example of "unbusinesslike" conduct.

In any event, legislators are unanimous in their desire for more information about the operation of academic programs. It would be deceptive to suggest that a policy of complete candor would work in every state; a few legislators might attempt to annihilate a perfectly sound educational program with the help of objective information furnished by the college. But legislatures feel that this is one of the gambles that higher education must take.

*Summary*

The multiple access of legislatures to universities has brought many attempts to control aspects of educational policy, but there is also an abundance of good will between legislators and college officials. Both groups are dedicated to the improvement of higher education in the states, although strong differences of opinion arise as to the proper sphere of authority for the legislature.

Although some states are replete with instances of overt political interference by individuals or groups of legislators who may decide to take educational matters into their own hands, in the main the disputes concern financial affairs. Aside from instances of detailed legislation affecting curriculum, official legislative activity is usually confined to tuition policy, enrollments, and details in the budget that touch on legislative interests. Legislatures have sometimes established university research programs without university consent, or slanted educational programs through their power over line items in the appropriation bill. Ordinarily, however, legislatures have followed the lead of professional educators in appropriating funds for higher education.

In the short run, the matter of upgrading or even holding the line on educational standards will be a critical area of concern for both educator and legislator. For anyone with an eye to standards of excellence in teaching and research, the ancient aphorism, "I ask not for larger gardens, but for finer seeds," takes on special significance. But the urgencies of the hour are bound to lead some to feel that any possible risk to educational standards must be taken in view of the broad public interest in making higher education available to broader segments of the community.

The elusive character of higher education should prompt

educator and legislator alike to be wary of crash programs that disrupt the balance of colleges and universities. Legislative earmarks that unduly restrict or direct the programming of university teaching and research do serious disservice to the mission of higher education. And if mistakes of this nature are written boldly across the face of the statute book, the damage may be irrevocable. This is the firm belief of American educators.

# CHAPTER XII

# The government of higher education

THE SWEEP of state controls examined in the preceding sections of this report could bring a profound alteration in the system of governing public institutions of higher education in this country. Traditionally, the government of American higher education, in the sphere of public as well as private colleges and universities, has been lodged in the hands of independent boards of trustees. These trustees come to public higher education through the political process either by appointment or election, but once established in office, they have served state colleges and universities as a principal line of defense against political interference.

The lay board of trustees has not been widely imitated outside of North America. As an institutional device it has

288

not escaped criticism. It is often belittled by state officials on the grounds that there are too many trustees who, having once been honored with an appointment, rarely attend board meetings and otherwise neglect their responsibilities. Academic critics, most notably Thorstein Veblen, have directed heavy fire at the lay board of trustees on the grounds that it puts control over higher education in the hands of men who are not professionally qualified to exercise this responsibility.

And yet it is doubtful if any other system of governing colleges and universities could have won as much freedom for American higher education as it now enjoys. Neither the British model of a university governed by its own faculty nor the Continental example of an institution run directly by the state suggests itself as an alternative more suited to the traditions of American life. The hierarchical tradition and awe of higher learning necessary to sustain a system of faculty government are simply not present in this society. And few would contend that the exercise of direct state control over colleges and universities would today find higher education freer than it has been under the government of independent boards of trustees.

Where the onset of state control—administrative as well as political—threatens to strip away the authority of independent governing boards, it contains a grave threat to the intellectual as well as the institutional independence of a university. These two phases of university freedom cannot be disassociated. Intellectual freedom originally sprouted in an environment of institutional autonomy.[1] It may well lose

[1] For a discussion of the relationship between intellectual and institutional freedom in the early history of the university see Richard Hofstadter and Walter P. Metzger, *The Development of Academic Freedom in the United States* (New York: Columbia University Press, 1955), pp. 9–11.

its vitality altogether if public colleges and universities are ever brought within the harness of conventional state administration. Preserving the authority of lay boards of trustees from state interference is as vital to the freedom of a university as the defense of freedom of teaching and research on the campus.

## The Governing Board in History

The government of the earliest European universities was radically different from the system which prevails in the United States today. The medieval universities were self-contained societies adhering to a form of representative democracy.[2] They were controlled either by students, as at the University of Bologna, or by masters, as was the case at the University of Paris. These medieval institutions had no trustees, and indeed little property that could be handled by a governing board. This gave the university a mobility which enabled it to migrate to more congenial surroundings when disputes developed with local officials.

There was no external secular control over the early universities—in fact, most institutions enjoyed papal immunity from civil restrictions. Of course, many of them had developed from "cathedral schools," and for a time the Church retained control over the selection of the university chancellor. The university convocation (of students or masters)

[2] Students flocked to universities from all over Europe. For self-protection and sociability they banded together according to the geographic areas from whence they came into "nations." The faculties were grouped by subject-matter disciplines, the main divisions being philosophy, law, and medicine. These groupings provided the governing units of the institutions. See Hastings Rashdall, *The Universities of Europe in the Middle Ages*, I (Oxford: Clarendon Press, 1895); and Charles H. Haskins, *The Rise of Universities* (New York: Henry Holt, 1923), especially Part I, pp. 3–36.

elected all other academic officials: the rector, procurators, counselors, deans, registrars, and treasurers.[3]

The church-appointed chancellor, at first a powerful figure with authority to grant degrees, appoint instructors, and order excommunication, soon came under fire from both faculty and students as a symbol of outside interference. Gradually he lost power to the university-elected rector, and by the fourteenth century the chancellor had dwindled to little more than a figurehead.

The rector was closely supervised by the legislative body of the university, the convocation. The powers of the rector were to some extent analogous to those of a modern university president. He convened and presided over the convocation and arranged the agenda. His disciplinary authority was extensive and was enhanced by the fact that the university conducted its own courts. The rector also exercised some financial powers and was the chief dignitary at public functions.

The British universities modified the early European pattern of self-government. As on the Continent, the first British institutions, Oxford and Cambridge, were under the direction of chancellors appointed by the church bishops. But in 1484 the chancellor of Oxford became a political appointee of the Crown, and by 1569 the state had solidly established its influence over the management of the university. The idea of the university as a gathering of scholars was now paralleled by the concept of an institution of higher education as a corporation established by charter from the state.

Eventually universities were to achieve considerable freedom from governmental control in Great Britain. This legal autonomy, reinforced by "old school ties" between government officials and the universities, has produced a climate

3 See Anatol Murad, "Democracy in European Universities," *The Educational Forum,* XIV (May, 1950), pp. 457–61.

of freedom for British and Scottish universities that is perhaps unequaled in the world today.[4]

On the Continent the medieval university also tended gradually to come under greater state control. In 1574 the Parlement of Paris declared the University of Paris to be a secular institution dependent upon royal power. The French Revolution saw the suppression of this university along with all other institutions of higher learning. In their place emerged a centralized educational system under the direct control of a ministry of state.

In Germany the first universities were founded and regulated by governmental action. As in Britain and France, German institutions were relatively free in their internal administration, selecting their own officials and retaining faculty jurisdiction over curriculum and discipline. This scholastic autonomy made the German university of the nineteenth century a landmark in the history of intellectual freedom. And yet it is true that the close connection between the state and the university was ultimately to place academic freedom on a fragile basis in Germany. After decades of internal autonomy, the university system offered little resistance to the efforts of the Nazi regime to mold it to the requirements of a totalitarian state. This same weakness was manifest elsewhere on the Continent:

> In the modern period, however, the university in continental Europe lost all prescriptive right to independence. It became a part of the administrative structure of the state and kept a measure of self-rule only as a branch

[4] It is only within the last decade that any serious question has arisen over the extensive autonomy of British institutions. Interestingly enough, the source of the questioning has been the Public Accounts Committee of Parliament—an agency of fiscal control. Thus far Parliament has refused to change the present system. As the universities move to improve their methods of financial operation, there appears little likelihood that the British government will apply restrictions over higher education. See Appendix B.

of the government and only on the sufferance of the higher authorities of the state . . . .

. . . From the start . . . Russian universities [that were] instituted . . . in the nineteenth century operated as agencies of the state. Thus in Russia the university conformed to the pattern of subordination to the state without even the remembrance of a previous autonomous status as an institution dedicated solely to the service of knowledge . . . . Though many individual professors resisted totalitarianism, the German universities succumbed without major resistance. The Nazi Regime needed only to disturb about 1/10 of the university professors in order to accomplish its purposes.[5]

## Boards of Trustees [6]

The American preference for lay boards of control can be

[5] Paul Farmer, "Nineteenth Century Ideas of the University: Continental Europe," in *The Modern University*, Margaret Clapp, ed., (Ithaca: Cornell University Press, 1950), pp. 6, 8, 24, and footnote 13. See also Frederick Lilge, *The Abuse of Learning: The Failure of the German University* (New York: Macmillan & Co., 1948).

[6] The various titles used by governing boards give no clear indication of their nature and duties. Among the most common titles are: Board of Regents; Board of Trustees; Board of Visitors; Board of Managers; Board of Curators; Board of Control; Board of Governors; and The Corporation. Boards supervising more than one institution (See Chapter IX) use the above or such titles as Board of Education, Board of Institutional Control, and Co-ordinating Board of Higher Education.

The common title "trustee" is somewhat a misnomer if literally interpreted, since board members are responsible for more than the management of funds. It is more appropriate to regard the office as one of public trust. See John D. Russell and Floyd W. Reeves, *The Evaluation of Higher Education*, Part VI, "Administration" (Chicago: University of Chicago Press, 1936); Edward C. Elliott, M. M. Chambers, and William A. Ashbrook, *The Government of Higher Education* (New York: American Book Company, 1935), pp. 25–26; and Morton Rauch, *College and University Trusteeships* (Antioch, Ohio: Antioch College Press, 1958). For an excellent statistical summary of data on governing boards, see U. S. Office of Education, *State Boards Responsible for Higher Education*, to be published in 1959.

traced directly to the first governing bodies established in this country, but American universities cannot lay claim entirely to the invention of the governing board device. In the words of James B. Conant:

> It is a matter of historical fact that during our colonial period the universities of Holland were managed by boards of lay governors. Leyden, Franeker, Groningen, and Utrecht, all founded before 1637, were established with boards of from three to six curators. . . . A similar arrangement was put into effect when Goettingen was founded in 1737, and was copied by certain of the older German universities in the late eighteenth century . . . .
> It may be that all of this contemporary academic history was unknown to the dwellers on the American continent. . . . and that the system of government of our institutions arose spontaneously. . . . I understand there is no record of . . . conscious plagiarism.[7]

Harvard applied the idea of board control in its original form of government in 1642, but the powers of the first Board of Overseers (six magistrates and six ministers) were subsequently shared with The Corporation (President and Fellows) in 1650. The charter granted Yale by the Connecticut General Assembly in 1701, for example, gave the "trustees, partners, or under-takers" complete authority to "erect, form, direct, order, establish, improve, and at all times in all suitable ways for the future to encourage" the college's growth. As it was amended in 1745, the charter created a Corporation consisting of the President [8] and Fellows who

---

[7] James B. Conant, *Academical Patronage and Superintendence*, Occasional Pamphlets of the Graduate School of Education, Harvard University, June, 1938. For further information on this topic, see Sir William Hamilton, *Discussions on Philosophy and Literature, Education and University Reform* (2d ed.; London: Longman's, 1853), pp. 362 ff.

[8] The term "president" came into the academic lexicon in 1650 when the Harvard Corporation of the President and Fellows was established. The teaching Fellows of the Corporation, who were elected by co-optation, were soon

were in the future to be selected by the board itself. Later, certain state officials served ex officio on the Yale board, but these officials were eventually replaced by six alumni-elected representatives. With the establishment of lay boards of control at Harvard, William and Mary, and Princeton, the pattern of governing private universities through a system of lay boards was firmly established.[9]

The use of independent boards of trustees as governing bodies was quickly followed in the establishment of public colleges and universities. In 1785 the University of Georgia was set up as one of the first purely public institutions of higher education in the country, and in 1789 it was placed under the control of a board of trustees appointed by the governor with the consent of the senate. North Carolina in 1789 and Vermont in 1791 also set up their state universities under lay boards of control.

Following the Dartmouth College case in which the United States Supreme Court held that royal charters to the older institutions were contracts not subject to violation by the state,[10] the legislatures were careful to stipulate in subsequent charters that the state had a right to amend or modify the powers of a public college or university. At this time also, legislatures began to stipulate the methods by which governing board members were to be selected.

By the time the Morrill Act of 1862 had launched the land-grant college movement, the lay board of control was the accepted form for governing virtually all institutions of

---

replaced by laymen. As the Corporation assumed vigorous leadership of Harvard, the first system of college government in this country found the governing body neither selected by nor directly responsible to the faculty or students.

9 In some present-day private colleges, e.g., Swarthmore and Black Mountain, there are institutional provisions for direct faculty participation in the government of the college. However, this system is atypical.

10 *Trustees of Dartmouth College* v. *William H. Woodward,* 4 Wheat. 518, 4 L. Ed. 629 (1819).

higher education,[11] and it was readily applied to the expanding state university system.

These early public boards possessed extensive powers. If incorporated, they had all the powers normally incidental to this status including the right to sue; to acquire, hold, and (in most cases) to dispose of property; to make contracts; to use a seal; to administer funds; to borrow money; to engage and dismiss employees; to set fees, and enact rules and regulations pertaining to the internal administration of the institution.

Governing boards that were regarded as instrumentalities of the state rather than corporate bodies were also granted a broad range of power. Both corporate and non-corporate boards usually had jurisdiction over discipline, the setting of salaries and conditions of employment, approval of budgets, and institutional planning and programming. In short, the powers of these early governing boards were by and large consistent with their responsibility for governing the institutions over which they exercised legal jurisdiction.

## The Trustee and the University

The tradition of governing higher education through lay boards of trustees thus finds firm support in American history. In the religious atmosphere of Colonial days this system served in good part to hold institutions of higher education within the bounds of denominational orthodoxy. In modern and more secular times it has become a means of keeping open channels of responsibility and support between

---

[11] Exceptions occur in Catholic institutions, which may be run by religious orders and in military academies under the command of military officers. In the case of both exceptions, however, advisory or visiting boards are frequently used to provide some of the functions normally rendered by governing boards.

the college and the community. The modern university, unlike its medieval predecessor, is to a large degree dependent upon the generosity of the community for financial assistance, and the lay board has become a means by which the public can assess the needs and appraise the performance of the institutions it is asked to support.

As has been noted, this system is not without its critics, even from within the academy. By some observers it has even been suggested that the lay board of trustees has had a predominantly negative influence upon the development of higher learning in America. Hofstadter takes what is perhaps an extreme point of view in this regard:

> The system of lay government has created special problems for free teaching and scholarship in America. The essence of lay government is that the trustees, not the faculties, are, in law, the college or university, and that legally they can hire and fire faculty members and make almost all the decisions governing the institution. This has hampered the development of organization, initiative and self-confidence among American college professors, and it has contributed, along with many other forces in American life, to lowering their status in the community.[12]

At the root of much of this criticism of lay boards of trustees is the belief that in the process of mediating between the academy and the community these boards are much more responsive to the pressures of the community than they are to the need for freedom, and it is not hard to find boards of trustees that have come under blistering indictment for their decisions on issues affecting academic freedom. The studies and investigations by the American Association of University Professors report numerous instances where trustees either initiated restrictions upon freedom or failed to offer

---

12 Hofstadter and Metzger, *op. cit.*, p. 120.

serious resistance to outside pressures upon the campus.[13]
This issue boils up most frequently and has posed the greatest difficulties where trustees are charged with the dismissal of faculty members whose views or activities have become controversial. A recent case involving the dismissal of two faculty members for alleged radicalism from Texas Technological College brought forth this comment from the *Dallas Times Herald:*

> Professors who think they have complete freedom usually find that they are mistaken. This is particularly true in tax-supported schools. Trustees of such institutions assume that they have the right to set standards of behavior for instructors and a large segment of the public agrees with them.[14]

In recent years a good many of these cases have been tied to the issue of communism, although of course it has always been possible for a faculty member to become an object of controversy in this country for his views on a varied range of topics, including atheism, evolution, and the nutrient value of oleomargarine. In many parts of the South today the tension surrounding the issue of race far surpasses that attached to any other issue or set of issues in the public mind.

On matters of this kind, regents are very much under the temptation to anticipate outside pressure by imposing in-

[13] The interest of the AAUP in this problem goes back to its first statement on academic freedom drafted in 1915. Periodically, reports of Committee "A" appear in the Association's *Bulletin* informing the membership of the Committee's findings in selected cases. Report of a Special Committee of the AAUP, "Academic Freedom and Tenure in the Quest for National Security," AAUP *Bulletin,* XLII, No. 1 (1956), pp. 96–97. For a good statement of the faculty point of view on academic freedom, see Fritz Machlup, "On Some Misconceptions Concerning Academic Freedom," AAUP *Bulletin,* XLI, No. 4, (1955), pp. 753–89.

[14] July 18, 1957. For a discussion of this case see the article from the Tulia (Texas) *Herald* inserted in the *Congressional Record* by Senator Ralph Yarborough, July 31, 1957, p. A 6167.

ternal restrictions before this interference can inflict griev-
ous damage upon the university. At both the University of
California and the University of Colorado, two institutions
that enjoy constitutional immunity from governmental control, boards of regents moved to head off legislative investigations by themselves imposing loyalty standards as a
prerequisite for employment at the university.[15] Both the attraction and the danger of these accommodations to outside
pressure have been well stated by the AAUP:

> The temptation to yield a little in order to preserve a
> great deal is strong, particularly when faculty members
> who cry out for protection seem wilfully unco-operative.
> Yet to yield a little is, in such matters, to run the risk of
> sacrificing all.[16]

Of course, the trustee system cannot be judged entirely by
its success in protecting freedom of teaching and research,
since trustees have other imperative functions as well.[17] But
with respect to their role in defending academic freedom, it
should be noted that trustees have not always yielded to community pressure. At times in fact they have resisted outside
coercion even in the face of threats to impose economic or
other sanctions against the university over which they preside. This is more true perhaps than is generally recognized,
since much of this coercion never becomes a matter of public
knowledge. To be sure, state colleges and universities may
not always be in as secure a position to assert this independence as some of the well-established private institutions of

15 AAUP *Bulletin*, XLII, No. 1 (1956), pp. 64–69.

16 *Ibid.*, pp. 96–97. Some faculty members have favored the existence of
alternative sources of appeal in cases involving academic freedom. A recent
controversy in Nevada was not settled by the governing board but by the state
legislature—an arrangement that met with considerable approval among faculty members. See Nevada Legislative Counsel Bureau, *The University of
Nevada: An Appraisal* (Carson City: State Printing Office, 1957), pp. 27–31.

17 For a discussion of these tasks, see *infra*, pp. 21–26.

higher learning.[18] But witness, for example, the University of New Hampshire, where the board of regents stood firmly behind the school's decision to allow a speaker on the campus who was under attack from both the legislature and the state attorney-general.[19]

Actually regents are in an exceptionally strong position to defend the tradition of intellectual freedom. Serving as trustees of the public interest within the academic family, regents can also be the university's most eloquent ambassadors within the community. For when a trustee speaks for academic freedom, he does so from the disinterested perspective of society's stake in the humane and material benefits of free inquiry. By contrast the faculty member's claim to academic freedom can never be entirely divorced from the fact that he is so directly involved in the process he is defending.[20]

## The Selection of Trustees

Across the country the necessity of reconciling the independence of the university with the need for responsibility to the community finds its clearest reflection in the process by which members of boards of trustees are selected. The states have taken many different paths in choosing their trustees, but each of the methods followed reveals an effort to

[18] See in this connection Robert M. MacIver, *Academic Freedom in Our Time* (New York: Columbia University Press, 1955), p. 82. MacIver notes that out of 19 institutions censured for violations of academic freedom between 1935 and 1950, 11 were state universities.

[19] As a result of its steadfast adherence to this policy, the University of New Hampshire received, in 1958, the first Alexander Meiklejohn Academic Freedom Award given by the AAUP.

[20] For a notable defense of academic freedom by a trustee (in this instance, of a private institution), see "Freedom at Harvard: An Exchange of Letters by Frank B. Ober, of Baltimore, President Conant, and Grenville Clark, Fellow of Harvard College," *Harvard Alumni Bulletin* (June 25, 1949).

achieve the dual and sometimes conflicting goals of relating higher education to the needs of the community, while protecting the university from capricious political interference.

Methods of sifting and winnowing candidates to fill board vacancies are numerous, and it is not unusual to find boards filled by a combination of different processes. However, a majority of board members are appointed by the governor, with or without the consent of the legislature.[21] Election to the board, the second most popular method, may be accomplished either by the voters of the state, by alumni or other special groups, or by the state legislature itself.

There are those who prefer that trustees be appointed rather than elected. This preference is based largely on the grounds that better qualified personnel are not inclined to run in an election campaign.[22] Yet experienced regents have reservations on this point. An Arizona regent observes: "Although we give lip service to the idea that appointments are not 'political,' in effect they are. It is rare for a governor to appoint a member from a party other than his own unless that individual has aided his campaign."

And yet across the country appointed boards have been remarkably successful in protecting higher education from political interference. In many places, of course, boards are assisted in their defense of the autonomy of higher education by the fact that it is not good "politics" for any administration to meddle with the schools. To avoid giving any appearance of political interference, governors sometimes go to great lengths to make conspicuously non-political appointments to governing boards.[23]

[21] For further discussion on the practice of gubernatorial appointments to the board, see Chapter X, pp. 238-242.

[22] Fred Englehardt, "The Administrative and Fiscal Control of State Universities and Colleges," *Proceedings of the Association of Governing Boards of State Universities and Allied Institutions*, 1930, p. 90.

[23] Some indication of the status of higher education may be found in a

Some observers, however, regard election at large as the only effective way of tying the university to the community.[24] A Michigan trustee puts it this way:

> The fact that we are elected rather than appointed gives the voters a more direct chance to have a voice in the determination of board membership than would be the case if we were appointed by the governor. The electoral method has served Michigan educational institutions well for a century or more.[25]

A contrary view regarding the value of elections in selecting board members comes from Colorado, where regents are listed on the ballot in alphabetical order and where the charge is frequently heard that the voters give their approval to the first names they encounter. As one Colorado board member noted:

> I believe appointment is more conducive to better board members than the elective system since only those with a last name beginning in "A," "B," or "C" ever are elected.

It is true that the only Republican regent at the University of Colorado who survived a recent Democratic party sweep in that state had a surname beginning with "B." There are, of course, exceptions to the rule, but they are infrequent.

Election by the legislature is justified, according to a North

---

survey of 70 state colleges and universities, which found approximately 40 institutions where the presidents' salaries were higher than the respective governors' pay, although in most of those states the governors had more expense funds and "fringe benefits." G. D. Humphrey, "Statutory Control of College and University Salaries," *School and Society* (May 25, 1957), pp. 185–86.

[24] Claude Eggertsen, "Composition of Governing Boards," in *Democracy in the Administration of Higher Education*, H. Benjamin, ed., (New York: John Dewey Society, 1950), pp. 117–26. See also Edward C. Elliott, "The Board of Control," in *Higher Education in America*, Raymond A. Kent, ed., (Boston: Ginn & Co., 1930) p. 617, footnote 21.

[25] In response to the Committee survey of members of the Association of Governing Boards of State Universities and Allied Institutions. Subsequent regents' quotations are also drawn from this survey.

Carolina regent, as a means of improving relations between the legislature and the university. And higher education in both North Carolina and Minnesota has prospered under a system of legislative election of trustees. However, some educators in South Carolina argue that exceptionally able candidates for the position of trustee have been rejected in the General Assembly when they refused to campaign among the legislators.

A similar problem cropped up in Iowa, where several experienced regents failed to win reconfirmation by the senate. These regents had taken a leading position in criticizing the array of fiscal controls that had blanketed the state colleges and universities in the wake of a "little Hoover Committee" report. It is believed in some quarters that the regents' outspoken views on state controls were largely responsible for the senate's failure to keep them on the board. It should be noted, however, that these regents were also caught in an intra-party test of strength between the governor and the legislature, and this helped to seal their doom as nominees. Ultimately, they had the satisfaction of seeing many of the fiscal controls against which they had fought removed by a succeeding legislature.

Selection of trustees by alumni of an institution is praised by some as a means of producing regents who have a strong personal interest and pride in the school. And co-optation— that is, the selection of new members by the board itself— is advocated by others who contend that it provides stability and continuity in educational policy. This method of selection is actually quite rare in public colleges. However, strong objections have been registered to both alumni election and co-optation as methods of selecting regents. Alumni members in some places have been primarily interested in the fortunes of the school's football team. The system of co-optation threatens to isolate the university from the community. An Alabama news editor, a staunch supporter of the state university, voiced doubts about the advisability of the self-perpetuating board which governs the university in that state. The board had, he said, a dangerous tendency to inbreed and produce "hyper-conservative" members.

Obviously, there is little unanimity as to the most appropriate method of selecting trustees. But the Committee survey did find an overwhelming majority of regents in favor of the method by which their own boards were selected. There is justification for this attitude, since each method has produced many eminently qualified trustees for higher education. However, it should be noted that no technique of selection can guarantee a high level of ability on governing boards unless there is a climate of opinion in the community which insists upon putting the affairs of higher education in the most capable hands.

Many governing boards at state colleges and universities contain a complement of ex-officio members. These members, automatically "selected" by virtue of the fact that they hold another public office, pose something of a problem in many states. On one hand, there are those who argue that the ex-officio member wins sympathy and support for higher education within the top echelons of state government. On the other hand, critics complain that ex-officio members tend to regard their board membership as either a relatively unimportant obligation or, what is worse, as an opportunity for engaging in political maneuvers with the affairs of higher education.[26] The Committee survey of regent opinion on the question of ex-officio membership turned up one clear find-

[26] Theodore Bilbo, when Governor of Mississippi, once boasted that as ex-officio head of the state board of education he fired three college presidents and hired their replacements within a space of a few hours. Robert M. Mac-Iver, *Academic Freedom in Our Time* (New York: Columbia University Press, 1956), p. 265, footnote 1.

ing. While boards having some type of ex-officio membership
are divided on the desirability of this arrangement, boards
without any ex-officio members definitely prefer not to have
any.

One rather common technique that is used to minimize
political interference through the selection process is the use
of staggered and relatively long terms of office for board
members. As a rule, only 10 to 20 per cent of the membership of boards turns over annually. The average term of
service is over five years, and through life membership or
continued reappointment some regents have served as long as
a quarter of a century and more. The practice of giving long,
staggered terms to board members provides no absolute guarantee against political interference, although it may serve to
sustain a spirit of independence by a governing board.

The practices followed in removing board members also
vary considerably among the states. Some boards retain this
power in their own hands (generally used against members
who are inactive), but in a large number of cases board members are subject to formal removal by the governor alone. In
a majority of cases, removal may take place "without cause,"
though in some instances a special reason (such as moral
turpitude) must be specified. Other methods of removal include judicial decision, legislative action, and popular recall.
A number of public boards (approximately 40 per cent) have
no formal machinery for removal at all.

In a number of states eligibility for board membership is
subject to specific legal stipulations. In part this represents an
effort to provide a governing board with representation
drawn from major interest groups within the community.
The attempt to make the governing board a mirror of the
constituency has been criticized on the grounds that it robs
the board of the disinterest that should be its primary qual-

ity. But by and large, boards do not regard these provisions as incompatible with effective operation.

The social status of board members has long been the subject of widespread interest.[27] Studies have shown that the clergy has been overshadowed by the business community as the group from which a majority of board members come. The Committee's own survey supports the belief that business and the professions now provide the bulk of the membership on boards of control. In some quarters it is believed that the socio-economic status of board members has an important bearing on the attitudes they take on issues involving academic affairs. But the truth of the matter may well be that board membership breeds an attitude and perspective that has little to do with the station in life from which the member enters upon his duties. On many boards there is a unity in pursuit of the goals of higher education and in defense of the university that obliterates previous distinctions among board members.

## The Role of the Trustee

Fixing the precise position of the trustee in the governing structure of higher education is a problem that has perplexed

[27] For analysis of changes in the social composition of governing boards, see George S. Counts, *The Social Composition of Boards of Education: A Study in the Social Control of Public Education* (Chicago: University of Chicago Press, 1927); Scott Nearing, "Who's Who Among College Trustees," *School and Society*, VI (1917), pp. 297-99; Earl J. McGrath, "The Control of Higher Education in America," *Educational Record*, XVII (1936), pp. 259-72; Hubert Beck, *Men Who Control Our Universities* (New York: Kings Crown Press, 1947); Myron F. Wicke, *Handbook for Trustees of Church-Related Colleges* (Nashville, Tennessee: Board of Education of Southern Methodist Church, 1957); Victor S. Bryant, *The Responsibilities of Trustees of a State University* (Chapel Hill, North Carolina: University of North Carolina, 1956); and Board of Educational Finance, *Manual for Boards of Regents* (Santa Fe, New Mexico: Board of Educational Finance, 1955).

many observers, including trustees themselves. Even after long experience in higher education, trustees like Willmarth Lewis, at Yale, have confessed that "The full duty of trustees is not evident even to trustees." [28] Nor has this uncertainty been altogether relieved by the publication of several manuals dealing with the subject of trusteeship in higher education. The quest for an authoritative statement on the position of the trustee is a perennial one.

In the case of a trustee who exercises jurisdiction over a state college or university, one part of his legal duty is quite clear. It is to insure that the funds appropriated by the state for the support of higher education are managed by the university in as wise and frugal a manner as possible and with responsiveness to the long-range needs of the people in the state. Competence to perform these tasks should be an important qualification for appointment to a position as trustee of a public college or university. For it has always been the American ideal to secure the state's interest in a highly competent and adequately responsive system of public higher education through the over-all supervision of colleges and universities by independent boards of trustees.

Perhaps the principal task of any statement on the rights and duties of trustees is that of arriving at a clear and distinct allocation of responsibility between the regents, on the one hand, and the president on the other. An obvious danger to be avoided in this area is that a board of trustees may devote so much time to the details of college and university administration that it neglects its own policy-making responsibility and severely limits the flexibility that administrators need to handle the day-to-day affairs of a university. A board cannot administer as effectively as a president, and a president can-

---

[28] As quoted in *The Role of the Trustees of Columbia University,* The Report of the Special Trustees Committee adopted by the Trustees, November 4, 1957, p. 71.

not administer at all unless he is given a broad grant of discretionary authority by a board.

While most trustees have sufficient wisdom or experience to recognize the necessity of this self-restraint, there is a constant turnover of membership on any board of trustees, and occasionally a new member will appear who is not immediately aware of the practical limits as well as the legal breadth of a board's authority. As a Columbia study on the position of the trustee has pointed out:

> The legal supremacy of trustees and their final authority to act is unquestioned, but the most experienced trustees are constantly warning their newer colleagues that overactivity in certain areas—particularly in the area of education itself—is as great a sin against the modern spirit as is neglect.[29]

The fact that the board must delegate so much authority into his hands necessarily makes the selection of a president the most important decision a board makes.[30] When the occasion arises, some regents may in fact spend an extraordinary amount of time at the task of recruiting a president—even taking time off from their occupations to fly around the country interviewing prospective candidates for the position. Convention requires that this process be hedged about with secrecy, so much so that a presidential candidate at one college came to look over the campus equipped with a beard and other accoutrements of disguise. His candidacy was not successful.

A board of trustees is also faced with the necessity of finding common ground with faculty members on such matters

---

[29] *Ibid.*, p. 9.

[30] In the performance of this basic task, boards have occasionally found themselves hamstrung by the power of other state officials. A Florida governor, who had the power to approve warrants, blocked the appointment of one president by threatening to withhold the payment of his salary.

of joint responsibility as admission, curriculum, and graduation requirements. In theory at least, the fact that trustees bear responsibility for the quality of an institution's educational performance could lead to situations where the lay judgment of trustees and the professional views of faculty members are set against each other. In practice, however, this issue is avoided at most institutions by the fact that the trustees and faculty members are able to arrive at agreement even in the absence of a tidy division of responsibility.[31]

State officials do not always recognize the necessity of this exercise of self-restraint by the regents, and consequently they sometimes justify their interference with the internal affairs of public institutions of higher education by arguing that, in policing the campus, they are performing a task that the regents have neglected. Essentially, this criticism reflects a misunderstanding of the fact that trustees in public as well as private institutions of higher education cannot themselves directly govern a college or university. And just as it would be a mistake for trustees to second-guess a president at every turn in his administrative decisions, so it is an egregious error for state officials to attempt to manage a university from a distance even further removed from the scene of operations than the trustees themselves.

The peculiarity of the trustee's position is, therefore, that he occupies a position of supreme legal responsibility in higher education, but if he exercises this authority in a pervasive way in the internal affairs of the university, he risks destroying the vitality and creative energy by which the in-

---

[31] M. M. Chambers adds an important qualification to the responsibilities of governing board members. "A member of a governing board," he noted in a letter to the Committee, "in his individual capacity has no legal authority whatever; and certainly he should scrupulously refrain from acting as though he were personally in command of the university or any part of it. While it is quite true that the board is legally all-powerful, it exercises this plenary power only as a collegial body assembled in a duly called session."

stitution is nourished. It is a great tribute to the good sense and judgment of the men who have served as trustees of America's public institutions of higher education that so many of them have recognized the necessity of refraining from capricious interference in either the administration or the academic policy of the institution over which they preside.[32]

Of course, this is an act of self-denial that is called for in other areas where part-time lay boards exercise policy-making authority. Legislatures, for example, customarily delegate broad grants of authority to administrative agencies, and this in effect represents a transfer of managerial power to professional personnel in the executive branch of government. Boards of directors of business corporations ordinarily leave the affairs of the company in the hands of a professional management staff. But in the case of higher education, the act of self-denial by a lay board of trustees rests on more than considerations of efficiency and expediency, since freedom is the distinguishing mark of a university in Western society. An administrative agency or business corporation might lose its freedom without sacrificing its essential identity as a social institution; a university could not.

## Summary

The independent governing board is a distinctive, even though not entirely American contribution to the governmental tradition of higher education. This indigenous device represents an attempt to harmonize the freedom of higher

[32] Regents sometimes complain that their president runs the institution single-handed, leaving the board with little more to do than nod in approval. It should be noted that a totally inactive board is a perfect target for aggressive state officials who are seeking to narrow the range of a president's discretion.

education with responsiveness to the public interest, by giving lay boards of trustees official responsibility for governing colleges and universities. Virtually everywhere in the United States these independent governing bodies are at the frontier of academic responsibility, serving as both moat and bridge between the university and the community.

Occasionally it is asked whether a legislative committee or some other state agency could not take over this task of representing the public interest in the government of state colleges and universities.[33] But the distinctive characteristic of the board device is that at its best it provides for continuous, experienced, and perceptive scrutiny of higher education by members of the community who are brought within the university family by their role as trustees. Regents are thus in a position to view the operations of institutions of higher education at close range and to pass judgment on educational policy with intimate awareness of the complexity of the issues involved.[34] This is a vantage point no other

[33] One college official made this observation in a letter to the Committee: "While it may well be true that the board of trustees at the state university is to some extent copied from the practice of early private institutions, the board represents public interest in higher education in a unique way. The board is the final instrument for the determination of policy which in other operations might well be determined by the state legislature and the governor. If the fundamentals of university policy are to be determined by the state legislature and by the governor and by central administrative agencies, then the board of trustees has lost its basic reason for being."

[34] It would of course be naive to suggest that all trustees live up to this ideal characterization. Upon reading this paragraph, one close observer of public higher education commented as follows:
"If the regents were really as competent about matters of higher education as the concluding paragraph indicates, state officials and legislators would feel less compelled to get in on the act. The sad fact of the matter is that in most states there are at least two or three state officials and legislators who have a more thorough understanding of statewide and regional problems of higher education than college and university trustees. And this group of ambitious and knowledgeable state officials and legislators is growing in membership.
"As evidence of this trend, one need only to note the number of conferences

state agency has, and it is a function no other state agency can perform.

and workshops on problems of higher education being sponsored for legislative groups and state officials. My personal experience has also been that these people actually read the literature on higher education, and when I send reports of studies to them, I can expect some questions. By comparison, the trustees' annual conference is a party affair and as a group they are unread and frighteningly provincial in their outlook on higher education. This latter is probably partly the fault of their presidents, some of whom I find prefer to keep their trustees ignorant and intellectually dormant."

CHAPTER XIII

# The efficiency of freedom

THROUGHOUT this study the question of overriding importance that has presented itself is the extent to which the
freedom of state colleges and universities is consistent with
the efficient performance of higher learning as a public function. This is the problem to which both state and college
officials return in all discussions of the relations between the
campus and the capitol. In this dialogue, governmental efficiency and educational freedom are commonly viewed as
competitive claims that must be weighed in the balance before enduring harmony can be achieved.

Yet the fact is that higher education very largely owes its
autonomous position in state government to the belief that
freedom promotes rather than limits its efficiency. To the
authors of early state constitutions, grappling with the task
of establishing the public university in the governmental
structure of the state, it seemed almost self-evident that it is
through freedom that higher education attains its highest

313

level of performance. It was for this reason that in the framing of the constitutions in Michigan, California, and in other states, the state university was given a status that set it apart as virtually an independent branch of government.

High on the list of factors contributing to this grant of autonomy was the belief that public institutions of higher learning had lagged behind the development of private universities because of their subjection to political interference or control. As long ago as 1849 the Michigan legislature asked itself why "no state institution in America has prospered as well as independent colleges with equal, and often with less means?" [1] The answer at which it arrived in those early days was similar to the conclusion drawn in other states. Private institutions enjoyed continuity of control by skilled personnel and were able to engage in long-range planning, whereas public universities, assimilated within the ordinary structure of the state, were all too often exposed to the fluctuating pressures and inhibitions of politics. Freedom was viewed as enhancing efficiency in higher education because it best enabled colleges and universities to achieve their basic purposes as social institutions—gathering, disseminating, and creating knowledge. It was for this reason that state colleges and universities were placed under the jurisdiction of independent boards of trustees, thus duplicating as far as possible the freedom of the private university.

## The Contribution of Higher Education

Over the years the preferred position of higher education has been amply justified by the scope of its contributions to

[1] As quoted in *Sterling* v. *Regents of University of Michigan*, 110 Mich. 369, 68 N. W. 253 (1896), a decision by the Michigan Supreme Court upholding the independence of the state university.

the economic and cultural development of each of the states. Of all public functions education is the most fundamental, since achievement in other areas of governmental activity ultimately depends upon the quality of the educational system. Without the skills developed in colleges and universities it would be impossible to construct or maintain highways, rehabilitate mental patients, or perform many of the other diverse tasks of modern state government.

Success in higher education thus undergirds the successful administration of all other state programs. Moreover, mistakes made in education are much more irredeemable than is the case with other state activities. While the reclamation of worn-out land poses great difficulties, the neglect of intellectual resources may never be repaired. Witness this observation by a college president:

> Highways can be changed (although it is an expensive proposition) if mistakes are made; it is even possible to restock lakes and woods if conservation programs lack effective and continuing leadership and support, but it is virtually impossible to re-educate a generation of several generations of citizens who have been deprived of their rights through an educational system that is cramped or given imbalance by a state government that does not recognize the necessity of giving freedom to colleges and universities.[2]

Nor is any other state activity as creative as higher education, which, unlike the elementary and secondary school systems, is concerned with the expansion as well as the trans-

[2] The statements from university presidents included in this chapter are drawn from the replies to a letter sent to state university presidents which asked, among other things, the following question: "What characteristics does higher education have which justify the special treatment it has received in the constitutions and laws of many of the states?"

We would like to take this opportunity to express our gratitude to the busy executives who gave so generously of their time and wisdom in responding to this letter.

mission of knowledge. This trail-breaking function gives the state university a unique place in the life of the state, and it is one that cannot be carried on efficiently except in a climate of freedom.

Creative research, by its very nature, requires freedom to move in a different direction if the facts uncovered require it. The farther away budget authority lies and the more time-consuming it is to get permission for such changes, the less will be accomplished. Research and instruction at the higher levels, are not services for which specifications can be written in advance, and for which one seeks the lowest bidder. They are venture capital investments where one successful strike in a multitude, either in the form of a new ideal, or a trained individual capable of producing them, may spell the difference between a forward-moving or a retrograding nation.

The "cutting-edge" function that a state university performs in the quest for knowledge necessarily exposes it to a good deal more criticism and controversy than is the case with more conventional state activities. One state college president noted that a really first-class university lives in "chronic tension with the society that supports it." New ideas always run the risk of offending entrenched interests within the community, and if higher education is to be successful in its creative role it must be guaranteed some protection against reprisal for any momentary unpopularity that innovation or the exposure of fallacy may bring.

Testimony to the innovating and creative role of the university in society is provided by the primacy totalitarian movements assign to the task of bringing the university under state control. "The citadel of learning," as Conant has pointed out,[3] must be taken if any society is to be brought

---

[3] James B. Conant, *The Citadel of Learning* (New Haven: Yale University Press, 1956), esp. pp. 2–4.

under authoritarian direction and control. Once captured, the university becomes merely an instrument for harnessing the mind of the young within the narrow confines of ideology.

The conception of a university as an instrument of indoctrination is altogether alien to the Western spirit of free inquiry. The quite different ideals which animate the free university have been eloquently summarized in the regulations of the University of California.

> The function of the university is to seek and to transmit knowledge and to train students in the processes whereby truth is to be made known. To convert, or to make converts, is alien and hostile to this dispassionate duty. Where it becomes necessary, in performing this function, to consider political, social, or sectarian movements, they are dissected and examined—not taught, and the conclusion left, with no tipping of the scales, to the logic of the facts.
>
> The University is founded upon faith in intelligence and knowledge and it must defend their free operation. It must rely upon truth to combat error. Its obligation is to see that the conditions under which questions are examined are those which give play to intellect rather than to passion.[4]

At its best, a university in its operations thus provides a model of the process by which the broader community of which it is a part can reach its decisions. The notion of education for democracy is a much used and much abused phrase, in so far as it carries with it the conception of ritualistic indoctrination in the formal machinery of free government. The truth of the matter rather is that the very style of life that a university embodies is itself an education in freedom. What could be better training for democracy than the spectacle of agile minds colliding in the free search for knowledge?

[4] University of California, University Regulations, No. 5 (revised), June 15, 1944.

No one has better described the symbolic role of the university in an open society than Ortega y Gassett:

> In the thick of life's urgencies and its passions, the university must assert itself as a major "spiritual power," higher than the press, standing for serenity in the midst of frenzy, for seriousness and the grasp of intellect in the face of unashamed frivolity.[5]

As Ortega points out, the university must be secure in treating "the great themes of the day from its own point of view: cultural, professional and scientific—an uplifting principle in the history of the Western world."

Ultimately, of course, the vitality of a free university in a democracy will wither unless it draws nourishment from the sustaining force of public opinion. Even the firmest of legal or institutional safeguards are of little avail against waves of public intolerance. Here is where the lay boards of trustees can be of supreme value in the relations with the community —explaining, justifying, and defending the intellectual freedom that is the birthright of the university. The freedom that public colleges and universities have traditionally enjoyed in American society has always depended upon public awareness that free institutions of higher learning are essential to the welfare and progress of the community.

In the future there is one point that colleges and universities will need to make to the public and its elected representatives very persuasively. This is simply that the goal of efficiency in higher education can be realized without non-educational officials intervening in the fiscal affairs of colleges and universities. For certainly generous public support for the continued independence of higher learning will be forthcoming only where there is public confidence in the budgeting, accounting, and reporting procedures of our schools.

[5] *Mission of the University* (Princeton: Princeton University Press, 1944), p. 99.

Under such conditions, overhead fiscal controls imposed upon higher education by the state will seem to be mere excess baggage. Freedom will itself be the mark of efficiency.

## The Limits of Centralization

No factor has contributed more to recent stress in the relations between the state and higher education than the widespread belief that centralized control over all state activity cheapens the cost while improving the services that are provided the public. And yet it is something of a paradox that the states have been moving to centralize control over their administrative structure at the same time that developments in management theory and practice elsewhere have been underscoring the value of deconcentrating decision-making authority wherever possible within institutional systems as complicated as state government.

As is common in the management field, private industry has led the way in this trend toward administrative decentralization. But during the last decade at least a small beginning in the same direction has become visible in government at the national level, particularly in the area of personnel administration. Animating this trend toward decentralization in both public and private administration is the belief that the broad range of functions carried on by any large and complex organization makes it impossible for all authority to be concentrated at a single center of control without a serious loss in both the speed and competence with which decisions are made. It has also come to be recognized that informed judgment in each area of administrative operations demands a specialized knowledge and experience that is only present in the agency that has immediate responsibility for performance.

Certainly there is no state activity other than higher education in which there is a greater need for leaving authority in the hands of those with immediate and intimate knowledge of its affairs. For the task of a university is infinitely more complex than that of conventional state activities. An institution of higher education engages in a wide range of teaching, research, and service activities in such diverse fields as law, medicine, engineering, agriculture, forestry, nursing, and the fine arts. No other state activity comes close to duplicating a college or university in the multiplicity of fields that it encompasses in its operations.

There are many other obstacles which confront any attempt to direct or control performance in higher education from the remote perspective of state bureaucracy. For one thing it is far more difficult to measure achievement in higher education than in other areas of state activity, given the intangible and immeasurable aspects of the educational function. In commenting on this difference between higher education and other state programs, the president of one leading university states:

> It is possible to measure far more precisely the number of miles of highways constructed, the number of patients cared for in a mental hospital, the number of planted fish caught from the lake, the reduction in the maternal death rate, the response of the crime rate to police measures, or the effect on traffic accident rates of law enforcement procedures. But the benefits of education are beyond such precise measurement and evaluation; they are often slow to develop, and then difficult to interpret or identify except in general terms. They are most often reflected in social, political, economic gains made over periods of decades, coming far too slowly and imperceptibly to be assayed critically by legislators working on year-to-year appropriations.

Higher education also differs from other state activities

with respect to the specialized nature of the resources that it uses. Colleges and universities employ a much higher percentage of professional personnel than is commonly the case in state administration. At one institution it was estimated that out of 575 employees, more than 60 per cent could be classified as professionals. In recruiting such skilled staff members, universities are obliged to enter into a national market in the face of competition from private as well as public institutions. If a state university is to maintain itself as a center of high-quality instruction, it must have sufficient discretion on matters of salary and working conditions to meet the widespread competition that exists for able faculty members.

The highly professionalized nature of its staff necessarily makes the task of running a university quite different from that of operating a conventional state agency. Travel restrictions, for example, can prove particularly burdensome for a university, hampering the process of communications among scholars upon which progress in research depends. A rigid interpretation of central purchasing requirements can seriously impede the operation of certain academic departments, especially in the physical sciences where there is a heavy demand for scientific equipment and laboratory apparatus. The problem of conforming to restrictions of this kind becomes acute when a university is located at some distance from the state capitol.

Moreover, the size of a university, at least in the case of the larger institutions, renders unnecessary many of the centralized services from which other state programs may benefit. A college president with long experience in state government has pointed this out:

> Most state universities are large enough as operational
> units to get all the benefits of "efficiency and economy"

that are commonly attributed to centralized purchasing, accounting, etc. A state system carried on and super-imposed upon accounting, purchasing and similar activities already established within state universities and colleges (and necessary for their own efficient operation) leads only to needless and costly duplication.

Actually, the best public colleges and universities lead rather than follow state government in adopting the most modern practices of business management.

In part the movement to bring state colleges and universities within the framework of uniform procedures and controls has been inspired by the belief that all state activities can be administered in exactly the same way. The truth of the matter rather is that any public function has certain unique requirements—in the case of higher education, the need for freedom—to which government procedures may need to adapt themselves. Budgeting, accounting, and auditing are not the purposes of government—they are the means by which those purposes are achieved. Higher education, mental health, and conservation—it is goals such as these that state agencies exist to attain and it is to their needs that all procedures should be subordinated.

The question is often asked—what has been the effect of controls upon colleges and universities? Have they, after all is said and done, had a seriously adverse effect upon the fundamental purposes of higher education? To this question, one college president has given eloquent reply:

> In my opinion, the state which considers close control as a desirable objective, and which asks a university to specify how each minor encroachment on freedom is going to affect achievement of the higher purposes of the institution is asking how many roots can be cut before a tree ceases to bear fruit, and becomes an ornamental dwarf.

However petty each instance of control may be, in cumulative effect a broad range of restrictions upon the operating freedom of institutions of higher education leaves very little room for the imagination and vitality by which truly creative institutions of higher learning are nourished.

# The state and higher education: a report from Michigan

JOHN W. LEDERLE, *Director,*
*Institute of Public Administration, University of Michigan*

> *This statement* \* *by John Lederle, formerly Controller of the state of Michigan, portrays relations between the state and higher education as they have developed in one of our principal states. It reflects a view that has gained increasing strength among state officials and students of administration —that there is much to be said for decentralization of authority in public as well as private administration.*

AT THE OUTSET I should like to express great sympathy for the objectives of your committee. I abhor any trend to extend governmental controls in such a way as to endanger the initiative and imagination of leaders of higher education. I oppose vehe-

\* Prepared for delivery before the Committee on Government and Higher Education, Baltimore, Maryland, on March 1, 1958.

mently a philosophy, seemingly held by some state budget officers, that all educational institutions should be cast in a common mold, subjected to standardization, and left no room for experimentation and differentiation.

I assume that you would want me to make some comments on the problems of government and higher education as seen from the government end of the spectrum. Toward the end of this discussion I will, of course, return to the university end of the spectrum and add additional Michigan examples of dissatisfaction with external controls.

It was quite an experience for me to go from the relatively quiet setting of a university professorship of public administration to the hot seat of Michigan state controller, responsible, under the governor, for preparing the state's budget, for exercising the various follow-up controls associated with budget execution, and for handling such central housekeeping functions as accounting, purchasing, motor transport, and capital outlay construction. An ex-professor controller suddenly discovers that higher education—hitherto the center of his universe—is only one of many state functions competing for the taxpayers' dollar. He is besieged for funds on all sides. The department of conservation wants 100 additional forest rangers and shouts that if it does not get them, there may be a conflagration which will destroy hundreds of thousands of trees, irreplaceable in our lifetime. The state police point to the mounting death toll on the highways and indicate the millions they must have to put an end to this holocaust. And the department of mental health—to hear this department's well-intentioned representatives talk, we must forthwith construct a roof over the entire state, since all citizens are on the verge of mental breakdowns and will need hospitalization. Basically sympathetic to higher education, the ex-professor controller suddenly finds himself forced to initiate decisions as between higher education and other worthwhile government services. Having done so his task is not over, for he must then make recommendations whereby the figure for all higher education is allocated among the various colleges and universities in the state system.

It is impossible to give higher education all that it ideally could use and requests. As the level of services which people demand of their state governments rises, the competition for limited revenues becomes more severe. In Michigan we have not only the competition between higher education and the demands of mental health, state police, and conservation, for example, but the decline of the real property tax at the local level has led to increasing competition for state funds between state agencies on the one hand and local school and municipal agencies on the other. Higher education faces particularly severe competition from the public secondary and elementary school people, who today draw substantial state support rather than rely wholly on local real property taxes. In this highly competitive atmosphere, state budget officers, governors, and legislators are understandably asking more and more detailed questions about the management and programs of public colleges and universities.

Michigan's two constitutionally independent universities have not readily accepted this situation. It seems to me that they have sometimes failed to appreciate their "public" character, one crucial aspect of which is public accountability and administrative life in a "goldfish bowl." The plain fact is that our universities are in "politics" and what they do is of concern to the outside public which foots the bills. As a political scientist this does not disturb me, for I view politics not as an evil thing but as an influence which can help universities to improve.

In Michigan there is mounting criticism of the veil of secrecy with which our constitutionally independent universities have often surrounded themselves. For a number of years the two university governing boards refused to open their meetings to the public. The press was critical of these closed sessions and alleged a "right to know." Belatedly the governing boards did give in. However, neither constitutionally independent institution makes its internal operating budget available to the public, or for that matter, to the budget office, governor, or legislature. Specific requests for information are promptly complied with, but the entire document, from which the whole picture of the educational operation could be gauged, is not available. This secrecy, unique to the two universities, does not set well with state officials and legislators, or with the press. One does not have to be around the state capitol for long before he hears numerous antagonistic comments about the "fourth branch" of state government. While there are great reservoirs of good will, some cracks are appearing.

Your staff has been accumulating nation-wide evidence which may indicate a more and more questioning attitude toward public colleges and universities generally. A past president of the Association of State Budget Officers told me recently that at their annual conferences there has been a hardening of critical comments by the membership. From an attitude of "Let's get together and work things out," which he says budget officers had a very few years ago, he now reports a change to an attitude that might be described as "You can't work with the colleges and universities, so let's go ahead on our own and knock them down to size." As Arthur Naftalin told you last year, budget people do not see higher education as unique. They are not likely to treat it as sacrosanct. They must allocate limited funds between competing services and are not for putting higher education on a pedestal.

Not only is higher education in severe competition with other governmental services, with the obligation of first establishing its over-all portion of state appropriations, but individual colleges and universities are in competition with each other for that portion of total funds to be allocated to higher education. The scramble for funds among the colleges and universities, always well publicized by the press, often hurts the prestige of higher education.

Because in Michigan our six separate boards governing nine institutions reach little, if any, advance agreement, the battle for funds sometimes has descended to the level of name-calling between competing institutions. On occasion clientele groups have been marshalled and the pressure on the legislature has been so severe that the legislative attitude has in a few instances become one of "a plague on all your houses." If public higher education in Michigan could agree and present a common front, some of the fumbling, inept questions raised by budget officers and legislators would never be asked. External investigators are particularly likely to look for duplication and waste when colleges and universities get away from their primary and unique function of teaching and research, into television, extension, and a variety of off-campus service activities. Single state boards of higher education to co-ordinate the separate institutions are not an absolute answer, any more than a single department of defense is the final answer to interservice rivalries. But colleges and universities in a particular state must maximize areas of agreement so as to present a common front. It is unseemly and ruinous to fight each other.

So much for comments on the way relations between government and higher education in Michigan look from the government end of the spectrum. Now let us turn to the opposite end. The two constitutionally independent universities, which receive their funds in a lump sum, have been singularly free to handle their own accounting, purchasing, and other administrative arrangements without external interference. However, in the capital outlay area, the legislature has more and more seen fit to tie up release of construction funds by requiring clearances from the state's building division. Also, self-liquidating projects which used to be authorized by the governing boards independently, now need legislative advance approval, even though they do not involve expenditure of state funds, and even though any taxpayer liability, should they go sour, would be moral rather than legal. However, up to now such approval has been automatic and perfunctory.

I should mention one new development, namely recent appeals to the legislature by each of the constitutionally independent universities for special projects which, when granted, come in the form of a line item. Beginning with a special agricultural marketing program at Michigan State University in 1954 there has followed a traffic administration center and a labor and industrial relations center at the same university. The University of Michigan, a little slow in the up-take and perhaps fearing the implications of the line item for special projects, has only this current year begun to push this approach in earnest. It has presented requests, which have been included in the governor's budget recommendations, for funds for an institute of labor and industrial relations, a Great Lakes research institute, a program of research and service for small business enterprise in Michigan, and an institute of science and technology. If, as some observers have felt, the University of Michigan and Michigan State have been unusually fortunate in having flexibility of educational management because of lump sum appropriations, we are witnessing a perceptible trend away from this in recent requests for special program items. One cannot be certain whether funds for these programs could only have been obtained on a line-item basis. Enthusiasm for line-item programs might dissipate rapidly if hindsight indicates them to be an incursion upon the concept of lump-sum appropriation. One gets the impression that some educators are going overboard on the salable, categorical programs at the expense of more central institutional objectives. Perhaps we are only witnessing here what has been true for a long time in the capital outlay area; namely, that it is easier to get a legislature to appropriate for medical and science buildings than for music and library buildings.

In contrast to the two constitutionally independent universities, the other institutions present requests for funds after submitting a detailed proposed operating budget which is gone over by budget officials and legislative committees. They receive their operating funds not in a lump sum but under the three headings of (1) salaries and wages, (2) contractual services, supplies and materials, and (3) equipment. When it comes to spending their funds, these schools are subject to central accounting procedures, centralized purchasing controls, and central motor pool surveillance. They do, of course, control their own personnel practices.

In preparing for today's session I took pains to ask a number of Michigan college administrators how central state controls look to them. Do these officials feel that they are being assisted or are they being improperly circumscribed? On the whole there can be no question that Michigan external controls are more wisely exercised than external controls in most states. I am convinced however that from the worm's eye point of view, rather than from the state controller point of view, there is plenty of room for improvement. There is many a slip between the statement of policy by the state controller, expressing sympathy for vesting large discretion in the educational institutions, and the actual carrying out of this policy by the personnel of the central controlling department. Time and again during my period in Lansing, when conflicts between departmental personnel and educational institutions were called to my attention, I found it necessary to reverse over-zealous centralist activities by my staff. Some staff members were real martinets. There are those who assert that there is a congenital tendency on the part of central purchasing, accounting, and budget people to get beyond their depth and to violate the principle of service which they avow as their reason for being. I believe there is much truth in this claim. External control personnel, particularly those in the lower ranks, tend to "go by the book" and frequently show little real judgment or discretion. Their frame of mind emphasizes negative values.

Let me briefly run over some of the headaches and criticisms which the institutions, other than the constitutionally independent schools, have brought out.

I believe the basic complaint is related to the legislative practice of appropriating under the three headings mentioned above. Even though the gross appropriation is adequate, the schools cannot transfer moneys from any one of these three major accounts to the other in the interest of efficiency and flexibility to meet changed conditions. In one of our smaller institutions, whose enrollment has more than doubled in five years, tight budgeting has consistently underestimated enrollments by as much as twenty per cent of total enrollment. The legislative policy for this institution encourages accepting all qualified applicants, but the school's administrators are handicapped by another legislative policy which prohibits transfers. Consequently, school officials hang on tenterhooks as they push through deficiency bills, not knowing until May of the fiscal year whether the legislative leaders will pick up the check for the deficit. As another example, one college controller told me that the "no-transfer" rule sometimes leads to spending $300 from the salaries and wages account to build a supply cabinet which could have been bought for $100 from the exhausted equipment account.

There is much complaint about unrealistic application of student-teacher ratio figures by budget personnel. Certainly Ferris Institute, with its extensive trade-technical program, and the University of Michigan, with its large graduate and professional program, should have student-teacher ratios which differ greatly from those suitable for schools where more traditional, essentially undergraduate, programs dominate. Yet budget examiners do not make those distinctions and many an attempt to quantify and compare institutions turns out to be a *non sequitur.*

There are complaints about capital outlay controls. All educators are very conscious that budget office cuts in totals for new buildings may be necessary in view of current limited state capital outlay resources. However, the students will shortly be in college; additional construction will be too late and at inflated prices.

While the schools generally like central motor transport facilities, they are less happy about the central purchasing unit. There are the usual complaints about long delays in receiving materials ordered. When central purchasers exercise their right to differ on specifications by adding a phrase permitting substitution of "or equal" products, the schools claim they get some pretty inferior substitutions. They are almost bitter over recent attempts by the state purchasing and accounting divisions to codify expenditures by materials groupings, and to apply these new account titles to all institutions, whether they be hospitals, prisons, state police posts, or educational institutions. In this way, instructional materials for pharmacy or chemistry classes are classified under the code as "hospital supplies," instructional materials used at the one institution teaching cosmetology are classified as "housekeeping supplies," and trade and industrial class materials are coded as "maintenance supplies." One college controller told me that he had to keep two sets of books with separate classifications, because the state-imposed classifications did not give the true picture of educational operations. I could go on. Suffice it to say that the climate is one of ferment—the relationship between educational institutions and external control agencies is uneasy, though not bitter as in some states.

I should like now to make some constructive suggestions on how higher education might proceed so as to secure improved relations with government. Your committee is doing a fine job of accumulating the criticisms and gripes. But this is essentially a negative approach. In the end you will no doubt wish to consider a positive program. Although I have not given this the years of thought that most of you have devoted to the subject, I would like to present four suggestions which I believe you might well include in any action program.

First, you should look at your campus educational role, and improve programs in public administration so as to raise the level of public service and turn out better potential government administrators.

Second, you should focus on the statutory jungle which governs external administrative control procedures in almost every state to the end of developing improved laws, if not model laws, for accounting, purchasing, budgeting and so forth.

Third, you should approach the national professional associations of state budget officers, purchasing officers, controllers, etc., talk over mutual problems, and in an atmosphere of frank discussion seek to improve relations.

Fourth, higher education itself should demonstrate a very real concern about economy and efficiency, rightly defined, which concern will make unnecessary many of the external controls presently being experienced. Let me now discuss each of these suggestions in greater detail.

Higher education can do much through its professional training programs to assure that we get better informed, professionally trained government officials. As I read the parade of horribles set forth in the early studies of the Committee, I am not so much depressed by the fact that these are improper interferences with higher education as I am by the fact that they represent violations of current administrative doctrine, whether applied to higher education or to any other function of government. The pressures for centralized purchasing, for co-ordination of state expenditures for higher education through central budget preparation and executing agencies, for central supervision of capital outlay construction, etc., were based on a desire to improve the economy and efficiency of state government and to put an end to evils associated with wide dispersion of authority. But when external control agencies hamper rather than promote, when they unduly delay, as seems so often the case, their rationale disappears.

What is needed is better trained professional purchasing agents, budget officers, accounting officials, who recognize that they are not the main reason for government, but necessary evils. Applied to higher education they must come to understand that education is one of the major functions of government and that purchasing or budgeting or accounting or personnel officials have a supporting rather than dominating role. Where there is a conflict between external control officials and those responsible for carrying out such a major governmental function as education, doubtful cases should be resolved in favor of the views of the major function officials. In cases of doubt, it is only with the greatest of temerity that the external control officials substitute their judgment for that of the major function officials who have the ultimate responsibility for getting the job done.

Of course, whether there is doubt, is often a question. Even within educational institutions there are frequent conflicts between central administrative officials and the functional departments which are engaged in teaching and research. If you question this, you should read the delightful book by William G. Morse, the former Harvard purchasing officer, entitled *Pardon My Harvard Accent*. In this book he describes with much humor the difficulties he experienced in attempts to economize and standardize and save money at Harvard. Professors have their idiosyncrasies and some are absolutely certain that they cannot write except with Venus lead pencils or with Parker ink, even though the purchasing officer contends that he can get off-brand products of equal quality at a much cheaper price. If the professor insists on a Zeiss microscope while the purchasing officer contends that a Bausch and Lomb microscope is just as good and costs much less, we get into a somewhat more doubtful realm. If I were the purchasing agent I would be inclined to overrule the professor on the pencils and ink but would be inclined to give him his head on the microscope, on the theory that *he* is doing the research and will have to live with the microscope through the years. But other purchasing officers would very likely consider his desires for the more expensive microscope as being an idiosyncrasy which should be overruled. Even ink may be a doubtful case for I have heard librarians complain about the ink that purchasing has wasted its money on.

Recent management literature has shifted the emphasis away from centralized managerial controls. Hierarchical values, while important, are being challenged by new concepts such as "Bottom-up Management." Present thinking is that we should decentralize, that the role of central control officials is to assist the departments and agencies and encourage them to develop their own control units. In purchasing, in budgeting, in personnel management, the new emphasis is to reverse the centralist trend of a few years ago. The federal Hoover Commission and most state Little Hoover Commissions have stressed decentralization.

Fifty years ago a U. S. forest ranger could not sell a cord of wood without advance clearance from Washington. Not so long ago there would be long delays in the settling of minor claims arising from collisions between army vehicles and civilian motor cars due to centralized control procedures. Today these matters are handled quickly in the field, without the frustrating delays and increased possibility of error that would have been involved under previous more centralized procedures. Maybe the present generation of state external control officials are out of touch with these trends. However, it is up to higher education to make sure that our future graduates, many of whom are bound to move into external control positions, acquire a proper understanding of the primary responsibility of the major function agency to resolve the doubtful questions. The trend away from centralization of managerial controls is a confirmation of the axiom that not all roads should lead to the state capital.

Turning now to my second suggestion, I have the impression

that the laws dealing with accounting, purchasing, capital out-lay, etc., laws which state officials are enforcing, are frequently outdated, inconsistent, and as unpalatable to these officials as they are to the universities and colleges. It seems to me that the time is ripe for a frontal attack with the objective of modernizing these laws in particular states or of developing model laws which might be adopted rather generally by the several states.

As Michigan's state controller, I discovered that much of our accounting legislation was very ancient, adapted more to the horse and buggy days, than to the present. But in my short tour of duty I found no way to marshal support for a complete face-lifting. Paradoxically, Michigan had created a shiny-new central department of administration with the hope of introducing sound business management in state government, but had left the new department with moss-encrusted accounting laws which proved a constant source of frustration. Well do I remember an attorney general's opinion, rendered late in the fiscal year, which suddenly informed all state agencies through the department of administration that it was no longer sufficient to order supplies and materials and encumber the appropriation within a fiscal year. There must be actual delivery of the ordered goods within the fiscal year. If there should be failure of delivery only for a few days beyond the end of the fiscal year the funds would lapse. A new request for funds would have to be justified and pushed tortuously through the legislature. This particular attorney gen-eral's ruling raised complete havoc. Yet no matter how sympa-thetic the state controller and his subordinates might be, it was necessary to apply the ruling to all agencies including the col-leges and universities.

In the purchasing area modern practice calls for delegating to the agency the authority to make small purchases within the local community without going through central competitive bid-ding procedures. Yet in many states the central purchasing peo-ple insist upon central handling of even the smallest purchases. While in some instances they may require this out of pure cussed-ness, I suspect that at other times their hands are tied by law. Not infrequently statutes governing competitive bidding eliminate all discretion. Your committee might well explore the legislative jungle which governs external control procedures to see what can be done about making a better statutory environment for relations between higher education and government.

As a third suggestion, it seems to me that there are many possibilities for improving relations between higher education and government through conversations with the professional associations of government officials. The state budget officers, state purchasing officers, and other groups have national organizations. It should be possible to get the viewpoint of higher education expressed by speeches at their national conferences. Joint committees to study common problems might be helpful. In a particular state, where there is a rather benighted state official riding herd on the colleges and universities, it may be possible to educate him through the admonitions or ribbing of his professional colleagues from the outside. After all, while he may not be willing to listen to complaints from university representatives from his own state, many times he will react to the comments of his professional colleagues from other states.

Finally, if there is any truth to the old adage that a good offense is the best defense, it seems to me that it may well have application in connection with the relations of higher education to external control officials. If the philosophy of decentralization, about which I have been talking, is actually to be implemented, it is up to the universities to demonstrate that they are as much concerned about efficient and economical management as are the advocates of external controls. Carping criticism will get nowhere in the face of strong public demand for economy and efficiency in state government. There can be no doubt that colleges and universities have much to learn. With no harm to institutional objectives they could save public funds by paying greater attention to modern business practices. While Michigan's two constitutionally independent universities are on the whole very efficiently run, they could learn much from studying procedures that have been developed by the state department of administration. The state motor pool, maintained by the department of administration, for example, makes cars available to operating agencies for 5½¢ a mile and is completely self-support-ing. As a professor at the University of Michigan, using the University of Michigan motor pool, my unit is charged 7¢ a mile. What are the reasons for this difference in cost? They are worth exploring. In these days of taxpayer concern about rising governmental costs, external controls over higher education are bound to expand unless leaders of higher education can convince the public that they have as much concern about operating costs as any external control official could ever have. This concern must be communicated to the public and internal administrative procedures must be tightened so as to reflect the concern.

Although the situation may look black at times, in any struggle between a prominent state university and state officials, never underestimate the power of the university. In Michigan, at least, it takes considerable temerity for a legislator to attack one or the other of the two major state institutions. The institutions have tremendous prestige, and their alumni, both of the real and of the synthetic variety, are likely to remember criticisms of their favorite school when voting at the next election. Of course, much of the interference with universities occurs in the less public atmosphere of bureaucratic decision-making, and hence, it is not always easy to crystallize support for the university's viewpoint. However, let me remind you that if you are on the university end, you are probably exaggerating your helpless situation. Believe me when you are on the external-control-end, you feel that the best cards are in the hands of the leaders of higher education. I have no doubt that if you take pains to get your story across, you will win the day.

# British universities and the state:

# a contrast with

# the American scene

ROBERT O. BERDAHL

*Social Science Division, San Francisco State College*

*In its relations with the state, the British university system furnishes an interesting comparison with public higher education in the United States. Particularly worthy of note is the University Grants Committee, which provides the university with a shield from the kind of fiscal and management supervision that is commonly practiced by state government in the United States.*

IF THERE IS SUCH a thing as a British "genius" for politics, it is nowhere more clearly manifest than in the way in which the university system in Britain has been successfully brought within the framework of national planning and subsidy without serious damage to educational autonomy. The complete story of how this delicate task has been accomplished is told in detail elsewhere.[1] Our purpose here is to show in brief compass the principal outlines of the British experience in order to acquaint those working in the area of higher education with an alternative way of reconciling the responsibilities of government with the freedom of the university.

Questions may be raised about the value of comparisons across national lines when the pattern of higher education in the two countries concerned is so different. It is true that in Britain the university system generally excludes many institutions (like technical colleges and teacher training colleges) that are an integral part of the American scene. It is also true that the British universities deal with a much smaller proportion of college-age youth than their American counterparts.[2] Finally, it is clear that completely private British universities are, in the unitary British state, in a much different legal position *vis-a-vis* public authority than state universities in the American federal system. Notwithstanding these differences in type, size, and constitutional context, there are many striking parallels between attempts of institutions in both countries to accept essential governmental aid without at the same time surrendering vital areas of university autonomy.

## The Background of Concern

The following table demonstrates the ways in which British universities differ with respect to antiquity, type, and size:

[1] See the author's *British Universities and the State,* University of California Publications in Political Science, VII (Berkeley: University of California Press, 1959).

[2] Opinions differ on the relative proportions of college educated youth in America and Britain, but it has been estimated that America's ratio is from six to ten times higher than that of Britain.

## The Type, Date of Chartering, and Number of Students (1954–55) of British Universities [3]

|  | Number of full-time students in 1954–55 |
|---|---|
| *2 Medieval Foundations* | |
| Oxford, origins in 12th century | 7,187 |
| Cambridge, origins in 13th century | 7,934 |
| *3 Nineteenth Century Federal Foundations* | |
| Durham, 1832 | 3,915 |
| London, 1836 | 18,201 |
| Wales, 1893 | 4,494 |
| *11 Modern English Provincial (civic) Universities* | |
| Birmingham, 1900 | 3,135 |
| Manchester, 1903 | 3,921 |
| Liverpool, 1903 | 2,919 |
| Leeds, 1904 | 3,398 |
| Sheffield, 1905 | 2,010 |
| Bristol, 1909 | 2,666 |
| Reading, 1926 | 1,110 |
| Nottingham, 1948 | 2,066 |
| Southhampton, 1952 | 1,100 |
| Hull, 1954 | 727 |
| Exeter, 1955 | 889 |
| Leicester, 1957 | 638 |
| *4 Scottish Universities* | |
| St. Andrews, 1411 | 1,820 |
| Glasgow, 1451 | 4,748 |
| Aberdeen, 1493 | 1,652 |
| Edinburgh, 1583 | 4,608 |
| *1 University College granting degrees* | |
| North Staffordshire, 1949 | 533 |
| *2 Technical Colleges receiving U. G. C. grants* | |
| Manchester College of Technology, 1955 | 719 |
| Royal Technical College, Glasgow, 1912 | 1,315 |
| Total: | 81,705 |

[3] University Grants Committee, *Returns from Universities and University Colleges* for the year 1954–55, p. 11. The Grants Committee is hereafter cited as U. G. C.

The essential fact to be noted about British universities is that they are all private institutions, possessing their own organs of government, regulating their own affairs, appointing their own teaching and administrative staff and, until recently, largely self-financing. This does not mean, however, that they are altogether beyond the reach of government control, for this has certainly never been the case. In the mid-nineteenth century, for example, the government of the day succeeded over strong opposition from Oxford and Cambridge in having the Crown appoint royal commissions of inquiry into the affairs of the two universities. The commissions subsequently established beyond doubt that the universities, although private agencies in the eyes of the law, were nevertheless "national institutions" with certain minimum obligations to society.

Since that time, the problem has largely been one of defining the content of those obligations in accordance with changing circumstances. The inauguration in 1889 of small state grants to the modern English and Welsh university colleges, the subsequent gradual increase in the scale of these awards, the formation in 1919 of a University Grants Committee to distribute the grants with a minimum of state regulations, and the inclusion of Oxford and Cambridge on the grant list in 1923—all these developments tended to bring the universities to the state's *continuing* attention sooner than might otherwise have been the case. But let it be understood: the grants were the *occasion* and not the *cause* of the state's increased interest in the universities, for this concern both pre-dates and transcends the question of grants. Few people in Britain today would seriously contend that, even if the universities were financially self-sufficient, the contemporary state could forego efforts to integrate their operations into the general framework of national planning. In the era of the Sputnik and the "dollar gap," the universities have become absolutely essential to the nation's economic viability and military security.

At the close of World War I, when the state indicated its growing interest in the universities by establishing a permanent committee to advise on grants to higher education, university leaders informed the government that such help would be welcome provided that it was not accompanied by government control. One vice-chancellor (the equivalent of an American university president) some years later described this university position: "No one but ourselves can have any idea of how that money can best be spent from time to time. The doors are open, and if we make fools of ourselves, you can take it away. Inspect freely, but there must be absolutely no control." [4]

## The University Grants Committee

Consequently, when the University Grants Committee (U. G. C.) was finally created, in 1919, the government made several concessions to university autonomy. First, the Grants Committee was given these very modest terms of reference: "to enquire into the financial needs of University education . . . and to advise the Government as to the application of any grants that may be made by Parliament to meet them." [5] Second, the government funds which were given to the universities were distributed by the U. G. C. in the form of block grants, to be spent according to the universities' best judgment. Finally, the new committee was placed, not under the Board (now the Ministry) of Education, as might have been expected, but under the Treasury. According to Sir Keith Murray, the present chairman of the U. G. C., this location was deliberate and one "which has been the source of much confidence in the Committee. [The Universities] have no fears that a Minister . . . who is likely to have theories or special interest in educational matters may question the objective advice of the Committee and exert undue influence on university affairs." [6]

The original University Grants Committee consisted of a part-time Chairman, Sir William McCormick, and ten other distin-

4 Sir Alfred Hopkinson, in "Universities and the State," in Third Congress of the Universities of the British Empire, *Report of the Proceedings* (1926), pp. 27-30.

5 Treasury Minute, July 14, 1919.

6 Sir Keith Murray, "The Work of the University Grants Committee in Great Britain," *Universiteit en Hogeschool,* I (1955), p. 250.

guished academicians not in the active service of any of the institutions entitled to grants. Members of the Committee were appointed by the Chancellor of the Exchequer after consultation with the President of the Board of Education (now the Minister of Education) and the Secretary of State for Scotland. The Committee was served by a full-time Secretary drawn from the Treasury as well as a clerical staff. An observer later remarked on the symbolic significance of the administrative pattern: "An academic Chairman, and a civil servant (usually of the Treasury) as Secretary; the one as it were facing to the Universities, the other to the Treasury." [7]

The University Grants Committee represented an attempt to co-ordinate government grants to universities both functionally and geographically by combining in one agency the government's earlier fragmented aid to higher education. In 1919 the sum voted by Parliament for the universities was £ 1,000,000, a figure considerably above the total of the grants that had previously been distributed among a varied range of projects and institutions. When Oxford and Cambridge Universities, following a Royal Commission of Inquiry into their fiscal conditions and policies, were added to the grant list in 1923, all the universities of England, Wales, and Scotland were for the first time placed on the same footing with the government. (Northern Ireland, after 1922, became a separate political jurisdiction.)

Although the grants were not provided on a five-year basis until 1925, when post-war financial conditions had eased somewhat, the University Grants Committee retained the practice of an earlier *ad hoc* grants committee in visiting each university and university college on the grant list at least once every five years. What U. G. C. members saw on these early visits was a most disparate system of universities and colleges, if indeed it could be called a "system" at all. Each institution had a tradition (albeit some a much longer one than others) of governing itself in splendid isolation of what went on in other areas. Notwithstanding some efforts at inter-university co-operation, the British

[7] Sir Hector Hetherington, *The British University System, 1914–1954*, Aberdeen University Studies No. 113 (1954), p. 6.

universities remained suspicious of any efforts to impose common national standards.

The early U. G. C. therefore walked lightly in order to avoid giving offense. Its first reports examined nearly all facets of university life and offered many suggestions for improvements. But it went no further in pursuing greater national co-ordination than to praise inter-university consultations, such as had taken place in 1921 regarding the raising of fees. In fact, the Committee insisted that

> . . . to different universities the same general problems will present themselves in different orders of urgency, determined by their peculiar histories and circumstances; . . . we must say at once that, even if we thought we could propound, as we are sure that we cannot, an ideal common policy for all our universities, we should not feel the slightest wish to press its adoption.[8]

What the U. G. C. did urge, however, was that each university and university college address itself to "the formulation of a definite policy, in the light of which the many problems of its future development over a period of years can be considered and decided, in due relation to its financial position and prospects." [9]

In 1935, in recognition of the increasing burden of U. G. C. responsibilities, the chairmanship (then held by Sir Walter Moberly) was made full-time. In the following year the annual grants to universities had reached £ 2,100,000. By the end of the thirties the U. G. C. had become a "clearing house for all the plans for the use of the Universities in the event of war." [10]

*War and Its Aftermath*

World War II, like its predecessor, had a dramatic impact on the universities. While university enrollments did not drop as sharply during the second world war, due to careful planning

[8] University Grants Committee, *Report* (1925), p. 12.
[9] *Ibid.*, p. 28.
[10] Sir Keith Murray, *op. cit.*, p. 282.

and the large scale deferment of students of science and medicine, university buildings suffered greater war damages and the evacuation of several universities from their exposed locations brought a plethora of unprecedented complications. Constituent colleges of London University, for example, were sent as far away as Aberdeen, St. Andrews, Swansea, and Exeter.

Otherwise, the universities faced the familiar wartime evils of spiraling inflation, heavy backlogs of plant maintenance and repair needs, and deferred construction. Furthermore, the large number of ex-servicemen waiting to be admitted to the universities meant an expansion in enrollment far beyond anything previously experienced. And since the tax rate continued very high after the war, it became obvious that university fees and the donations of private benefactors could no longer continue as major sources of university income; state aid had to be increased above its pre-1939 proportion of approximately one-third of total university income in Britain.

Accordingly, the U. G. C. submitted to the Treasury in January 1945, a memorandum outlining tentative university plans for the following ten years and pointing out that "the universities had reached a critical point in their history and that the expansion and improvement of facilities for university education which the public interest demanded could be achieved only with the aid of largely increased subventions from the Exchequer." [11]

Sir John Anderson, Churchill's Chancellor of the Exchequer, then accepted the U. G. C. recommendation that the national grants to universities should be raised for a period of two years to £ 4,149,000 annually, with a further £ 1,000,000 a year included to meet the costs of improvements in medical education recommended by the Goodenough Committee of 1944. Furthermore, a Treasury assurance was given in general terms that these grants would be substantially increased during the remaining years of the decade.

When university enrollments doubled within three short years, the government grants were accordingly raised to nearly £ 9,000,-

[11] U. G. C., *University Development from 1935 to 1947* (1948) (hereafter cited as *Univ. Devel. 1935–1947*), p. 76.

000 in the year 1947–48. The Education Act of 1944 had resulted among other things in a much larger number of students who were qualified to matriculate at the universities. Moreover, during this period reports of various official committees on such fields as medical, dental, veterinary and agricultural education, social and economic research, scientific manpower, and technological education [12] had recommended an expansion of university facilities in a wide range of fields.

The growth in state financial assistance resulting from the need to expand the universities is reflected in the table on p. 348.

The huge increase in national grants to universities and the increased importance of higher education to the nation's security and economic viability combined to raise a question as to whether the Grants Committee should play a more positive role in distributing state aid. One influential body, the Barlow Committee on Scientific Manpower, wrestled with this problem in 1946:

> We are unanimously opposed to any infringement of the cherished independence of the Universities, even if it could be justified on the grounds that it would facilitate the execution of [our recommended] expansion programme.
> We do not, however, believe that the maintenance of the Universities' independence is in any way incompatible with the extension and improvement of the machinery for adjusting their policy to the needs of the country. . . . The State has perhaps been over-concerned lest there should be even a suggestion

[12] Committee on Agricultural Education in Scotland, (Alness) *Report* (1945), Cmd. 6704; Committee on Higher Agricultural Education in England and Wales, (Loveday) *Report* (1946), Cmd. 6728; Committee on Scientific Manpower, (Barlow) *Report* (1946), Cmd. 6824; Committee on Social and Economic Research, (Clapham) *Report* (1946), Cmd. 6868; Committee on Veterinary Education in Great Britain, *Second Report* (1944), Cmd. 6517; Foreign Office, Inter-departmental Commission on Oriental, Slavonic, East European, and African Studies, (Scarbrough) *Report* (1946); Inter-departmental Committee on Dentistry, (Teviot) *Report* (1946), Cmd. 6727; Ministry of Education, Special (Percy) Committee on Higher Technological Education, *Report* (1945); Ministry of Education, (McNair) Committee on Teachers and Youth Leaders, *Report* (1944); Ministry of Health and Department of Health for Scotland, (Goodenough) Committee on Medical Education, *Report* (1944).

## Sources of University Income

Analysis of University Income for Selected Years since 1920

| | | Analysis by source, in per cent of total income | | | | | |
|---|---|---|---|---|---|---|---|
| Year | Total income of universities | Parliamentary grants | Grants from local authorities | Fees | Endowments | Donations and subscriptions | Other sources |
| 1920–21 | £3,020,499 | 33.6 | 9.3 | 33.0 | 11.2 | 2.7 | 3.3 |
| 1923–24 | 3,587,366 | 35.5 | 12.0 | 33.6 | 11.6 | 2.5 | 4.8 |
| 1928–29 | 5,174,510 | 35.9 | 10.1 | 27.8 | 13.9 | 2.4 | 6.9 |
| 1933–34 | 5,953,320 | 35.1 | 9.2 | 32.8 | 13.7 | 2.4 | 6.8 |
| 1938–39 | 6,712,067 | 35.8 | 9.0 | 29.8 | 15.4 | 2.6 | 7.4 |
| 1946–47 | 13,043,541 | 52.7 | 5.6 | 23.2 | 9.3 | 2.2 | 7.0 |
| 1949–50 | 22,009,735 | 63.9 | 4.6 | 17.7 | 5.7 | 1.7 | 6.4 |
| 1953–54 | 31,112,024 | 70.5 | 3.6 | 12.0 | 4.3 | 1.6 | 8.0 |
| 1955–56[13] | 36,894,000 | 72.7 | 3.1 | 10.8 | 3.8 | 0.9 | 8.7[14] |

[13] For a projection of the anticipated grants for the years 1957–58 to 1961–62, by the Chancellor of the Exchequer, see the *Manchester Guardian*, March 15, 1957.

[14] "Other income" in 1955–56 included £1,478,000 from grants for research and £818,000 from income receivable under research contracts.

of interference with the independence of the Universities. . . . We think that circumstances demand that it should increasingly concern itself with positive University policy. It may be desirable for this purpose to revise [the University Grants Committee's] terms of reference and strengthen its machinery.[15]

To this was added the statement of another influential body, the Committee of Vice Chancellors and Principals. This group is the private organ of inter-university co-ordination operating parallel to the U. G. C. Although it has no formal power to take decisions binding its constituent members, the Vice Chancellor's

[15] *Op. cit.*, p. 21.

Committee has nevertheless become the most effective means of inter-university collaboration. It was of major significance, therefore, when these university spokesmen stated that:

> . . . the universities entirely accept the view that the Government has not only the right, but also the duty, of satisfying itself that every field of study which in the national interest ought to be cultivated in Great Britain is, in fact, being adequately cultivated in the university system, and that the resources which are placed at the disposal of the universities are being used with full regard both to efficiency and economy . . . The universities may properly be expected not only individually to make proper use of the resources entrusted to them, but also collectively to devise and execute policies calculated to serve the national interest, and in that task, both individually and collectively, they will be glad to have a greater measure of guidance from the Government than until quite recent days they have been accustomed to receive.[16]

Shortly thereafter, on July 30, 1946, the Chancellor of the Exchequer told Parliament that since the universities had entered a new phase of rapid expansion and planned development, he was anxious that the Grants Committee serve a more positive and influential function than it had in the past. He then announced that in addition to its original duties the U. G. C. would be asked to "assist, in consultation with the universities and other bodies concerned, in the preparation and execution of such plans for the development of the universities as may from time to time be required in order to ensure that they are fully adequate to national needs." [17]

The U. G. C. envisaged its new relationship with the universities as a "form of partnership," maintaining that "the principles of central planning and of academic autonomy are not opposites." [18] Soon steps were taken to expand the scale of its activities.[19] First, government grants to agricultural, veterinary and

[16] "A Note on University Policy and Finance," as quoted in *Universities Quarterly*, I (1947), p. 188.

[17] *Parl. Debates*, House of Commons, Vol. 426, col. 129 (July 30, 1946).

[18] *Univ. Devel. 1935–1947*, p. 82.

[19] This expansion of U. G. C. activities did not extend to the administration

forestry education were brought under the Grants Committee. Second, several new university colleges were added to the grant list. Third, the U. G. C. (due to the huge increase in non-recurrent capital grants) became involved in university building programs to an extent not experienced before. And finally, in response to the recommendations of several of the official committees cited earlier, a series of earmarked grants was instituted alongside the traditional block grants for the period 1947–1952, in order to bolster development in certain specified areas.

The additional work necessitated by these and other new duties led to an enlargement of the U. G. C. membership and administrative staff and the creation of a number of specialist sub-committees, made up partly of experts co-opted from outside, to advise the parent Committee in a variety of fields. The practice of excluding men or women actively engaged in university teaching or research from Committee membership had already been modified in 1943, and the average age of the Committee accordingly became younger with succeeding appointments. The Committee was enlarged to eighteen members, each appointed for a five year period, but often asked to serve a second term. According to Sir Keith Murray,

> . . . the members are not selected as representatives of any particular interest; the over-ruling consideration is that they should personally carry the confidence of the Chancellor [of the Exchequer] and of the Universities, though attention is also paid to achieving some balance in the academic membership both geographically and with reference to the most important interests in University teaching and research.[20]

The Committee in 1956 included nine members in active university service; one retired and two active heads of colleges; three men of affairs from industry and commerce; a chief educa-

---

of state scholarships, which remained with the Ministry of Education, nor was any attempt made to centralize control of the research grants made to the universities by various government agencies (e.g. Department of Scientific and Industrial Research, the Medical Research Council, and the Agricultural Research Council).

20 Sir Keith Murray, *op. cit.*, p. 254.

tion officer of one of Britain's largest cities; and the headmaster of a famous grammar school.

Aside from the above changes in scope of activities and in internal organization, the U. G. C. continues to operate in its traditional pattern: visits ("in no sense inspections or cross-examination" [21]) to each institution on the grant list at least once a quinquennium, on the basis of which, along with less formal contacts, judgments are made of the universities' individual and collective needs for the next five year period. The Grants Committee then advises the Chancellor of the Exchequer on the total sum which it recommends be made available for the next quinquennium, making no breakdown of its request into grants for individual universities. After consultations between the Treasury and the U. G. C., the Chancellor decides, in the context of the nation's over-all financial situation, what over-all sum he will ask Parliament to vote for the universities. (In these days of disciplined party voting in the Commons, the Chancellor's "request" is tantamount to a decision.) The Grants Committee then allocates the individual university grants from whatever appropriation the Chancellor has seen fit to approve. According to the present chairman, these allocations

> cannot be made under any set of regulations or on any hard and fast formulas. The number of variables is great—they must include recognition of numbers of students, differences in cost of different types of subjects, the balance of teaching and research, the relative importance of the various proposals for expansion, the institution's access to other sources of money, administrative efficiency and numerous other factors, both tangible and intangible.[22]

In former years, after the period of visitation and allocation had ended, the U. G. C. lapsed into relative idleness. But with the expansion of its duties, the Committee now holds eleven meetings per year to deal with current problems and to plan for the future. Agenda are prepared for these meetings at which a variety of issues may be discussed, from major policy to minute

21 *Ibid.*, p. 256.
22 *Ibid.*, pp. 257–58.

details of building programs. The Committee is often guided by memoranda from its sub-committees, particularly on such highly technical matters as the capital building program. The U. G. C. also employs the device of *ad hoc* sub-committees, such as the one appointed in 1957 to report on the nature and importance of residence halls in the education of university students.

### The Scope of State Control

With the state thus becoming so intricately involved in university finances, in educational policy, in capital expansion, and in scholarships and research, it is perhaps inevitable that questions should arise with regard to the nature of the relationship which has evolved between universities and the government. On the one hand there are those who feel that though the universities' exemption from the usual controls surrounding the spending of public funds was justifiable when their grants from the state were mere pittances, it is imperative that a closer state scrutiny be exercised now that these grants have reached £ 50,000,000 a year.

On the other hand, many people associated with the universities are uneasy about the ever increasing shadow which the state is casting over the universities. To what extent, they ask, should the state have the right to influence the development of university policy? At what point does legitimate state influence become illegitimate state control? Have the universities, so gradually that they don't realize it, sold their souls for a mess of pounds?

Compared to the situation which exists in many parts of this country, British universities are remarkably free of direct control. Outside of a few Regius Professorships and three of four Scottish Principalships which are appointed by the Crown "with a good deal of regard for university opinion," [23] higher education is subject to state control only through the intervention of the University Grants Committee. There is neither a "governor's budget" nor line-item appropriations. The university's recurrent

[23] Sir Walter Moberly, *The Crisis in the University* (1949), p. 227.

grants are voted in a lump sum. The state undertakes neither a pre-audit nor a post-audit of expenditures made by the universities under these grants. There is no requirement that the universities use state agencies for central purchasing or for the recruitment of non-academic personnel.

When the University Grants Committee is included in the picture, however, the idyllic situation just described is modified in several ways. In the first place, while the universities literally have no direct relations with the Treasury concerning their budgets, and while they do get the bulk of their recurrent state grants in block form, the reality behind the appearance is that they are obliged to supply financial information to the U. G. C. in the form requested by the Committee, and are under substantial commitment to spend their block grants for the programs they have previously outlined to the Committee.

In addition, the universities are very closely supervised in their capital building programs by the Grants Committee, which has an elaborate system of control differentiating in its severity between major and minor projects.[24]

Notwithstanding the existence of the Grants Committee controls described above, there has been unrest in some parliamentary circles about the possibility of waste or extravagance in the expenditure of the university grants, particularly with respect to non-recurrent capital expenditures, and proposals have accordingly been made to extend the scrutiny of the Comptroller and Auditor General to the non-recurrent grant records of either the universities or the U. G. C. itself.

Although the rise of relatively disciplined parties in Britain has lessened the Commons' earlier importance in deciding questions of state policy, it has not at all diminished the lower chamber's role in checking on the legality and economy of public expenditure. For, once a Government had determined on a course of action and the majority party has duly translated this

[24] For full details of the Grants Committee's controls over the capital building programs, see the Gater Committee Report: U. G. C., *Methods Used by Universities of Contracting and of Recording Expenditure* (1956), Cmnd. 9, Appendix C.

into legislation, it is in the interests of all parties to devise the most efficient and economic procedures possible for its implementation. It is in connection with this function that parliamentary unrest over some aspects of university grants has arisen.

The two committees of Parliament most deeply involved in this issue are the Select Committees on Estimates and on Public Accounts. While in the theory of parliamentary procedure these committees have separate jurisdictions (based on the distinction between the "economy" and "legality" of expenditures), in practice their interests often overlap, and such is indeed the case with respect to university grants. While both committees are precluded by their terms of reference from considering questions of policy, they each pay a great deal of attention to the working of "Treasury control," co-operating with the Treasury to see that internal fiscal regulations are being followed by the operating departments and agencies of government. To recommendations of the committees bearing on Treasury control, the Treasury usually replies in a Treasury Minute (printed in a subsequent committee report), either agreeing to undertake the recommended change or explaining politely the Exchequer's reasons for disagreeing.

It is against this background of essential harmony that the controversy between the Treasury and the committees about university grants must be viewed. What commenced in 1947 as an exchange of views on the question of statutory authorization for the U. G. C. turned in later years into a series of requests for more information about the Grants Committee's Estimates, for the right of access by the Comptroller and Auditor General to university records relating to non-recurrent building grants, and finally, for the same right regarding the U. G. C.'s records. Although some differences of opinion still remain after ten years of "dialectics" between the parliamentary committees and the Treasury, most points of contention have been eliminated with the help of concessions from both sides. On all major issues but the very last cited above, the parliamentary committees have either obtained satisfaction or have abandoned their recommendations.

The question of statutory authorization was raised by the Public Accounts Committee (P. A. C.) in conjunction with a long-standing agreement with the Treasury that statutory authorization should be expressly provided for any continuing activity involving substantial charges on public funds. According to this interpretation, Parliament's annual vote on the funds in question is not of itself sufficient, for "strictly speaking, the Appropriation Act grants and appropriates money for a service [but] does not say that the service may be provided." [25]

Since the University Grants Committee was created simply by a Treasury Minute in 1919, it was one of the agencies to which the P. A. C. called attention in 1947 and 1948 as requiring a statutory basis.[26] Legislation for this purpose, it was maintained, would give Parliament

> . . . the opportunity of reviewing the need for the continuance of this expenditure on the present scale and of determining whether the administrative organisation, which was established at a time when the expenditure was on a limited scale and without any assurance of continuance, is equally well adapted for the control and disbursement of the continuing and very substantial sum now involved.[27]

The Treasury, in reply, agreed again to the general principle, but felt there were "strong reasons" for making the University Grants Committee an exception. "It had never been the policy of any Government that the universities should be subject to statutory regulations or that academic policy should be controlled by the State." [28] Furthermore, no formula could be devised "which would automatically measure the extent of assistance needed because academic standards, on the maintenance of which any grants must be based, were hardly susceptible of statutory definition." [29]

25 Sir Ivor Jennings, *Parliament* (Cambridge, Cambridge University Press, 1939), p. 285.

26 P. A. C., *Third Report*, 1946–47, H. C. 122, and *Second Report*, 1947–48, H. C. 199.

27 P. A. C., *Second Report*, 1947–48, H. C. 199, para's. 16–17.

28 P. A. C., *Third Report*, 1948–49, H. C. 233, para's. 1–3.

29 *Ibid.*

The Public Accounts Committee admitted being "impressed by the arguments advanced by the Treasury . . ." and abandoned, therefore, its recommendation "in the circumstances now prevailing." [30] The Select Committee on Estimates (S. C. E.), in a later study of the university grants in 1952, similarly concluded that "there are certain non-Governmental bodies which derive the main part of their finances from Government sources and which yet should be allowed, in the public interest, to retain the maximum degree of independence." [31]

Although the Public Accounts Committee and the Select Committee on Estimates agreed that statutory authority would not be required for the U. G. C., neither committee was satisfied with the type of information available concerning the estimates (i.e. the formal request to Parliament for funds) for the university grants. The P. A. C., for example, urged the Treasury to consider "whether without impairing the independence of the Universities, any further means can be adopted to inform Parliament more precisely how the grant-in-aid proposed . . . is to be spent and to assure Parliament that grants made to the Universities are wisely used." [32]

When the Treasury reply was inconclusive, the P. A. C. "felt it necessary to pursue . . . the question," insisting that Parliament had a right to ensure that the grants were administered "with a due regard for economy." The information then being supplied to Parliament did not, in the opinion of the P. A. C., enable it to form an opinion on the subject.[33]

The Minutes of Evidence on the P. A. C.'s various hearings on university grants reveal basic differences of attitude on the part of the P. A. C. and the Treasury over the procedure to be followed in dealing with the universities. These differences go far toward explaining the inability of the disputing parties to agree on the details of university grants administration. As an example, the Treasury, justifying its lack of detailed information concerning

[30] *Ibid.*, para. 4.
[31] Select Committee on Estimates, *Fifth Report,* 1951–52, H. C. 163, para. 27.
[32] P. A. C., *Third Report,* 1948–49, H. C. 233, para. 4.
[33] P. A. C., *Fourth Report,* 1949–50, H. C. 138, para. 40.

the university grant Estimates prepared by the U. G. C., explained that "only in exceptional cases would the Treasury seek to disturb the balance of the [U. G. C.'s] recommendations . . . the inquiries made by the U. G. C. are extremely thorough, very careful and painstaking and carried out with a full sense of responsibility." [34]

Captain Waterhouse of the P. A. C. felt, however, that such a Treasury attitude invited waste; it was beyond his powers of belief that the U. G. C. never put forward anything but the bare minimum of its requirements:

> Anybody who is an enthusiast about something nearly always puts up a figure and thinks, "We will try this." What I should like to be certain of was that the try-on has never succeeded, their having got a good deal more than they thought they might have got. [35]

Sir Edward Bridges, Permanent Secretary to the Treasury, replied that the universities valued their independence so much that they did their utmost to see that the system did in fact work well and economically. He had argued earlier that a "defence in depth" system, by which the Treasury would cut requests at every stage of review, would merely encourage the universities to submit bloated requests in the expectation that these would be heavily chopped. In view of the delicate question of academic freedom, Sir Edward said he much preferred giving the universities and the U. G. C. the responsibility for submitting requests limited to the absolute essentials. [36]

On the other hand, the Treasury said that the last thing they wanted to do was give the impression that they were "anxious to hide anything" for, in their view, "independence did not imply secrecy." [37] Thus, when the Select Committee on Estimates joined its voice [38] to that of the P. A. C. in urging more information on the university grant estimates and on the reasons for increases

[34] P. A. C., *Fourth Report,* 1950–51, H. C. 241, Minutes of Evidence, Q. 7095.
[35] *Ibid.*
[36] P. A. C., 1948–49, *op. cit.,* Minutes of Evidence, Q's. 249–50.
[37] S. C. E., *Fifth Report,* 1951–52, H. C. 163, para. 35.
[38] *Ibid.*

therein, the Treasury moved quickly to comply. The annual volume of statistical *Returns* from the universities were recast in a more comprehensible form; a brief interim report on the first four years of the quinquennium was published in order to aid the parliamentary review of the next quinquennial estimates; and more information of a general nature was provided to explain the basis of the recurrent grants.[39] Another divisive issue was thus solved—this time by virtue of the readiness of the Treasury and the University Grants Committee to satisfy the wishes of the parliamentary committee.

However, the Select Committee on Estimates in the same 1952 report made another recommendation, subsequently taken up by the P. A. C., which did not find the Treasury in such an acquiescent frame of mind. The S. C. E., noting a 1951 exchange between the P. A. C. and the Treasury agreeing to the general principle that the books and accounts of bodies receiving the greater part of their income from public funds should normally be open to inspection by the Comptroller and Auditor General,[40] recommended that "this practice . . . be extended to cover all money issued by way of non-recurrent grant to the Universities for capital development." It did not appear to them that this would in any way "encroach on the freedom of the Universities since this money is voted annually for specific purposes." [41]

The P. A. C. agreed with this recommendation in its 1951–52 report, arguing that "the present system of controlling [building] grants, which stops short at an examination of plans and estimates, is less than Parliament is entitled to . . . where such appreciable amounts of voted monies are involved." [42] (These grants had amounted to £ 7,300,000 in the academic year 1950–51.)

Once again Treasury officials urged that the universities should constitute a legitimate exception to a principle otherwise enjoying general Treasury approval. In this instance, they argued that existing procedures offered sufficient safeguards against waste

39 S. C. E., *Eleventh Report,* 1951–52, H. C. 289, p. 20.
40 P. A. C., 1950–51, *op. cit.,* and Treasury Minute, Nov. 29, 1951.
41 S. C. E., *Fifth Report,* 1951–52, H. C. 163, para. 37.
42 P. A. C., *Third Report,* 1951–52, H C. 253, para. 41.

and that the Comptroller's inspection of university records would inevitably impinge on questions of academic policy, which by definition were excluded from government control. If evidence of the universities' correct application of non-recurrent grants was desired, this information could be found in the reports of the universities' own auditors.[43]

When the Public Accounts Committee, pointing out that neither the Treasury nor the U. G. C. was aware of the instructions issued by the universities to their auditors, renewed its recommendation the following year,[44] other voices in the body politic rose to the defense of the Treasury, the U. G. C., and the universities. Such august journals as *The Times,* the *Observer,* the *Manchester Guardian,* and *The Economist* spoke in justification of university independence. *The Times,* for example, called the P. A. C. proposal to bring in the Comptroller the "thin end of a wedge" which might upset the existing "admirably but delicately balanced relationship" between the state and the universities. As *The Times* put it: "The special trust placed in the Universities is a natural incitement to those who watch over the public purse. They find a closed door and they would have it open. But it is a public interest that it should remain shut." [45]

When the Treasury, after consulting the universities, made the conciliatory gesture of appointing a committee of inquiry (the Gater Committee) into university administrative procedures relating to capital development, the P. A. C. agreed to hold further recommendations regarding access to university records until after this new committee's report.[46] In the interim, it advanced a different proposal which opened a new area of disagreement.

Noting that neither the Treasury nor the Comptroller had access to the Grants Committee's records, the P. A. C. recommended that the Comptroller be allowed to inspect such documents of the U. G. C. as relate to non-recurrent grants. This

43 Treasury Minute, November 18, 1952.
44 P. A. C., *Third Report,* 1952–53, H. C. 203, paras. 1–4.
45 August 6, 1953, p. 7.
46 P. A. C., *Third Report,* 1953–54, H. C. 231, para's. 31–32.

practice, the P. A. C. reasoned, would ensure "due economy" in the capital development programs without necessitating "any contact with the Universities." [47]

On this occasion *The Times* was moved to speak of the "thick end of the wedge," pointing out that such a step would threaten the independent status of the U. G. C. and make it difficult to recruit the best men to serve as members.[48] The Treasury in its reply to the P. A. C. stated that this proposal could not be dissociated from the larger question of access to the university accounts themselves, and expressed the hope that the P. A. C. would not press its new point until the Gater Committee had reported.[49]

The Gater Committee submitted its findings to the U. G. C. in January 1956, and the Grants Committee subsequently published the report, with a few minor qualifications, in its own name. The Gater investigation had indicated that there was "no evidence in the universities of a lack of appreciation of the need for economy," but the Committee felt nevertheless "bound to stress the risk that 90–100% grants-in-aid from public funds may weaken the sense of financial responsibility." [50] The U. G. C. passed on this report to the universities, stating that it was "of great importance that [they] should in the future comply with the recommendations . . . as qualified." The U. G. C. asked to be informed to what extent the universities were taking steps to bring this about.[51]

However, the P. A. C. while "welcoming the report of the Gater Committee and the steps which the U. G. C. have taken to ensure that its recommendations are complied with," stated that the report did "nothing in itself to secure greater Parliamentary control over the expenditure of public money." [52] It therefore "reiterate[d] most strongly" its earlier recommendation to give

47 *Ibid.*

48 September 8, 1954, p. 7.

49 Treasury Minute, January 31, 1955.

50 U. G. C., *Methods Used by Universities of Contracting and of Recording Expenditure, op. cit.*, para. 9 (see footnote 24).

51 *Ibid.*, Annex II.

52 P. A. C., *Sixth Report*, 1955–56, H. C. 348, para. 14.

the Comptroller access to U. G. C. books and papers relating to non-recurrent grants.

Once again the leading journals sprang to the defense of the Treasury and the U. G. C. *The Times,* particularly incensed at the P. A. C.'s expressed doubt "whether the University Grants Committee are themselves in a position fully to satisfy themselves" regarding the elimination of waste, etc. in non-recurrent grants, commented:

> This comes so near to a declaration of no confidence in the University Grants Committee and their procedures that it is necessary to say unequivocally that this body of highly responsible and experienced men and women have the confidence of everybody else . . . [Parliament] must keep the implied contract there has always been that the Committee shall be in fact as well as in name a true watertight bulkhead between the State and the academic world.[53]

Notwithstanding such support, the Treasury in its reply reflected the impact of the P. A. C.'s insistent campaign; for although no concession was made on the major point of Comptroller access, a series of procedural revisions relating to non-recurrent grants was announced which went far in the direction desired by the P. A. C. In the first place, it was stated that the universities had all agreed to notify their auditors of the capital grants received and the purposes for which they were made, and to request these auditors to certify in general terms that every such grant was duly applied to its proper purpose.[54]

Second, the Treasury listed a whole new set of procedures by which the U. G. C. would keep the Treasury more fully and more currently informed of the details of the capital development programs, and which would require the Committee to seek prior Treasury approval for any substantial (i.e. more than 10%) alterations in the proposed distribution of non-recurrent grants.

Finally, the Treasury agreed to present the proposed major and minor capital development programs as separate items in the Appropriation Account, thus requiring the U. G. C. to obtain

[53] August 17, 1956, p. 9.
[54] Treasury Minute, January 31, 1957, p. 7.

Treasury permission for any transfer of funds between the two categories.

The Treasury Minute concluded with the hope that "the Committee will agree that the existing practice, as now amended, gives a reasonable assurance that this expenditure will be properly controlled and properly administered." [55] The P. A. C seemed impressed with this series of actions taken by the Treasury, and its 1957 report agreed to suspend judgment on the issue for three years while the new procedures were given a fair trial.[56]

There the matter rests—at least for the moment. Two comments seem appropriate to American readers. First, the extent of Parliamentary criticism of the handling of university grants should not be over-estimated. Neither the Public Accounts Committee nor the Select Committee on Estimates has been able to arouse much interest in Parliament in their campaign to extend technical controls over the universities' expenditure of public funds. Furthermore, both of these committees, while expressing reservations about certain phases of Treasury and Grants Committee operations, have been explicit in their praise of the general worth of the Grants' Committee. The S. C. E., for example, stated that "the continued existence of the University Grants Committee seems to be the best solution to the problem of maintaining control." [57] The P. A. C., for its part, felt that ". . . current arrangements for control are a reasonable compromise between the general desire to maintain the independence of the Universities and the need for the exercise of proper financial control both by the University Grants Committee and by Parliament." [58]

Second, for all the subtleties of argument between the Treasury and the Public Accounts Committee regarding greater fiscal supervision over university grants, the central issue really is whether or not it would be possible to separate the controls desired by the P. A. C. and the S. C. E. from questions of academic policy. In 1953 the chairman of the Public Accounts Committee wrote a

55 *Ibid.*
56 P. A. C., *Third Report*, 1956–57, H. C. 243, para. 11.
57 S. C. E., *Fifth Report*, 1951–52, H. C. 163, paras. 48–49.
58 P. A. C., *Third Report*, 1951–52, H. C. 253, para. 39.

letter to *The Times* in which he insisted that academic policy would in no way be involved in the Comptroller's audit or the P. A. C.'s subsequent investigation of non-recurrent building grants—"not even the necessity for, or desirability of, [any] building in question." It was merely a matter, he continued, of judging, as was done with government buildings, whether the methods of contracting and of recording and controlling expenditure were reasonably designed and properly applied to ensure effective safeguards against waste and extravagance or other abuse.[59]

The chairman's letter to *The Times* was, however, implicitly contradicted by one of his fellow committeemen at a later meeting between the P. A. C. and representatives of the Treasury and Grants Committee, but no one from either "side" called attention to this fact. Mr. Hoy of the P. A. C., after some fairly rigorous questioning of the Secretary of the U. G. C., raised a question about the justification for building new examination halls at Edinburgh University, stating, "I am told when these halls are completed at this considerable cost, they will stand empty for most of the year." When the U. G. C. Secretary replied that the halls were used for other purposes as well, Hoy continued: "My information is that they are not and there is considerable perturbation about it . . . this Committee should be assured . . . that . . . Government money which is being spent has been put to the best possible use." [60] This seems like a reasonable desire, except that it is obviously a question of academic policy whether examination halls are more necessary to Edinburgh University than other of its proposed buildings.

In retrospect, then, one can see that what has happened has been a variation on a familiar British theme, namely the slow operation of forces to bring about substantial changes in a situation without causing any break in its outer appearance. In this instance, if, as seems likely to the writer, the Public Accounts Committee ultimately accepts the latest Treasury position, the

59 August 13, 1953, p. 7.
60 P. A. C., *Sixth Report*, 1955–56, H. C. 348, Minutes of Evidence, Q's 6304-6305.

situation will be as follows: on the one hand, neither the universities' nor the U. G. C.'s records will be subject to inspection by the Comptroller, and the U. G. C. will continue to operate without a statutory basis; on the other hand, Parliament will, in contrast to the 1940's, find itself supplied more quickly with more complete information on the university grants. Moreover, the administrative procedures between the Treasury and the U. G. C., between the latter and the universities, and within the universities will have been tightened, especially with respect to nonrecurrent grant practices.

Thus, whether or not the P. A. C. foresaw such a result when it initiated its campaign, and whether or not the outcome could have been achieved by less strenuous means, the give-and-take which stemmed from the P. A. C.'s assumption of the role of "watch-dog" has improved the safeguards on the expenditure of a sizeable sum of public funds without doing mortal damage to the universities' freedom from direct state financial control.

*The Grants Committee as a*
*Model for Higher Education*

Several factors need to be borne in mind in appraising the suitability of the Grants device for export. First, it is a fact of the highest significance that the top figures of virtually every British Cabinet as well as the U. G. C. staff and the Treasury have been educated at the universities (Oxford and Cambridge in particular) and have demonstrated sympathetic understanding of the essential purposes and problems of higher education. As President Dodds of Princeton University has pointed out,

> The success of the U. G. C. rests fundamentally upon unwritten conventions and personal and social relations of a homogeneous community of university men, in and out of government, who share common tastes and a common outlook.[61]

[61] H. W. Dodds, L. Hacker and L. Rogers, *Government Assistance to Universities in Great Britain* (New York, Columbia University Press, 1952), pp. 102-107.

A second factor which accounts for the success of the Grants device is the absence of partisan controversy over university issues. Not since Parliament in 1923 debated the burning issue of whether Cambridge University should be forced to admit women to full and equal status have university affairs been a source of serious political conflict. The fact that British universities serve such a relatively small proportion of college-age youth in Britain has acted, perhaps, to lessen lay interest in the controversy. Moreover, the fact that the nature of the minority which does receive a university education is changing from a social elite to an intellectual elite tends to muffle criticisms from the Labour Party about the problem of equalitarianism.

A third and obvious source of strength for the Grants Committee is a healthy Exchequer; for the absence of financial duress means that the state does not need to demand the absolute rationalization of all the institutions whose work it subsidizes. Moreover, a Treasury which is able to support not only projects favored by the state but also many sponsored by the universities is likely to enjoy good relations with these institutions.

In a comparison of British and French universities made in 1947, an observer praised the greater "slack" in state policy, and the consequent flexibility permitted British institutions, but pointed out that this was a much more costly arrangement:

> . . . [in Britain] very little positive planning has been done in the past to avoid duplication or an excessive dispersion of limited resources, or to encourage common standards in appointments, examinations, and exchanges of staff or information between universities. . . . The Chancellor may not forever be able to keep the Exchequer tap running so freely. And if so, the universities of Britain may have much to learn from the more positive allocation of resources, the greater possibilities of guidance and economic distribution of talent and money which can be organised under a more co-ordinated system.[62]

However, the case for rationalizing university education holds little appeal in Britain "where centralisation may still be carped

62 E. Layton, "French Universities in 1947," *Universities Quarterly*, I (1947), pp. 391–92 and 398–99.

at and *Gleichschaltung* is an obscene word." [63] It is tempting nevertheless to speculate over what would happen to university-state relations in Britain if an extreme financial crisis were to bring forth another economy committee similar to the Geddes Committee which made drastic budget cuts in the early 1920's.

The procedures followed by the University Grants Committee have also gone a long way to promote harmony. One of the chief values of the U. G. C. is its self-restraint; it tries not to invoke more than the minimum power necessary to accomplish its goals, and it relies as much as possible on university initiative. Sir Walter Moberly has described the role of the Grants Committees as a goad to long-range planning within the universities: "It is a stimulating influence, always inciting the universities to plan for themselves somewhat more fully than they might do if they were left to themselves." [64]

But it needs to be remembered that the U. G. C. as an administrative device is not without its faults. Two chief criticisms could be levelled against this British co-ordinating board. These are, first, its potential rigidity in the face of situations requiring an unorthodox response, and second, its availability as an instrument of possible future abuse if changed conditions should alter the present harmonious university-state relations.

Regarding the first point, a writer in the *Times Educational Supplement* raised the following queries:

> How does a strong committee of the academically orthodox come to a state of mind when it is willing to commit large sums of public money to support an experiment which at the time is academically unorthodox? . . . If Lord Lindsay of Birker had not been a power in the Labour Party, would the University College of North Staffordshire, with its original curriculum, ever have come to the light of day? And if Lord Cherwell had not had the ear of Sir Winston Churchill, would so great a

---

[63] H. Wiseman, "Parliament and the University Grants Committee," *Public Administration,* Vol. 34 (1956), p. 75.

[64] Sir Walter Moberly, in "Government and the Universities," in Sixth Congress of the Universities of the Commonwealth, *Report of the Proceedings* (1948), p. 16.

sum have been now devoted to the development of the Imperial College of Science and Technology? [65]

On the basis of its more recent policies, particularly those regarding the place of technology in the universities, it is possible to wonder whether the Grants Committee actually suffers from this rigidity. Nevertheless, regret over the decline of multiple sources of financial support for educational proposals involving risk is understandable. The spectre of the Public Accounts Committee demanding its pound of flesh for a costly educational gamble gone wrong is enough to make any public figure think twice. But in Britain the decline in independent sources of wealth and the necessity of keeping university tuition fees low in order not to drive away students without scholarships, combine to leave little alternative to the Grants Committee and its subsidies.

The second source of misgiving regarding the Grants Committee is more significant, for although nearly all commentators stand in admiration of the Committee's enlightened personnel and practices, the danger must be faced that it has acquired formidable power to interfere with academic affairs. Sir Walter Moberly has related the problem of possible state control over the universities to the broader issue of an informed public interest in university freedom: "The tacit understanding that has hitherto existed between the universities and the governing class must now be extended to a much wider public." [66] Sir Walter sees the increasingly representative selection of university students from all grades of society and the universities' extra-mural education programs as hopeful steps in that direction.

Dr. D. W. Logan, Principal of London University, is not so optimistic on this score:

65 February 10, 1956, p. 154.
66 The Rede Lecture, Cambridge University, November 18, 1948. *The Times* expressed a variation of this same theme: "Academic freedom depends on an informed public opinion which believes that for universities to be left free is right in principle and justified at the same time by the strictest canons of utility." Nov. 6, 1952.

In the outside world there is, I fear, a great lack of understanding of what the University is, what it stands for and what
it does. The responsibility for this sad state of affairs rests
largely on the University itself which could justly be accused
of going out of its way to hide its light under a bushel. It is
vitally necessary that the problems with which the University
is faced—and they are many and complex—should be more
fully comprehended and the points at issue more clearly
grasped than is at present the case.[67]

It is unnecessary to dwell further on the obvious need for universities in a democracy to interest the widest possible segment
of public opinion in the broad values of academic freedom.

In summary it is clear that the fast-growing financial needs of
public and private universities and colleges in the United States
will necessitate a variety of experiments in providing public
funds for institutions of higher education without suffocating the
creative spark of the universities and colleges. It is not inconceiv-
able that variations of the University Grants Committee system
might prove workable in some areas, particularly in larger states
where a university and state college system compete for limited
state funds.

A factor on the horizon which would make the Grants Committee model even more pertinent is the possibility that increased
public funds may have to be voted to sustain private colleges and
universities where their services are deemed vital to the public
interest. Many states presently have constitutional provisions for-
bidding gifts to private institutions, but it is reasonable to expect
a closer examination of the possibility of aiding such establish-
ments with public funds in lieu of founding expensive additional
public centers of higher learning. The Grants Committee model
would be valuable under these circumstances, for it provides a
means of knitting together the activities of private as well as
public institutions.

If limited state resources do have to be spread among competing institutions of higher education, nothing would be more
harmful to these schools than a ruthless, public competition for

[67] University of London, *Report by the Principal*, 1956–57, p. 3.

favor. Battles may be won by one side or the other, but the war will most assuredly be lost by all, for legislatures have typically imposed political solutions when university and college leaders have been unable to reach professional agreement. If master boards or their equivalent become increasingly necessary in order to settle institutional differences behind closed doors upon the basis of professional criteria, it is important that such boards keep well in mind the British Grants Committee and its practice of self-restraint. Otherwise they may tend to pre-empt the powers of the participating institutions' governing bodies.

The British experience suggests several principles that may serve as guides wherever democratic institutions are required to harmonize the interests of the state and higher education. Society has a legitimate interest in the over-all policies of its universities, whether these are public or private institutions and whether or not public funds are involved. Universities should form educational policy with sensitivity for community needs, and if the schools are subsidized by public funds, after consultation with responsible government officers. In cases of disagreement between the state and the university, the judgment of the latter should prevail, subject always to ultimate government intervention in the face of a major breakdown in higher education.

While the indigenous social institutions and traditions of other democratic societies preclude the creation of an exact replica of the Grants Committee and its informal mode of operation, the general application of many of the principles enumerated above could lead to Britain's ultimately being regarded not only as the home of parliamentary government, but also as the source of the most enlightened principles of state conduct toward universities.

# Some notes on research strategy

ANYONE WHO has worked in the labyrinth of state government can testify to the difficulty of making generalizations about practices across the country. This is a particular problem in dealing with state-supported higher education, for within each state there may be wide variations in the legal status or public stature of individual colleges and universities.

A short period of exploration made it clear that personal interviews would have to bear the greatest burden in the collection and analysis of data. Library research or detailed questionnaires could only begin to uncover the more subtle aspects of the state-higher education relationship. Little has been written on the subject of state controls and most of the available data has long since been outdated.

In the search for an accurate picture of campus-state relations, two steps were immediately taken.

First, sample interviews were conducted in Michigan, Minnesota, and California in an effort to obtain a preliminary picture of the problems besetting campus and state officials.

Second, an attempt was made to gather all the information available in published form—provisions in state constitutions affecting higher education, court cases, official documents, and general surveys of higher education and state government.

371

*The Use of Questionnaires*

The staff also prepared a series of questionnaires designed principally to elicit factual information from state and college officials. These questionnaires included:

1. *A checklist of state controls.* This was mailed to the business officers of 344 publicly supported institutions of higher learning. It sought to discover the nature and extent of state control over higher education in such areas as budgeting, purchasing, building construction, personnel, publications, as well as related information on the activities of legislative staff agencies. With a ninety per cent return from these questionnaires, it was possible to develop a rather complete picture of the extent of formal controls over higher education.

2. *A letter to attorneys general.* To obtain as much documentary information as possible, the attorney general of each of the states was asked to supply copies of formal opinions and legal decisions in their states bearing on the status of higher education. With gratifying co-operation nearly all attorneys general responded with helpful information.

3. *Checklist for governors.* One problem was that of obtaining a perspective on current trends in state administrative organization. A checklist sent to governors determined the years in which many states set up centralized departments of administration, and furnished related data on the composition of these centralized agencies.

4. *Letter to presidents of small colleges.* As the study progressed it quickly became apparent that the problems of the small college often differ markedly from those of the large university. A series of questions designed to clarify these differences was mailed to the presidents of 241 institutions which could reasonably be classified as "colleges" or at least not as major state universities. Over sixty per cent of the presidents replied, many with helpful comments about their present situation. As might be expected, most replies were carefully guarded. College officials

are understandably reluctant to commit their grievances to writing.

5. *Letter to major university presidents.* One question took on particular importance as the study moved along. How does higher education differ from other activities of the state? Is it really distinctive enough to require special treatment, or should it be treated as any other state agency? Existing discussions of this subject were in short supply. Upon the assumption that state university presidents had thought about the problem on more than one occasion when they confronted legislatures and executive agencies, ninety-three presidents were asked to present their views on the distinctive features of higher education. Many of the letters were long, carefully prepared statements that obviously involved the work of the best minds on the campus. Some of the thinking of these presidents has been cited in the final chapter of this report, which compares higher education with other state activities.

6. *Questionnaire for college and university trustees.* In order to obtain more recent information on the social composition and methods of selecting governing board members, a questionnaire was sent to 345 trustees of state colleges and universities. The returns on these were rather low—just over fifty per cent—which can be attributed to two factors: the questionnaire itself was complex and required information that was difficult to provide, and lay trustees are not as likely to feel at home with questionnaires as college officials who deal with such documents as part of their daily routine. The responses to this questionnaire proved to be of considerable value in appraising the trustee's concept of his own responsibilities in higher education.

*Interviews*

Over a period of seventeen months extending from March, 1957, until December, 1958, staff members travelled across the nation to discuss campus-state relations with college presidents, business officers, deans, professors, trustees, governors, legislators, budget officers, purchasing officers, auditors, newspaper editors, and reporters who cover the statehouse or the university. When it was over, the tally stood at 39 states visited, with 440 interviews. This was an average of over eleven interviews for each state, although in some cases twenty or thirty interviews were necessary. In addition to on-the-spot visits to the states, staff members were able to attend a number of meetings [1] of educators or state officials, where they succeeded in talking with representatives from the nine states not actually visited (Arizona, Idaho, Maine, Missouri, Montana, North Dakota, Pennsylvania, Vermont, and Washington). All other states were touched in the staff itinerary. (Neither Alaska nor Hawaii were in the union before research was completed and computations have been made on the basis of forty-eight states.)

In selecting states for interviews, an attempt was made to strike a balance at each stage of the research between states which were reportedly having difficulty in campus-state relations, for example, Massachusetts, and those which are commonly regarded as having a harmonious relationship, such as Oklahoma.

The interview procedure was generally of an informal nature. It was determined that the most rewarding approach would be for the interviewer to describe to an official the general outlines of the study, indicating the types of problems being studied, and then ask the official to describe his own situation. An attempt

---

[1] Among the national meetings attended were the meetings of the National Association of State Budget Officers, the Western Association of College and University Business Officers, the Western Interstate Conference on Higher Education, the Association of Land-Grant Colleges and Universities, the National Association of State Universities, the American Council on Education, the Association of Higher Education of the National Education Association, the American Association of Colleges for Teacher Education, the Southern Association of Colleges and Secondary Schools, a workshop of governing board members sponsored by the Southern Regional Education Board, and the Association of Governing Boards of State Universities and Allied Institutions. In all cases the officers and members of the associations were extremely helpful and displayed deep interest in the problems of state control over higher education. In addition the Committee was assisted by the Council of State Governments in sponsoring a workshop attended by a number of legislators from across the country.

was also made to give each official an opportunity to discuss the problems that were actually on his mind rather than presupposing that his difficulties necessarily fit into preconceived patterns. Of course, if the interviewer had advance information about a particular problem that he knew involved the official he was interviewing, he would usually bring up the matter during the course of conversation.

Extensive notes were made at the conclusion of each interview, but usually not in the presence of the respondent. It was found that officials were inclined to be reticent in their discussions if notes were taken during an interview. (Naturally, an exception was made when especially detailed matters were being discussed, such as a complicated budget formula where percentages and figures were essential to the discussion.)

Later, the interview notes were distributed into topical and state-by-state files. Then, when time permitted, an analytical summary was prepared of the situation in each state visited by the staff.

Looking back over the 440 interviews, it is possible to see three general categories of response:

First, most state and educational officials spoke freely but not intimately, and demonstrated an obvious desire to present a complete picture of campus-state relations. Many would furnish the interviewer with extensive factual materials to back up their statements, and were willing to answer even the toughest questions.

A second group of respondents used the interview as an opportunity to "tell all" about their problems. Some, for example, would assume, despite the interviewer's initial statement of neutrality, that the interviewer was on their side. Others chose to tell all because of their assumption that the interviewer might already have damaging information from adversaries. A typical reaction in this case would be to smother the interviewer with information in the hope that any statements received from other officials would be neutralized. Respondents of this kind were inclined to exaggerate their stories heavily, and the interviewer had to check carefully the accuracy of the stories.

Finally, there were those who obviously had much to say but declined to provide information because of their fear that its publication, even without identifying the source, would do violence to the status of the official or the cause he served. Thus a number of college presidents insisted that their relations with the state could not be improved upon, even when it was obvious from other sources that the president had been engaged in fierce dispute with particular agencies. College officials tend, incidentally, to be much more candid in talking about their relations with state officials than their relations with their own governing boards.

One fact seems clear. The frankness of state and college officials depends heavily on the existing condition of state-campus relations. Respondents talked most freely when there was genuine harmony and when candor could not occasion embarrassment. But they also talked openly when there had been an open break between the college and the statehouse and hostility was the order of the day. In the latter situation both state and college officials often decided that their case can only be strengthened by public disclosure of their problems. Hence in Kentucky, Massachusetts, and West Virginia, to cite only three examples, college officials who had given up much hope of working out their problems by negotiation with state officials, spoke out openly of the problems they faced.

By contrast, officials were most reticent to discuss their problems in states where serious problems existed but had not yet reached the stage of open hostility. Any publicity given to the problems was likely to upset careful negotiations that were constantly going on. This is the case in several of the southern states, where interviewers were often told that no real problems existed even though it was readily apparent that heavy pressures were being applied on the college campuses.

# Selected references

*General*

Addis, Wellford. *Federal and State Aid to Education.* United States Bureau of Education. Washington, D.C.: Government Printing Office, 1898.

American Council on Education. *Higher Education in Maryland; A Report of a Survey with Recommendations of the Maryland Commission on Higher Education.* Washington, D.C.: the Council, 1947.

Angell, Robert C. *The Campus, a Study of Contemporary Undergraduate Life in the American University.* New York and London: D. Appleton & Company, 1928.

Arkansas Commission on Higher Education. *State Controlled Higher Education in Arkansas.* Little Rock, Ark.: the Commission, 1951.

Blair, Lyle and Kuhn, Madison. *A Short History of Michigan State.* East Lansing: Michigan State College Press, 1955.

Boozer, Howard A. "A Limited Review of Institutional Planning for the Future." Unpublished staff study, American Council on Education, Washington, D.C., 1955.

Brewton, John E. et al. *Higher Education in Mississippi: a Digest of the Survey Report.* Jackson, Miss.: Mississippi Board of Trustees of State Institutions of Higher Learning, 1954.

———. "Public Higher Education in West Virginia." *Higher Education,* XII (May, 1956), pp. 141-144.

Brooks, Robert P. *The University of Georgia, 1785-1955.* Athens: University of Georgia Press, 1956.

Brown, Francis J. and Sellin, Thorsten (eds.). "Higher Education Under Stress," *Annals of the American Academy of Political and Social Science,* cccı (September, 1955).

Brumbaugh, Arthur J. "Higher Education in Louisiana," *Journal of Higher Education,* xııı (November, 1956), pp. 33-36.

Bryce, James B. "American State Universities," *Transactions and Proceedings of the National Association of State Universities,* 1909, pp. 68-72.

Burton, Earnest D. *Education in a Democratic World.* Chicago: University of Chicago Press, 1927.

Carmichael, Oliver C. *The Changing World of Higher Education.* New York: Macmillan, 1949.

Carr-Saunders, Alexander M. and Wilson, P. A. *The Professions.* Oxford: The Clarendon Press, 1933.

Charlesworth, James C. and Sellin, Thorsten. "Bureaucracy and Democratic Government," *Annals of the American Association of Political and Social Science,* ccxcıı (March, 1954).

Clapp, Margaret A. (ed.). *The Modern University.* Ithaca: Cornell University Press, 1950.

Coffman, Lotus D. *State University, its Work and Problems.* Minneapolis: University of Minnesota Press, 1934.

———. *Freedom Through Education.* Minneapolis: University of Minnesota, 1939.

Commission on Financing Higher Education. *Nature and Needs of Higher Education; The Report of the Commission on Financing Higher Education.* New York: published for the Commission by Columbia University Press, 1952.

Conant, James B. in *Functions of a Modern University; Proceedings of the First Symposium sponsored by the State University of New York.* Albany: State University of New York, 1950, pp. 11-17.

Council of State Governments. *The Book of the States.* 1945-1959. Chicago: Council of State Governments.

———. *Reorganizing State Government.* Chicago: Council of State Governments, 1950.

———. *Public Authorities in the States.* Chicago: Council of State Governments, 1953.

Cowling, Donald F. and Davidson, Carter. *Colleges for Freedom; A Study of Purposes, Practices and Needs.* New York: Harper & Bros., 1947.

Cushman, Robert E. *Civil Liberties in the United States; a guide to current problems and experience.* Ithaca: Cornell University Press, 1956.

Eddy, Edward D., Jr. *Colleges for Our Land and Times.* New York: Harper & Bros., 1956.

Edens, Arthur H. "The Governor and the Budget in Massachusetts, 1910-1941." Unpublished Ph.D. dissertation, Harvard University, 1949.

Fernald, Merritt C. *History of the Maine State College and the University.* Orono: University of Maine, 1916.

Flexner, Abraham. *Universities: American, English, German.* New York: Oxford University Press, 1930.

Foerster, Norman. *The American State University; Its Relation to Democracy.* Chapel Hill: The University of North Carolina Press, 1937.

———. "Lowering Higher Education: State Universities Face an Acid Test," *Scribner's Magazine,* XCIX (June, 1936), pp. 368-370.

Frischknecht, Reed L. *The Government and Financing of Higher Education in Utah.* Salt Lake City: Utah University Institute of Government, Bulletin Number 9, 1950.

Gary, Raymond. Governor of Oklahoma. *The Executive Budget in Brief for the Fiscal Years ending June 30, 1958-1959.* Oklahoma City, 1957.

Gideonse, Harry D. "Academic Freedom: A Decade of Challenge and Clarification," *Annals of the American Academy of Political and Social Science,* CCCII (November, 1955), pp. 75-85.

Governors Conference. *Proceedings of the Governors Conference, 1956.* Chicago: The Governors Conference, 1956.

Graves, W. Brooke. *American State Government.* Fourth Edition. Boston: Heath, 1955.

Gray, William S. *Current Issues in Higher Education.* Chicago: University of Chicago Press, 1937.

Griswold, Alfred W. *Essays on Education.* New Haven: Yale University Press, 1954.

Hancher, Virgil, "The Most Wonderful Work." The Shepard Lecture, Ohio State University, May 4, 1955. (Mimeographed.)

———. "The State University and the American Dream." National Association of State Universities Meeting, May 3-4, 1954. (Mimeographed.)

Haskins, Charles H. *The Rise of Universities.* New York: Henry Holt, 1923.

Hofstadter, Richard and Hardy, C. DeWitt. *The Development and Scope of Higher Education in the United States.* New York: published for the Commission on Financing Higher Education by Columbia University Press, 1952.

Hofstadter, Richard and Metzger, Walter P. *The Development of Academic Freedom in the United States.* New York: Columbia University Press, 1955.

Hollis, Ernest V. *Higher Education Looks Ahead; a Roundup on Postwar Planning on Higher Education.* Federal Security Administration. Office of Education. Washington, D.C.: Government Printing Office, 1945.

Hutchins, Robert M. *Education for Freedom.* Baton Rouge: Louisiana State University Press, 1943.

———. *The University of Utopia.* Chicago: University of Chicago Press, 1953.

———. "Freedom of the University," *Ethics,* LXI (January, 1951), pp. 95-104.

Illinois University. *Ferment in Education; the Problems, Responsibilities, and Opportunities of Universities in this Time; a Symposium at the Installation of George Dinsmore Stoddard as President at the University of Illinois.* Urbana: University of Illinois Press, 1948.

Indiana Survey Commission on State-Supported Institutions of Higher Learning. *Report of a Survey of the State Institutions of Higher Learning in Indiana.* Indianapolis, 1926.

Institute of Public Administration. *State Administrative Consolidation in Maine, Report of a Survey of the State Government Conducted for Governor Gardiner.* New York: Institute of Public Administration, 1930.

Kansas State Department of Administration. *Report.* Topeka: the Department, January, 1956.

Kelly, Frederick J. "Virginia Report on Higher Education," *Higher Education,* viii (October 1, 1951), pp. 25-26.

Kent, Raymond A. *Higher Education in America.* Boston: Ginn and Company, 1930.

Kirk, Russell. *Academic Freedom; an essay in definition.* Chicago: Henry Regnery Company, 1955.

Lindsay, Julian I. *Tradition Looks Forward—the University of Vermont; a History, 1791-1904.* Burlington: University of Vermont and State Agricultural College, 1954.

Long, Norton E. "Power and Administration," *Public Administration Review,* ix (Fall, 1949), pp. 257-264.

McCamy, James. "Responsiveness vs. Efficiency in Public Service," *Annals of the American Academy of Political and Social Science,* ccxcii (March, 1954), pp. 30-38.

McConnell, T. R. et al. *A Restudy of the Needs of California in Higher Education.* Sacramento: California State Department of Education, 1955.

Macdonald, Austin F. *American State Government and Administration.* 5th rev. ed. New York: Crowell, 1955.

Machlup, Fritz. "On Some Misconceptions Concerning Academic Freedom," *American Association of University Professors Bulletin,* xli (December, 1955), pp. 753-784.

MacIver, Robert M. *Academic Freedom in Our Times.* New York: Columbia University Press, 1955.

Massachusetts Commission on Administration and Finance. *Report.* Massachusetts Public Document No. 140. Boston, 1926.

Merton, Robert K. *Social Theory and Social Structure.* Glencoe, Ill.: Free Press, 1949.

—— et al. (eds.). *Reader in Bureaucracy.* Glencoe, Ill.: Free Press, 1952.

Michigan Council of State College Presidents. *Future School and College Enrollments in Michigan: 1955 to 1970.* Ann Arbor: J. W. Edwards Publisher, Inc., 1954.

Michigan, the Survey of Higher Education in Michigan (John Dale Russell, Director). *Preliminary Report,* March, 1957.

——. Staff Studies, Numbers 1-12, June, 1957-July, 1958.

——. *Higher Education in Michigan,* Final Report of the Survey of Higher Education in Michigan, September, 1958.

Minnesota Commission on Higher Education. *Higher Education in Minnesota*. Minneapolis: University of Minnesota Press, 1950.

Mississippi Board of Trustees of State Institutions of Higher Learning. *Mississippi Study of Higher Education, 1945*. Jackson, Mississippi: the Board, 1945.

Monroe, Walter S. (ed.). *Encyclopedia of Educational Research*, revised edition. New York: Macmillan, 1941.

Morison, Samuel E. *The Founding of Harvard College*. Cambridge, Massachusetts: Harvard University Press, 1935.

Murad, Anatol. "Democracy in European Universities," *The Educational Forum*, xiv (May, 1950), pp. 457-461.

National Conference on Higher Education, Chicago, 1947. *Current Problems in Higher Education; Official Group Reports*. Washington, D.C.: National Education Association of the United States, Department of Higher Education, 1947.

National Conference on Higher Education, Chicago, 1951. *Addresses on Current Issues in Higher Education, 1951*. Washington, D.C.: National Education Association of the United States, Department of Higher Education, 1951.

Nebraska Legislative Council. *State Supported Institutions of Higher Education in Nebraska*. Lincoln, Nebraska: Nebraska Legislative Council, Research Department, 1942.

New Hampshire University. *History of the University of New Hampshire, 1866-1941*. Durham, N.H.: The Record Press, Inc., 1941.

New Republic, The. "A Special Report on the Universities: Freedom, Solvency and Survival," *The New Republic*, cxxvi (October, 1951), pp. 11-21.

Neilson, William A. and Wittke, Carl F. *The Function of the University*. Evanston, Illinois: Northwestern University, 1943.

Nock, Albert J. *The Theory of Education in the United States*. Chicago: Henry Regnery Company, 1949.

Ortega y Gasset, José. *Mission of the University*. Translated with an introduction by Howard L. Nostrand. Princeton: Princeton University Press, 1944.

Parsons, Mary B. "The Legislative Branch and Assisting Services." Study prepared for the New Hampshire Legislative Council, Concord, New Hampshire, 1956. (Mimeographed.)

Perkins, John A. *The Role of the Governor in Michigan in the Enactment of Appropriations*. Michigan Governmental Studies No. 12. Ann Arbor: Michigan University Bureau of Government, 1943.

———. "Reflections on State Reorganizations," *American Political Science Review*, xlv (1951), pp. 509-510.

Porter, Kirk H. *State Administration*. New York: F. S. Croft and Company, 1958.

Porter, Noah. *The American Colleges and The American Public*. New Haven: Chatfield and Company, 1870.

Rand, Frank P. *Yesterdays at Massachusetts Agricultural College, 1863-1933*. Amherst: The Associate Alumni, Massachusetts State College, 1933.

Ransone, Coleman B. *The Office of Governor in the United States.* University: University of Alabama Press, 1956.

Rashdall, Hastings. *The Universities of Europe in the Middle Ages.* 2 vols. Oxford: Clarendon Press, 1895.

Riesman, David. *Constraint and Variety in American Education.* New York: Doubleday Anchor Books, 1958.

Rogers, Francis M. *Higher Education in the United States, A Summer Review.* Cambridge, Massachusetts: Harvard University Press, 1952.

Ross, Earle D. *Democracy's College, the land-grant movement in the formative stage.* Ames: The Iowa State College Press, 1942.

Russell, John D. *Emergent Responsibilities in Higher Education.* Chicago: University of Chicago Press, 1946.

———. "Control of State Tax-supported Higher Education in Illinois," *Higher Education,* VII (March 1, 1951), pp. 145-147.

———. "Ohio Survey of Higher Education," *Journal of Higher Education,* XXVII (October, 1956), pp. 367-370.

Sayre, Wallace S. "The Triumph of Techniques Over Purpose," *Public Administration Review,* VIII (Spring, 1948), pp. 134-137.

———. "Trends in a Decade of Administrative Values," *Public Administration Review,* XI (Winter, 1951), pp. 1-9.

Seeley, Reginald. *The Function of the University.* Toronto: Oxford University Press, 1948.

Shaw, Wilfred B. (ed.). *The University of Michigan: An Encyclopedia Survey,* I. Ann Arbor: University of Michigan, 1942.

Simon, Herbert A. "Staff and Management Controls," *Annals of the American Academy of Political and Social Science,* CCXCII (March, 1954), pp. 95-103.

Simon, Herbert A., Smithburg, Donald W., and Thompson, Victor A. *Public Administration.* New York: Knopf, 1950.

Sindler, Allan P. *Huey Long's Louisiana.* Baltimore: The Johns Hopkins Press, 1956.

Smith, Huston. *The Purposes of Higher Education.* New York: Harper & Bros., 1955.

Smith, T. V. *The Legislative Way of Life.* Chicago: University of Chicago Press, 1940.

Stemmons, Walter. *Connecticut Agricultural College—A History.* Storrs, Connecticut, 1931.

Stene, Edwin O. *American Administrative Theory.* Lawrence: University of Kansas Bureau of Government Research, 1950.

Stoddard, George D. "Illinois, Illinois," *School and Society,* LXXIX (April 3, 1954), pp. 97-101.

Strayer, George D. *A Digest of a Report on a Survey of the University System of Georgia.* Atlanta: University of Georgia, 1950.

Strayer, George D. and Klein, Arthur J. *Report of a Survey of the Institutions of Higher Education in the State of Iowa.* Des Moines: State Board of Education, October, 1950.

Tewksbury, Donald G. *The Founding of American Colleges and Universities Before the Civil War.* New York: Columbia University Teachers College, 1932.

Texas Legislative Council. *A Source Book on Public Higher Education in Texas.* Austin: the Council, 1951.

Thwing, Charles F. *A History of Higher Education in America.* New York: D. Appleton and Company, 1906.

Trevor, Arnett. *Recent Trends in Higher Education in the United States.* New York: General Education Board, 1940.

Ulich, Robert. *Fundamentals of Democratic Education.* New York: American Book Company, 1940.

U.S. Bureau of the Census. *Compendium of State Government Finances in 1957.* Washington, D.C.: Government Printing Office, 1958.

U.S. Office of Education. *Education Directory.* Part III. Washington, D.C: Government Printing Office, 1958.

———. *A Study of the Organization and Functions of Higher Education in Louisiana, 1941.* Baton Rouge: Louisiana Educational Survey Commission. 1942.

———. *Public Higher Education in Kentucky; Report to the Committee on Function and Resources of State Government,* prepared under the direction of the Division of Higher Education. Frankfort, Ky.: Legislative Research Commission, 1952.

———. *Survey of Land-Grant Colleges and Universities,* directed by Arthur J. Klein, Chief, Division of Collegiate and Professional Education. U.S.O.E. Bulletin 1930, No. 9. 2 vols. Washington, D.C.: Government Printing Office, 1930.

U.S. President's Commission on Higher Education. *Higher Education for American Democracy, A Report.* Washington, D.C.: Government Printing Office, 1947.

Utah University. *The State University and American Education; Centennial Commemoration Proceedings,* University of Utah. Salt Lake City: University of Utah Press, 1950.

Western Regional Conference on Education Beyond the High School. "Facing the Critical Decade," *Proceedings* of the Conference, April 9-11, 1957. Boulder, Colo.: Western Interstate Commission for Higher Education, 1957.

White, Leonard D. *Trends in Public Administration.* New York: McGraw-Hill, 1933.

Williams, Robert L. "Financial Support of State-Supported Colleges and Universities," *Michigan Education Journal,* xxvii (November, 1949), p. 211.

Wilson, Logan. *The Academic Man, a study in the sociology of a profession.* New York: Oxford University Press, 1942.

Wilson, Woodrow. "The Study of Administration." *Political Science Quarterly,* ii (June, 1887), p. 197-222.

Works, George A. and Morgan, Barton. *The Land-Grant Colleges,* prepared for the Advisory Committee on Education. Staff Study No. 10. Washington, D.C.: Government Printing Office, 1939.

Young, William H. "The Development of the Governorship," *State Government*, XXXI (Summer, 1958), pp. 178-183.

Zeller, Belle (ed.). American State Legislatures, *Report of the Committee on American Legislatures of the American Political Science Association*. New York: Crowell, 1954.

——. "Pressure Groups and the State Legislatures," *State Government*, XI (July, 1938), pp. 121-122, 124.

Zimmer, Agath. (Brother). *Changing Concepts in Higher Education in America Since 1700*. Washington, D.C.: The Catholic University of America Press, 1938.

Zook, George F., Lotus D., and Mann, A. R. *Report of a Survey of State Institutions of Higher Learning in Kansas*. U.S. Office of Education. Washington, D.C.: Government Printing Office, 1923.


*Legal Relations—the University and the State*

Ashbrook, William A., Chambers, Merritt M., and Elliott, Edward C. *The Government of Higher Education*. New York: American Book Company, 1935.

Bartlett, Lester W. *State Control of Private Incorporated Institutions of Higher Education as defined in decisions of the United States Supreme Court, laws of the states governing incorporation of institutions of higher education, and charters of selected private colleges and universities*. New York: Columbia University Teachers College, 1926.

Beu, Frank A. *Legal Basis for the Organization and Administration of Publicly Supported Normal Schools and Teachers Colleges in the Territory of the North Central Association*. Minneapolis: Burgess Publishing Company, 1937.

Blackwell, Thomas E. *Current Legal Problems of Colleges and Universities, 1950-1951*. St. Louis: Washington University, 1953.

Brody, Alexander. *The American State and Higher Education: The legal, political and constitutional relationships*. Washington, D.C.: American Council on Education, 1935.

Brown, Elmer E. *The Origins of American State Universities*. Berkeley: The University of California Press, 1903.

Carey, James C. "University or Corporation," *Journal of Higher Education*, XXVII (November, 1956), pp. 440-444.

Chambers, Merritt M. and Elliott, Edward C. *The Colleges and the Courts*. New York: Carnegie Foundation for the Advancement of Teaching, 1936.

Chambers, Merritt M. *The Colleges and the Courts, 1941-1945*. New York: Carnegie Foundation for the Advancement of Teaching, 1946.

——. *The Colleges and the Courts, 1946-1950*. New York: Columbia University Press, 1952.

——. "Constitutional Provisions regarding State Universities," *Education Law and Administration*, II (April, 1933), pp. 30-39.

————. "Judicial History of Certain Mid-West State Universities," *Proceedings of the Association of Governing Boards of State Universities and Allied Institutions,* Eleventh Annual Meetings, 1933, pp. 57-65.

————. "Litigation Regarding Free Tuition and State Scholarships in Universities and Colleges," *Education Law and Administration,* III (May, 1934), pp. 42-46.

Dunlap, E. T. "The History of Legal Controls of Public Higher Education in Oklahoma." Unpublished Ph.D. dissertation, Oklahoma Agricultural and Mechanical College, Stillwater, Oklahoma, 1956.

Fleischer, Robert D. "The Development of the Relationship of Legal Fiscal Controls to the Extent of State Aid for Education as Applied to Pennsylvania, 1921-1953," *Journal of Educational Research,* L (October, 1956), pp. 81-90.

Florida Council for the Study of Higher Education in Florida. "Provisions of State Constitutions for Higher Education." Study prepared for the Council. (Mimeographed, n.d., n.p.)

Gardiner, George K. "Liberty, the State, and the School," *Law and Contemporary Problems,* XX (Winter, 1955), pp. 184-195.

Henderson, Algo D. "State University Legislation in New York," *Higher Education,* IV (May 15, 1948), pp. 214.

Henry, Jerome E. et al. *Annotated Compilation of Laws of Oklahoma as to Institutions of Higher Education.* Langston, Oklahoma: Langston University School of Law, 1948.

Hollis, Ernest V., Land, William G., and Martorana, S. V. *Survey of State Legislation Relating to Higher Education, July 1, 1956 to June 30, 1957.* Circular No. 511, Department of Health, Education, and Welfare, Office of Education, Washington, D.C.: Government Printing Office, 1957.

Humphrey, George D. "Statutory Control of College and University Salaries," *School and Society,* LXXXV (May 25, 1957), pp. 185-186.

Kettleborough, Charles (ed.). *The State Constitutions.* Indianapolis: B. F. Bowlen & Company, 1918.

Little, J. Kenneth. "State Institutions of Higher Learning," Madison: University of Wisconsin, 1948. (Mimeographed.)

Martorana, S. V. "Legal Status of American Public Junior Colleges" in *American Junior Colleges,* Bogue, Jesse P. (ed.). Third Edition, Washington, D.C.: American Council on Education, 1952, pp. 18-26.

Peabody, Charles W. "Legal Status of the University of Maine," *Maine Law Review,* XIII (June, 1920), pp. 187-197.

Thorpe, Francis N. (ed.). *Federal and State Constitutions, compiled and edited under Act of Congress.* 59th Congress, 2d Session. 7 vols. Washington, D.C.: Government Printing Office, 1909.

Verhaalen, Roman F. *Legislation and Higher Education; The Laws and By-Laws Affecting the Government of Public Institutions of Higher Learning.* Laramie: Bureau of Educational Research and Service, University of Wyoming College of Education, 1950.

Wildermuth, Ora L. "Legal Status of State Universities," *Proceedings of the Governing Boards of State Universities and Allied Institutions*, Eighteenth Annual Meeting, 1940, pp. 53-75.

Wooden, William P. "Recent Decisions," *Michigan Law Review*, LV (1957), p. 728.


*University and State Administrative and Fiscal Relations*

Adams, Charles K. *State Aid to Higher Education*. Address delivered at the twenty-second anniversary of The Johns Hopkins University. Baltimore: The Johns Hopkins Press, 1898.

Ader, Emile B. "State Budgetary Controls of Federal Grants-in-Aid," *Public Administration Review*, x (Spring, 1950), pp. 87-92.

Agger, Eugene E. *The Budget in American Commonwealths*. New York: Columbia University Press, 1907.

Allen, Harry K., and Axt, Richard G. *State Public Finance and State Institutions of Higher Education in the United States*. New York: Columbia University Press (for the Commission on Financing Higher Education), 1952.

Appleby, Paul. "Role of the Budget Division," *Public Administration Review*, XVII (Summer, 1957), pp. 156-158.

Arkansas State Comptroller. *General Accounting Procedure for State Agencies for the Disbursement of State Funds, Effective July 1, 1957*. Little Rock: the Comptroller, 1956.

――――. *State Travel Regulations, Effective July 1, 1957*. Little Rock: the Comptroller, 1956.

Arkansas Legislative Auditor. *Biennial Report*. Little Rock: the Auditor, November 30, 1956.

Association of Land-Grant Colleges [and Universities]. "Report of Special Committee on Centralized Financial Control," *Proceedings*, Thirty-seventh Annual Convention, 1923, pp. 463-480.

――――. Report of Special Committee on State Fiscal Policies," *Proceedings*, Thirty-ninth Annual Convention, 1925, pp. 377-378.

Atkinson, Carroll. "Watchdog of the Treasury," *Nation's Schools*, XXVI (November, 1940), p. 62.

Axt, Richard G. *The Federal Government and Financing Higher Education*. New York: Columbia University Press for the Commission on Financing Higher Education, 1952.

Ball, Irving. "Centralized Control and Budgetary Procedure of Public Higher Education in the United States to 1935." Unpublished Ph.D. dissertation, University of Texas, 1935.

Bane, Frank. "Government Control of State Supported Higher Education," *Proceedings* of the Thirty-second Annual Meeting, Association of Governing Boards of State Universities and Allied Institutions, 1954, pp. 32-38.

Barth, Harry A. *Financial Control in the States, with emphasis on control by the governor.* Philadelphia: Westbrook Publishing Company, 1923.

Bell, George A. *State Budget Administration in Maryland.* College Park: University of Maryland Bureau of Governmental Research, 1957.

Benson, George C. S. *Financial Control and Integration: A Study in Administration with special reference to the Comptroller-General of the United States.* New York: Harper & Bros., 1934.

Blackwell, Thomas E. "Power of the Legislative Auditor to Control Disbursement of Colleges," *College and University Business,* x (February, 1951), pp. 31-34.

———. "Legality of Revenue Bonds Issued for Building Dormitories," *College and University Business,* xi (September, 1951), pp. 49-50.

———. "Deposit of University Funds with State Treasurers," *College and University Business,* viii (March, 1950), pp. 48-49.

Bosworth, Karl A. "The Politics of Management Improvement in the States," *American Political Science Review,* xlvii (March, 1953), pp. 84-99.

Brookings Institution, The. "Financial and Salary Survey of State-Controlled Institutions of Higher Education, July 1, 1937," South Dakota State Planning Board, 1937. (Mimeographed.)

Browns, Vincent J. *The Control of the Public Budget.* Washington, D.C.: Public Affairs Press, 1949.

Bruer, Henry. "The Budget as an Administrative Program," *Annals of the American Academy of Political and Social Science,* lxii (November, 1915), pp. 176-191.

Buck, Arthur E. *Public Budgeting, a discussion of budgeting practice in the national, state and local governments of the United States.* New York: Harper & Bros., 1929.

———. *The Budget in Governments of Today.* New York: Macmillan, 1934.

———. *The Reorganization of State Government in the United States.* New York: Published for the National Municipal League by Columbia University Press, 1938.

Bunbury, Sir H. N. "Efficiency is an Alternative to Control," *Journal of Public Administration,* vi (April, 1928), pp. 97-98.

Burdette, Ross B. "Critical Present Day Issues in Administration of State Higher Education," *Addresses and Proceedings of the National Education Association of the United States,* 1917. Pp. 305-313.

Burkhead, Jesse V. *Governmental Budgeting.* New York: John Wiley & Sons, 1956.

———. "Budget Classification and Fiscal Planning," *Public Administration Review,* vii (Fall, 1947), pp. 228-235.

Chamber of Commerce of the United States. *State and Local Budgetary Methods: Report of the Committee on State and Local Taxation and Expenditures,* Washington, D.C.: Chamber of Commerce of the U.S., 1935.

California Department of Finance. "The Faculty Staffing Formula of the California State Colleges." Sacramento, January, 1957. (Mimeographed.)

Cannon, Joseph G. *The National Budget*. Washington, D.C.: Government Printing Office, 1919.

Campbell, W. V., et al. *Current Operating Expenditures and Income of Higher Education in the United States, 1930, 1940, 1950*. New York: Columbia University Press for the Commission on Financing Higher Education, 1952.

Chamberlain, Leo M. "Survey of Salaries in State Universities and Land-grant Colleges," *School and Society*, LXV (June 28, 1947), pp. 481-482.

Chambers, Merritt M. *Some Features of State Educational-Administrative Organization*. Washington, D.C.: American Council on Education, 1936.

Chandler, A. D., Jr. "Management Decentralization—an Historical Analysis," *The Business History Review*, XXXIX (June, 1956), pp. 111-174.

Christopherson, Victor A. "Dilemmas of Administration in Higher Education," *Journal of Higher Education*, XXVI (April, 1955), pp. 210-214.

Clark, F. B. "Disciplinary Action Controlling Agencies of Publicly Supported Educational Institutions," *School and Society*, LXVI (December 6, 1947), pp. 433-437.

Cleveland, Frederick A. "Evolution of the Budget Idea in the United States," *Annals of the American Academy of Political and Social Sciences*, LXII (November, 1915), pp. 15-35.

———. Popular Control of Government: "Three Schools of Opinion in the United States with Respect to Budget-Making," *Political Science Quarterly*, XXXIV (June, 1919), pp. 237-261.

Cleveland, Frederick A. and Buck, Arthur E. *The Budget and Responsible Government*. New York: Macmillan, 1920.

Coker, Francis W. "Dogmas of Administrative Reform, as exemplified in the recent reorganization in Ohio," *American Political Science Review*, XVI (August, 1922), pp. 399-411.

Collett, Merrill J. "The Role of Budget Planning and Personnel as Staff Services," *Public Administration Review*, X (Summer, 1945), pp. 226-232.

Committee on Public Administration. *Research in Public Budget Administration*. New York: Social Science Research Council, 1941.

Connecticut Department of the Comptroller. "Standard Classification of Revenues and Expenditures," *Bulletin Number One*, Hartford: the Comptroller, 1953.

Council of State Governments. *A State Department of Administration*. Chicago: Council of State Governments, 1957.

———. *Purchasing by the States*. Chicago: Council of State Governments, 1956.

Deming, George H. *The New Hampshire Budgetary Process*. Incidental Publications Number 1. Durham, New Hampshire: University of New Hampshire Bureau of Governmental Research, n.d.

Devine, Carl T. "Cost Accounting and Higher Education," A Memorandum prepared for the Committe on Government and Higher Education, February, 1958. (Typewritten.)

Eastern Association of College and University Business Officers. "Business

Administration and Budget Controls," *Proceedings of the Association,* 1939, pp. 45-56.

Edwards, William H. "The Public Efficiency Experts," *Southwestern Political and Social Science Quarterly,* x (December, 1929), pp. 301-312.

——. "Has State Reorganization Succeeded?" *State Government,* xi (October, 1938), pp. 183-184, 192-193.

Englehardt, Fred. "The Administrative and Fiscal Control of State Universities and Colleges," *Proceedings of the Association of Governing Boards of State Universities and Allied Institutions,* Eighth Annual Meeting, 1930, pp. 90-98.

Ensley, Grover W. *The Role of Budgeting in Government.* New York: The Tax Foundation, 1941.

"Finances and Administration, University of Nevada," *Nevada Tax Review,* July, 1950 (entire issue devoted to a summary of a study made October, 1949-February, 1950).

Garber, L. O. "This Question of State School Building Authorities," *Nation's Schools,* LII (August, 1953), pp. 67-68.

Gaus, John M. *Reflections on Public Administration.* University, Alabama: University of Alabama Press, 1947.

——. "The Budget in the Growth of State Government." Paper presented at Annual Meeting of the National Association of State Budget Officers, Boston, May 23, 1950. (Mimeographed.)

Greenleaf, W. J. "Financial Support of Colleges," *Journal of Higher Education,* I (May, 1930), pp. 254-260.

Gulick, Luther H. *Evolution of the Budget in Massachusetts.* New York: Macmillan, 1920.

Hatton, Augustus R. and King, Clyde L. (eds.). "Public Budgets," *Annals of the American Academy of Political and Social Science,* LXII (November, 1915).

Heady, Ferrel. "States Try Reorganization," *National Municipal Review,* XLI (July, 1952), pp. 334-338, 345.

Hyneman, Charles S. "Administrative Reorganization: An Adventure into Science and Theology," *Journal of Politics,* I (February, 1939), pp. 62-75.

Irvin, Oscar W. *State Budget Control of State Institutions of Higher Education.* Contributions to Education Number 271, New York: Columbia University.

Johnson, W. L. "Let's Untie Operating Officials," *Public Personnel Review,* XI (April, 1950), pp. 60-64.

Johnston, Paul A. "New Budget Procedures in North Carolina," *State Government,* XXXI (June, 1958), pp. 106-109.

Jones, Victor. *Legislature and the Budget.* Legislative Problems Number 5. Berkeley: University of California Bureau of Public Administration, 1941.

Kaufman, Herbert. "Emerging Conflicts in the Doctrines of Public Administration," *American Political Science Review,* L (December, 1956), pp. 1057-1073.

Kentucky Council on Public Higher Education. "Agreement on Uniform Classification of Accounts for Kentucky State Colleges, July 9, 1957." Frankfort: the Council, 1957. (Mimeographed.)

————. Kentucky College Budget Formula. Frankfort: the Council, 1956. (Mimeographed.)

Kentucky Department of Finance. A Guide to Real Estate and Construction Procedures. Frankfort: Division of the Budget, January, 1957.

Kenyon, Howard A. "Budgeting in a Democracy," State Government, xxi (December, 1948), pp. 251-252.

Key, V. O., Jr. "The Lack of a Budgetary Theory," American Political Science Review, xxxiv (December, 1940), pp. 1137-1144.

Kilpatrick, Wylie. "Classification and Measurement of Public Expenditures," Annals of the American Academy of Political and Social Science, clxxxiii (January, 1936), pp. 19-26.

Laing, B. M. "The Legislative Functions of Government Departments," Public Administration (London), viii (July, 1930), pp. 335-348.

Landers, Frank M. and Hamilton, Howard D. "A Survey of State Budget Agencies," Public Finance, viii (July, 1953), pp. 399-413.

Lederle, John W. "The State and Higher Education: A Report from Michigan," Statement prepared for the Committee on Government and Higher Education, March 1, 1958. Published as Appendix A in this book.

Lewis, Vernon. "Toward a Theory of Budgeting," Public Administration Review, xii (Winter, 1952), pp. 42-54.

Logan, John W. and Donaho, John A. "The Performance Budget and Legislative Review," State Government, xxvi (July, 1953), pp. 185-187.

Lowrie, S. Gale. The Budget. Madison: Wisconsin State Board of Public Affairs, 1912.

————. "The Proper Function of the State Budget," Annals of the Academy of Political and Social Science, lxii (November, 1915), pp. 47-63.

McLaury, F. "Budgetary Weakness," in Toward Better Budgeting, Papers of the Twenty-ninth and Thirtieth Conferences of the Governmental Research Association, Chicago: Public Administration Service, 1941, pp. 9-10.

McNeeley, John H. Authority of State Executive Agencies over Higher Education. United States Office of Education. Bulletin 1930, No. 15. Washington, D.C.: Government Printing Office, 1936.

————. Fiscal Control Over State Higher Education. Federal Security Agency, United States Office of Education. Bulletin No. 8, 1940. Washington, D.C.: Government Printing Office, 1940.

Massachusetts Commission on Administration and Finance. Subsidiary Accounts and Expenditure Code Numbers for Budgetary Control. Boston: the Commission, April, 1954.

————. Rules and Regulations Governing Purchasing. Revised. Boston: the Commission, 1933.

Martin, James W. and Briscoe, Vera. "Some Statutory Provisions for State Budgets," State Government, xviii (September, 1945), pp. 162-167.

Martin, James W., Kentucky Commissioner of Finance. "Finance Administration as a Tool of Management with special reference to recent Kentucky experience," Unpublished speech at Southeast Institute on Public Administration, University of Georgia, 1957.

Mauck, Elwyn A. "Some Problems in State Budgetary Administration," *State Government*, XXVI (February, 1953), pp. 40-42, 55-56.

Merriam, Charles E. "Observations on Centralization vs. Decentralization," *State Government*, XVI (January, 1943), pp. 3-5, 18.

Michigan Department of Administration. "Selected Questions on State Budgeting and Higher Education," Lansing: Budget Division, September, 1957. (Mimeographed.)

————. *Budget Detail, Capital Outlay and Operating Expenses, 1957-1958*. Lansing: Budget Division, 1956.

Michigan State Board of Education. *Building for Tomorrow Through Self-Liquidating Projects*. Lansing: the Board, 1956.

Michigan University. *University Hospital, 5 Year Capital Outlay Program and 1957-1958 Appropriation Request*. Ann Arbor: University of Michigan, 1956.

————. *University of Michigan 5 Year Capital Outlay Program and 1957-1958 Appropriation Request*. Ann Arbor: University of Michigan, 1956.

Middlebrook, William T. "University Budget and the State Government," *Minutes of the Twenty-fourth Annual Meeting of the Association of University and College Business Officers*, 1934, pp. 71-76.

————. *How To Estimate the Building Needs of a College or University: a Demonstration of Methods Developed at the University of Minnesota*. St. Paul: University of Minnesota Press, 1958.

Miller, F. E. "What's Wrong With Supervision," *Personnel Administration*, May, 1950, pp. 21-23.

Mitchell, George W. "Recent Trends in State Budget Practices," *Remarks at the Annual Meeting of the National Association of State Budget Officers*, Miami Beach, Florida, September 12, 1955, pp. 4-5.

Moncewicz, Fred A. "Comments: Allotments, Encumbrances, Budgetary Control and Fund Systems of the Commonwealth of Massachusetts," Boston: Office of the [Massachusetts] Comptroller, Commission on Administration and Finance, 1956. (Mimeographed.)

Morey, Lloyd "Finance and Business Administration in Institutions of Higher Education," *Review of Educational Research*, X (April, 1935), pp. 143-147.

Mosher, Frederick. "The Executive Budget, Empire State Style," *Public Administration Review*, XII (Spring, 1952), pp. 73-84.

Municipal Finance Officers Association. *Performance Budgeting and Unit Cost Accounting for Governmental Units*. Accounting Publications Series Number 11-2. Chicago: the Association, May 1, 1954.

————. *Budgeting with Special Reference to Capital Outlay Budgeting*. Chicago: the Association, 1956.

Murphee, A. A. "The Relations of the University to the State Budget Commission," *Transactions and Proceedings of the National Association of State Universities, 1927*, pp. 63-68.

National Committee on the Preparation of a Manual on College and University Business Administration. *College and University Business Administration.* Washington, D.C.: American Council on Education, 1952.

New Hampshire Legislative Budget Assistant. *Report of Audits of State Departments, Institutions and Agencies.* Concord: the Assistant, January, 1955.

New York State Department of Public Works. *Procedure to be Followed by Associate Architects in the Planning of State Projects.* Albany: Division of Architecture, January 7, 1957.

Norlin, George. "Standardizing Agencies and Their Interference with Normal University Development," *Transactions and Proceedings of the National Association of State Universities*, 1938, pp. 12-21.

North Carolina Department of Administration. *Budget Policies of the Department of Administration.* Raleigh: the Department, March 4, 1958.

Oklahoma Executive Department. *Fiscal and Accounting Procedures to be Followed in Preparing Documents to be Presented to the State Budget Office.* Oklahoma City: Division of the Budget, 1955.

Oklahoma Governor's Joint Committee on the Reorganization of the State Government. *Oklahoma and Higher Education: Some Comparative Tables and Comments.* Oklahoma City: the Committee, 1952.

Perloff, Harvey S. "Modern Budget Policies: a Study of the Budget Process in Present-day Society." Unpublished Ph.D. dissertation, Harvard University, 1939.

Pinney, H. "Institutionalizing Administrative Controls," *American Political Science Review*, xxxviii (February, 1944), pp. 79-88.

Prescott, Frank W. "The Executive Veto in American States," *Western Political Quarterly*, iii (March, 1950), pp. 98-112.

Price, Richard R. *The Financial Support of State Universities.* Cambridge, Massachusetts: Harvard University Press, 1924.

Redfern, Leo F. "State Budgets and State Universities in New England," Unpublished Ph.D. dissertation, Harvard University, 1957.

"Regional Cooperative Conferences on Library Building Programs," *School and Society*, lxxiii (April 14, 1951), p. 235.

Robbins, Rainard B. "State Barriers to Planning Retirement Income for Public Employees," *Association of American Colleges Bulletin*, xxxiii (December, 1947), pp. 678-687.

Sebastian, C. R. "Preparation of State Budget," *Report of Twenty-fourth Annual Convention of the National Association of State Auditors, Comptrollers and Treasurers*, 1939, pp. 42-48.

Sly, John F. "Principles Which Underlie Governmental Reorganization," Lecture at the Administrative Process Seminar, Harvard University, February 12, 1940. (Mimeographed.)

Smith, Harold D. "The Budget as an Instrument for Legislative Control and

Executive Management," *Public Administration Review,* IX (Summer, 1944), pp. 181-188.

Smithies, Arthur. *The Budgetary Process in the United States.* New York: McGraw-Hill, 1955.

Solomon, S. R. "The Governor as Legislator," *National Municipal Review,* XL (November, 1951), pp. 515-520.

Stahl, O. Glenn. "The Horizons of Personnel Administration," *Public Personnel Review,* XIII (1952), p. 102.

Steiner, Gilbert Y. "A State Building Authority: Solution to Construction Needs?" *Current Economic Comment,* XVII (February, 1955), pp. 22-30.

Stene, Edwin O. "Administrative Integration," *Annals of the American Academy of Political and Social Science,* CCXCII (March, 1954), pp. 111-119.

Stockburger, Arlin E. "The Preparation and Control of a State Budget," *Report of the Twenty-Third Annual Convention of the National Association of State Auditors, Comptrollers and Treasurers,* Biloxi, Mississippi, November, 1938, pp. 43-57.

Stourm, Rene. *The Budget.* Translated by Thaddeus Plazinski. New York: D. Appleton and Company for the Institute for Government Research, 1917.

Strickland, Vernon L. "Mill Tax for State Educational Institutions," *School and Society,* XXIV (September 4, 1926), pp. 302-304.

Studenski, Paul. *Costs and Financing of Higher Education: A Report of the Temporary Commission on the Need for a State University.* New York Legislative Document Number 34. Albany: the Commission, 1948.

Sundelson, Jacob W. *Budgeting Methods in National and State Governments; Special Report of the State Tax Commission,* Number 14. Albany: J. B. Lyons Company, 1938.

"Symposium," *Public Personnel Review,* XIV (1953), pp. 129-131.

Tannery, Fladger F. *State Accounting Procedures.* Chicago: Public Administration Service, 1943.

Texas Commission on Higher Education. "Materials Pertaining to Formulas for Appropriations Purposes and Role and Scope of Institutions," Austin: the Commission, n.d. (Mimeographed.)

Texas Research League. *Purchasing Functions of the Texas State Board of Control.* Austin: the League, January, 1957.

Turner, Glen C. "In Defense of Ivied Towers," Reprint from Address to the Western Association of College and University Business Officers, April 21, 1958. (Mimeographed.)

U.S. Commission on Organization of the Executive Branch of Government. *Budgeting and Accounting.* Washington, D.C.: Government Printing Office, 1949.

———. *Personnel and Civil Service: a Report to the Congress, February, 1955.* Washington, D.C.: Government Printing Office, 1955.

Vandermuelen, Alice (Mrs.). "Guideposts for Measuring the Efficiency of Governmental Expenditures," *Public Administration Review,* X (Winter, 1950), pp. 7-12.

Van Hise, Charles R. "Central Boards of Control," *Transactions and Proceedings of the National Association of State Universities,* 1911, pp. 62-104.

Vermont Auditor of Accounts. *Audit Report of the Auditor of Accounts,* 1955. Montpelier: the Auditor, 1955.

Virginia Auditing Committee of the General Assembly and the Auditor of Public Accounts. *Purchasing for the State of Virginia.* Richmond: the Committee, n.d.

Wells, R. H. "The Item Veto and State Budget Reform," *American Political Science Review,* XVIII (November, 1924), pp. 782-791.

Western Interstate Commission for Higher Education. *Proceedings* of the Legislative Workshop on Financing Higher Education. June, 1958.

Williams, Robert L. "Appropriations to the State Supported Institutions of Higher Education in Michigan," *Michigan Education Journal,* XXX (February, 1953), pp. 341-342.

Willoughby, William F. *The Movement for Budgetary Reform in the States.* Institute for Government Research Studies in Administration, Number 4. New York: D. Appleton and Company, 1918.

Wood, Robert C. "The Metropolitan Governor: State Executive Management." Unpublished Ph.D. dissertation, Harvard University, 1955.

*Higher Education and the State*

Adams, Herbert B. *The State and Higher Education.* Washington, D.C.: Government Printing Office, 1889?

American Association of University Professors—University of Kentucky Chapter. *Relationships Between the State Government and the University of Kentucky.* Lexington: the Chapter, 1951.

Arkansas University. *Recommendations for Legislative Relations Program.* Fayetteville: Office of the President, April 11, 1957.

Association of Governing Boards of State Universities and Allied Institutions. "Securing Legislative Appropriations:"
  (a) A Legislator's Viewpoint—Michigan Senator James Milliken, pp. 41-50.
  (b) An Administrator's Viewpoint—University of Wyoming President George D. Humphrey, pp. 51-56.
  (c) The Regent's Viewpoint—Secretary Charles D. Byrne of the Oregon State Board of Higher Education, pp. 57-63. *Proceedings, Twenty-seventh Annual Meeting,* 1949.

Blackwell, Thomas E. "Legislative Control of Tax Supported Universities," *College and University Business,* XXVI (September, 1956), pp. 34-35.

Bolman, Frederick de Wolfe, Jr. "Does Public Money Threaten Higher Education?" *Journal of Higher Education,* XXIV (April, 1953), pp. 169-176.

Brandon, Arthur L. (ed.). *The State and Public Education.* Austin: the University of Texas, 1940.

Brownell, Baker. *The College and the Community; A Critical Study of Higher Education.* New York: Harper & Bros., 1952.

Cangelosi, Theo. "Universities and Political Authority," *Proceedings of the Association of Governing Boards of State Universities and Allied Institutions,* Thirty-First Annual Meeting, 1953, pp. 111-117.

Carmichael, Oliver C. "State University: its problems and prospects," *Transactions and Proceedings of the National Association of State Universities,* 1954, pp. 28-34.

"Carnegie Corporation Study of State Universities to Weigh Effects of Government Support," *School and Society,* LXV (June 14, 1947), pp. 437-438.

Chamberlain, Leo M. "What Are the Significant Developments in this Relationship of Higher Education to State Governments," in *Current Issues in Higher Education, 1955-1956,* Smith, G. K. (ed.). Tenth-Eleventh Annual Conference of the National Conference on Higher Education. Washington, D.C.: National Education Association Department of Higher Education, 1956, pp. 236-242.

Chambers, Merritt M. "Position of the University Governing Board in the Total Scheme of State Government," *Proceedings of the Association of Governing Boards of State Universities and Allied Institutions.* Ninth Annual Meeting, 1931, pp. 63-76.

College and University Personnel Association. *Personnel Practices in Colleges and Universities.* Champaign, Illinois: the Association, 1958.

Committee on Education. *Responsibility of the States in Education.* Washington, D.C.: Chamber of Commerce of the United States, April, 1947.

Conant, James B. "Higher Education in a Democracy—Official Report," *Proceedings of the American Association of School Administrators,* 1938, pp. 122-128.

Committee on Legislative Processes and Procedures. *Our State Legislatures.* Revised edition, Chicago: Council of State Governments, 1948.

Council of State Governments. *Higher Education in the Forty-Eight States, A Report to the Governor's Conference.* Chicago: the Council, 1952.

———. *Reports on Higher Education: An Annotated Bibliography of Recent Reports of State Study Commissions and Other Official Agencies.* Chicago: the Council, March, 1958.

Cowley, W. H. "Governmental Trespassing," *Journal of Higher Education,* VIII (April, 1937), pp. 225-226.

Davidson, Carter. "Government Support of Private Colleges and Universities," *Annals of the American Academy of Political and Social Science,* CCCI (September, 1955), pp. 112-122.

Doudna, Edgar G. "Teachers Colleges and State Legislatures," in *American Association of Teachers Colleges Seventeenth Yearbook,* 1938, pp. 79-84.

Edwards, William H. "Politics and Higher Education in New Mexico," *American Association of University Professors Bulletin,* XXVIII (October, 1942), pp. 452-464.

"Freedom Crusade of the University of Massachusetts," *Educational Record*, XXXVIII (April, 1957), pp. 100-111.

Gibson, Harold E. "Should the Federal Government Guarantee Higher Education Through Grants to Colleges and Universities?" *School Activities*, XXVII (November, 1955), pp. 97-100.

Henderson, Algo D. "The Role of the State in Higher Education," *Educational Record*, XXXII (January, 1951), pp. 64-69.

Herter, Christian A. "A Legislator Views the Administrative Process," Lecture at the Administrative Process Seminar, March 27, 1939. Harvard University. (Typewritten transcript.)

Hill, David S. *Control of Tax-Supported Higher Education in the United States.* New York: Carnegie Foundation for the Advancement of Teaching, 1934.

Hollis, Ernest V., et al., "State Controlled Higher Education in Arizona; report of a survey authorized and sponsored by the Board of Regents of the University and state colleges of Arizona, prepared under the direction of the Division of Higher Education, United States Office of Education," 1954. (Mimeographed.)

Hoover, Herbert C. *Higher Education and the State Government.* Washington: Allied Printing Trades Council, 1926.

Horack, H. C. "Politician and the Education Buzz-Saw," *Journal of Higher Education*, XIV (April, 1913), pp. 171-174.

Horner, Harlan H. *The State and Higher Education.* Albany: University of the State of New York, 1939.

Illinois Higher Education Commission. *Illinois Looks to the Future in Higher Education.* Chicago: the Commission, 1957.

Jones, Lewis W. "Responsibility of the State University," *Journal of Higher Education*, XVIII (November, 1947), pp. 401-406.

Kelly, Frederick J. and McNeely, John H. *The State and Higher Education; Phases of Their Relationship.* New York: Carnegie Foundation for the Advancement of Teaching, in cooperation with the United States Office of Education, 1933.

Klopsteg, Paul E. "Role of Government in Basic Research," *Science*, CXXI (June 3, 1955), pp. 781-784.

Lilge, Frederic. *The Abuses of Learning: The Failure of the German University.* New York: Macmillan, 1948.

Lipson, Leslie. *The American Governor from Figurehead to Leader.* Chicago: University of Chicago Press, 1939.

———. "Has Executive Reorganization Increased the Governor's Legislative Power?" *State Government*, XI (August, 1938), pp. 141-142, 155.

———. "The Executive Branch in New State Constitutions," *Public Administration Review*, IX (Winter, 1949), pp. 11-21.

Louisiana Commission on Higher Education. "What Does Louisiana Face in Publicly Supported Higher Education?" Baton Rouge: the Commission, 1955. (Mimeographed.)

McAllister, Charles E. *Inside the Campus: Mr. Citizen Looks at His Universities.* New York: F. H. Revell, 1948.

McGee, Vernon A. "A Legislative Approach to State Budgeting," *State Government,* xxvi (August, 1953), pp. 200-204.

McNeely, John H. *Supervision Exercised by States Over Privately-Controlled Institutions of Higher Education.* United States Office of Education. Bulletin 1934, No. 8. Washington, D.C.: Government Printing Office, 1934.

———. *Higher Educational Institutions in the Scheme of State Government.* United States Office of Education. Bulletin 1939, No. 3. Washington, D.C.: Government Printing Office, 1939.

———. "Riders on Appropriation Acts," *School Life,* xxii (September, 1936), pp. 7-8.

———. "Governor's Power of Removal," *School Life,* xxiv (April, 1939), pp. 211-212.

———. "Control of Higher Education." *School Life,* xxv (March, 1940), p. 183.

———. "New State Policies," *Journal of Higher Education,* vii (October, 1936), pp. 363-377.

Maine Legislature. *Hearings of the Special Legislative Committee on the University of Maine to Inquire into the Just Obligations of the State to the University.* Augusta, 1906.

Massachusetts Special Commission on Audit of State Needs. *Needs in Massachusetts Higher Education.* House Document No. 3035, March 26, 1958.

Miles, R. E. "The Budget and the Legislature," *Annals of the American Academy of Political and Social Science,* lxii (November, 1915), pp. 34-46.

Millett, John D. *Financing Higher Education in the United States.* New York: Columbia University Press for the Commission on Financing Higher Education, 1952.

Morey, Lloyd. "Governmental Control of Public Higher Education," *Transactions and Proceedings of the National Association of State Universities,* 1955, pp. 30-41.

Russell, John D. *The Financing of Higher Education.* Revised Second Edition. Chicago: University of Chicago Press, 1954.

———. *Higher Education in the Post-War Period.* Chicago: University of Chicago Press, 1944.

———. "The States in Higher Education," *State Government,* xxii (May, 1949), pp. 135-139, 147.

Scace, Homer E. *The Organization of the Executive Office of the Governor.* New York: Institute for Public Administration, 1950.

Scott, E. M. and Zeller, Belle. "State Agencies and Lawmaking," *Public Administration Review,* ii (Summer, 1942), pp. 205-220.

Special Committee of the American Association of University Professors, "Academic Freedom and Tenure in the Quest for National Security," *American Association of University Professors Bulletin,* xl (March, 1956), pp. 49-107.

398 THE CAMPUS AND THE STATE

Stevenson, Adlai E. "Wanted: A Statewide Concept of Higher Education," *Illinois Education*, XL (December, 1951), p. 136.

Strand, A. L. "Land-Grant Colleges and the State," *Proceedings of the Association of Land-Grant Colleges and Universities,* Sixty-seventh Annual Convention, 1953, pp. 221-225.

Ten Brook, Andrew. *American State Universities, Their Origin and Progress.* Cincinnati: R. Clark, 1875.

Tennessee Legislative Council. *Public Higher Education in Tennessee.* Report to the Education Survey Subcommittee. Nashville: the Council, 1957.

Morrill, J. L. "The Place and Primacy of the State University in Public Higher Education," *Transactions and Proceedings of the National Association of State Universities,* 1958, pp. 15-22.

Mort, Paul R. and Sheerer, F. W. *State Support for Public Education.* Washington, D.C.: National Education Association, Department of Superintendence, official Report, 1934.

Mowat, Charles L. "State University and the Public," *American Association of University Professors Bulletin,* XXXV (June, 1949), pp. 216-223.

Naftalin, Arthur. "Fiscal Independence for Higher Education," Memorandum prepared for the Committee on Government and Higher Education, September 27, 1957. (Typewritten.)

North Carolina Commission on Higher Education. *State Supported Higher Education in North Carolina.* Raleigh: the Commission, 1955.

Perkins, John A. "Higher Education and the State Government," *School and Society,* LXVI (November 8, 1947), pp. 353-358.

————. "Government Support of Public Universities and Colleges," *Annals of the American Academy of Political and Social Science,* CCCI (September, 1955), pp. 101-111.

Plock, Richard H. "Issues in State Control of Higher Education." Reprint of remarks at the Western Regional Conference on Education Beyond the High School, San Francisco, April 10, 1957. Burlington, Iowa: Association of Governing Boards, May 1, 1957.

Reynolds, J. H. "State Policy in Higher Education," *Association of American Colleges Bulletin,* XX (November, 1934), pp. 429-433.

Texas Commission on Higher Education. *Report to the Honorable Allan Shivers, Governor of Texas, and the Legislature of the State of Texas,* December 1, 1956. Austin: the Commission, 1956.

Thompson, William O., Hill, A. R., and Kinley, D. "Report of the Committee on University Control," *Transactions and Proceedings of the National Association of State Universities,* 1931, pp. 122-141, also appeared in *School and Society,* XXXVI (August 13, 1932), pp. 214-222.

Tigert, John J. "University's Place in the State," *Review of Reviews,* LXXXVII (May, 1933), pp. 37+.

Washington (State) University Board of Regents. *Communism and Academic*

*Freedom: The Record of the Tenure Cases at the University of Washington.* Seattle: University of Washington Press, 1949.

Weeks, Ila D. "Principles Governing Legislative Requests for Educational Institutions," *School and Society,* LXXVII (March 28, 1953), pp. 193-194+.

Wilbur, R. L. "University and the State," *Frontiers of Democracy,* VI (February, 1910), pp. 137-138.

*Governing Boards and University Management*

Arnett, Trevor. *College and University Finance.* New York: General Education Board, 1922.

Beck, Hubert P. *Men Who Control Our Universities; the economic and social composition of governing boards of thirty leading American universities.* New York: Kings Crown Press (Columbia University), 1947.

Benjamin, Harold (ed.). *Democracy in Administration of Higher Education.* Tenth Yearbook of the John Dewey Society. New York: Harper & Bros. 1950.

Bigelow, Karl W. "American teachers college," *Journal of Education,* CXXXVII (January, 1955), pp. 13-14.

Bokelman, W. Robert. *Higher Education Planning and Management Data, 1957-1958.* Circular Number 517. Department of Health, Education, and Welfare, Office of Education. Washington: Government Printing Office, 1958.

Bryant, Victor S. *The Responsibilities of Trustees of a State University.* Chapel Hill: University of North Carolina, 1956.

Burress, Julian A. *A Study of the Business Administration of Colleges, based on an examination of the practices of land-grant colleges in the making and using of budgets.* Chicago: University of Chicago Libraries, 1921.

Cain, J. H. "Budgets for Institutions of Higher Education," *Educational Business,* XXI (June, 1938), pp. 4-6.

Capen, Samuel P. *The Management of Universities.* Edited by Oscar A. Silverman. Buffalo: Foster and Stewart Publishing Corporation, 1953.

Cattell, James McKeen (ed.). *University Control.* New York and Garrison, New York: The Science Press, 1913.

Chambers, Merritt M. "Functions of Lay Control in Higher Education," *School and Society,* XLVIII (October 22, 1938), pp. 532-535.

———. "How to be a Better Trustee; obligations of a University trustee," *Proceedings of the Association of Governing Boards of State Universities and Allied Institutions,* Twenty-eighth Annual Meeting, 1950, pp. 45-47.

Christensen, John C. "Unit Costs," *Journal of Higher Education,* XII, December, 1941, pp. 464-468, 500.

Coffman, Lotus D. "Higher Education: New Administrative Adjustments," *Addresses and Proceedings of the National Education Association of the United States,* 1924, pp. 876-882.

College and University Personnel Association. *Employee personnel practices in Colleges and Universities, 1951-1952.* Champaign, Illinois: the Association, 1952.

Columbia University Trustees. *The Role of the Trustees of Columbia University, Report of the Special Trustees Committee of Columbia University.* New York: the Trustees, 1957.

Conant, James B. *Academical Patronage and Superintendence.* Occasional Pamphlets of the Graduate School of Education, Harvard University, June, 1938.

Counts, George S. *The Social Composition of Boards of Education: A Study in the Social Conduct of Public Education.* Chicago: University of Chicago Press, 1927.

Cowley, W. H. "Academic Government," *Educational Record,* xv (January, 1951), pp. 217-229.

Dewey, John. "Control of Universities," *School and Society,* xi (November, 1915), p. 673.

Dibden, Arthur J. "Role of Administrators and Trustees: a faculty view," *Association of American Colleges Bulletin,* xliv (December, 1958), pp. 536-544.

Donovan, Herman L. "The State University Presidency: 1955," *Transactions and Proceedings of the National Association of State Universities,* 1955, pp. 15-30.

————. "Changing Conceptions of the College Presidency," *Association of American Colleges Bulletin,* xliii (March, 1957), pp. 40-52.

Duffus, Robert L. *Democracy Enters College; a study of the rise and decline of the academic lockstep.* New York: C. Scribners Sons, 1936.

Eggertsen, Claude. "Composition of Governing Boards," in *Democracy in the Administration of Higher Education.* Benjamin, Harold (ed.). Tenth Yearbook of the John Dewey Society. New York: Harper & Bros., 1950, pp. 117-126.

Elliott, Edward C. "The Board of Control," in *Higher Education in America.* Kent, Raymond A. (ed.). Boston: Ginn and Company, 1930, pp. 600-632.

Faulkner, Donald. "What Are the Functions of Internal Administration?", *Journal of Higher Education,* xii (October, 1941), pp. 378-385.

Fessler, James W. "The Functions of Board of Trustees," *Transactions and Proceedings of the National Association of State Universities,* 1924, pp. 61-66.

Gordon, J. E. "The President," *Journal of Higher Education.* xxiv (March, 1953), pp. 133-140.

Graves, Frank P. *The Administration of American Education, with special reference to personnel factors,* New York: Macmillan, 1932.

Hart, James B. "How Shall They Be Governed," *Texas Outlook,* xxxvi (May, 1952), pp. 22-23.

Hawley, Robert D. "The Business Administration and Financial Management of a Land-Grant College," *Educational Business,* xxi (October, 1938), pp. 6-7, 16-18.

Hill, David S. and Kelly, Frederick. *Economy in Higher Education.* New York:

Carnegie Foundation for the Advancement of Teaching in cooperation with United States Office of Education, 1933.

Hooker, Grover C. "Board of Control for a State University," *School and Society*, XXXVII (May 27, 1933), pp. 689-691.

Hughes, Raymond M. *Manual for Trustees of Colleges and University*. Revised Edition. Ames: Iowa State College Press, 1945.

———. "The Functions of Boards of Trustees," *Transactions and Proceedings of the National Association of State Universities*, 1924, pp. 67-74.

———. "College and University Trustees and Their Responsibilities," *Educational Record*, XXVI (January, 1945), pp. 27-32.

Hungate, Thad L. *Finance in Educational Management of Colleges and Universities*. New York: Bureau of Publications, Teachers College, Columbia University, 1954.

Institute for College and University Administrators. *Annual Report for 1957*. Boston: the Institute, 1958.

Jastrow, Joseph. "The Administrative Peril in Education," in *University Control*. Cattell, James McKeen (ed.). New York and Garrison, New York: The Science Press, 1913, pp. 315-348.

Jessup, John H. and Wadleigh, Kenneth R. "Governing Boards of State Universities," *Kadelphia Review* (now *The Educational Forum*) XV (March, 1936), pp. 237-244.

Keppel, Francis P. "Administrative Organization of the University," *Educational Review*, XL (October, 1919), pp. 292-299.

Kirkpatrick, John E. *Academic Organization and Control*. Yellow Springs, Ohio: The Antioch Press, 1931.

———. *The American College and Its Rules*. New York: New Republic Incorporated, 1926.

Knight, Edgar W. *What College Presidents Say*. Chapel Hill: University of North Carolina Press, 1940.

Knight, George W. *History and Management of Land-grants for Education in the Northwest Territory*. New York: G. P. Putnam Sons, 1885.

Leavenworth, P. E. "Financial Statements as a Means of Control," *American School Board Journal*, LXXVIII (March, 1929), pp. 43-44.

Lindsay, Ernest E. and Holland, E. O. *College and University Administration*. New York: Macmillan, 1930.

Louisiana State University. *Discussion of the Income and Expenditures of Louisiana State University*. Monograph Series, 1942, No. 1. Baton Rouge: Louisiana State University, 1942.

McGrath, Earl J. "Community Colleges," *Junior College Journal*, XXII (February, 1952), pp. 305-306.

———. "The Control of Higher Education in America," *Educational Record*, XVII (April, 1936), pp. 259-272.

McNeely, John H. and McCabe, Martha R. *Good References on Higher Education; control, organization, and administration*. United States Office of

Education. Bibliography No. 49. Washington, D.C.: Government Printing Office, 1936.

McNeely, John H. *University Unit Costs.* United States Office of Education. Bulletin 1937. No. 21. Washington, D.C.: Government Printing Office, 1938.

———. "Governor as Member of Boards." *School Life,* xxv (November, 1939), p. 56.

McVey, Frank L., and Hughes, Raymond M. *Problems of College and University Administration.* Ames: Iowa State College Press, 1952.

Morey, Lloyd. *University and College Accounting.* New York: John Wiley and Sons, 1930.

Nearing, Scott. "Who's Who Among College Trustees," *School and Society,* vi (September 8, 1917), pp. 297-299.

Nevada Legislative Counsel Bureau, *The University of Nevada: An Appraisal.* Carson City: State Printing Office, 1957.

New Mexico Board of Educational Finance. *Manual for Boards of Regents.* Santa Fe: the Board, 1955.

Page, Charles H. "Bureaucracy and Higher Education," *Journal of General Education,* v (January, 1951), pp. 91-100.

Perkins, John A. "Public Administration and the College Administrator," *Harvard Educational Review,* xxv (Fall, 1955), pp. 214-224.

Reeves, Floyd D. and Russell, John D. *The Evaluation of Higher Education.* Part VI, "Administration." Chicago: University of Chicago Press, 1936.

Reisner, Edward H. "The Origins of Lay University Boards of Control in the United States," *Columbia University Quarterly,* xxiii (March, 1931), pp. 63-69.

Sattgast, Charles R. *The Administration of College and University Endowments.* Contributions to Education No. 808. New York: Columbia University Teachers College, 1940.

Smith, Edgar W. "The Government of Public Education," *Proceedings of the Association of Governing Boards of State Universities and Allied Institutions,* Thirty-Second Annual Meeting, 1954, pp. 68-72.

Stoke, Harold W. *The American College President.* New York: Harper & Bros., 1959.

Sullivan, Richard H. "Administrative-Faculty Relationships in Colleges and Universities," *Journal of Higher Education,* xxvii (June, 1956), pp. 308-326.

Tead, Ordway. *Trustees, Teachers, Students: Their Role in Higher Education.* Salt Lake City: University of Utah Press, 1951.

Texas University Board of Regents. *Rules and Regulations of the Board of Regents for the Government of the University of Texas.* Austin: the University of Texas, 1943.

Thwing, Charles F. *The College President.* New York: Macmillan, 1926.

United States Office of Education, *Higher Education, Administration and Organization; Annotated Bibliography, 1940-1950.* Division of Higher Education. Washington, D.C.: Government Printing Office, 1951.

————. *State Boards Responsible for Higher Education.* To be published in 1959.

Veblen, Thorstein V. *The Higher Learning in America; a Memorandum on the Conduct of Universities by Businessmen.* New York: B. W. Huebach, 1918.

Wells, Harry L. "Standards and Service in University Management," *Annals of the American Academy of Political and Social Science,* CCCI (September, 1955), pp. 175-183.

Wicke, Myron F. *Handbook for Trustees of Church-Related Colleges.* Nashville: Board of Education of the Southern Methodist Church, 1957.

Wildermuth, Ora L. "University Trustee Views the Academic Profession," *American Association of University Professors Bulletin,* XXXV (June, 1949), pp. 233-239.

Williams, Lloyd P. "Some Heretical Reflections on Educational Administration," *Journal of Higher Education,* XXVII (April, 1956), pp. 182-188.

Woodburne, Lloyd S. *Faculty Personnel Policies in Higher Education.* New York: Harper & Bros., 1950.

Works, George A. "Types of Institutional Organization for Higher Education: Bibliography." *Proceedings of the Institute for Administrative Officers of Higher Institutions,* 1939, pp. 1-11.


*The Problem of Coordination*

American Council on Education. *Cooperation and Coordination in Higher Education—an exploratory study of the problems of cooperation, coordination and regionalization in higher education.* Washington, D.C.: the Council, 1938.

Armstrong, Wesley E. and Beach, Fred F. "State Teachers College in the State Structure for Education," *Journal of Teacher Education,* VI (June, 1955), pp. 105-113.

Beu, Frank A. "Single State Board," *Illinois Education,* XL (January, 1952), pp. 182-184.

Boles, Donald E. "The Administration of Higher Education in Wisconsin," *Journal of Higher Education,* XXVII (November, 1956), pp. 427-439.

Browne, Richard G. "Why Not an Autonomous Teachers College?" *Illinois Education,* XXXVIII (March, 1950), p. 264.

————. "Let's Have an Autonomous Teachers College Board," *The Alumni Quarterly of Illinois State Normal University,* November, 1949, p. 5.

Brumbaugh, Arthur J. and Sugg, Redding S., Jr. "Recent Developments in State and Regional Planning of Higher Education," *Annals of the American Academy of Political and Social Science,* CCCI (September, 1955), pp. 32-40.

Bulton, D. E. "State University of New York," *State Government,* XXVI (April, 1953), pp. 123-124, 127.

Byrne, Charles D. *Coordinated Control of Higher Education in Oregon.* Stanford: Stanford University Press, 1940.

Caldwell, John T. "Organizing State Supported Higher Education," *State Government,* xxvi (November, 1953), pp. 256-260, 272.

California Department of Education. *Study of Public Administration in California State Colleges: A Committee Report by Elliott W. Guild, Chairman, State College Public Administration Curriculum Committee, 1950-1951.* Sacramento: the Department, Division of State Colleges and Teacher Education, 1951.

Capen, Samuel P. "An Incomparable Challenge," *Journal of Higher Education* (entire issue devoted to coordinating higher education), iv (March, 1933), pp. 107-111.

Chambers, Merritt M. "Centralization in State Educational Administration," *Proceedings of the Association of Governing Boards of State Universities and Allied Institutions,* Tenth Annual Meeting, 1932, pp. 60-67.

"Coordination of State Supported Higher Education," *Journal of Higher Education,* xv (March, 1944), pp. 141-145.

Doran, Adron, "The Work of the Council on Public Higher Education in Kentucky," Unpublished Ph.D. dissertation, University of Kentucky, 1950.

Durham, G. Homer. *The Administration of Higher Education in Montana: a Study of the University of Montana System.* Helena: Montana Legislative Council, 1958.

Florida Legislative Reference Bureau. *Florida's University System: a Survey of State Supported Higher Education in Florida As Reported to the Legislative Council.* Tallahassee: the Bureau, 1953.

Frey, Fred C. and Pettiss, John O. "State Organization of Higher Education in the Eleven States of the Southern Association," *Southern Association Quarterly,* viii (November, 1944), pp. 486-490.

Georgia Board of Regents of the University System. *A Report of a Survey of the University System of Georgia.* Atlanta: the Board, 1949.

Glenny, Lyman. Forthcoming study of coordination and fiscal procedures to be published in 1959.

Hall, Gertrude M. "Needed: More Cooperation, or a State Board for All, Not Simply for Higher Education," *Illinois Education,* xl (March, 1952), p. 266.

Harger, Charles M. "Confusion in State College Control," *Education,* lviii (May, 1938), pp. 565-567.

Headley, John W. *An Analysis of the Report on Certain Aspects of Public Higher Education in South Dakota.* College Station: Office of the President of South Dakota State College, 1954.

Holy, Thomas C. and Semans, Hubert H. "Coordination of Public Higher Education in California," *Journal of Higher Education,* xxvi (March, 1955), pp. 141-147.

Hunter, Frederick M. and Frasier, George W. "Should All Higher Education, including Teacher Training, be administered through a Single State Agency?" *School Life,* xxv (June, 1940), pp. 272-274.

Hunter, Frederick M. "Case of Unification," *School and Society,* LII (October 26, 1940), pp. 383-388.

Johnson, Eldon L. "Coordination: the viewpoint of a political scientist," *Annals of the American Academy of Political and Social Science,* CCCII (November, 1955), pp. 136-142.

Klonower, Henry. "State Teachers Colleges Rehabilitated Through General State Authority," *Pennsylvania School Journal,* LXXXVII (November, 1938), pp. 77-78.

Louisiana Joint Legislative Committee on Higher Education. *Special Report.* Baton Rouge: the Committee, 1958.

Louisiana State University Alumni Federation. *The Super Board and the Freedom of Louisiana State University: A Report.* Baton Rouge: the Federation, 1958.

MacBride, Thomas H. "Duplication in Schools of Higher Learning, Supported by the State," *Transactions and Proceedings of the National Association of State Universities,* xxxx, 1914, pp. 163-182.

McNeely, John H. *The Problem of Duplication as Attacked in Certain State Surveys of Higher Education.* United States Office of Education. Bulletin 1934, No. 19. Washington, D.C.: Government Printing Office, 1935.

———. "State Councils of Higher Education," *School and Society,* XLIV (October 17, 1936), pp. 511-515.

Michigan, the Survey of Higher Education in Michigan (John Dale Russell, Director). Staff Study No. 12. *Control and Coordination of Higher Education in Michigan,* July, 1958.

Oklahoma State Coordinating Board for Higher Education. *A System for Higher Education for Oklahoma.* Oklahoma City: Oklahoma State Regents for Higher Education, 1942.

Oklahoma House of Representatives. *An Act making appropriations for regional cooperation with other southern states.* H.B. 672, April 10, 1957.

Pulliam, R. "Regard: Central Boards," *Journal of Higher Education,* xv (March, 1944), p. 152.

Russell, John D. "New Mexico Board of Educational Finance," *Higher Education,* IX (January 1, 1953), pp. 97-99.

———. *Control and Coordination of Higher Education in Michigan.* Staff Study Number 12 prepared for the Michigan Legislative Study Committee on Higher Education. Lansing: The Survey of Higher Education in Michigan, 1958.

Sage, J. R. "Centralized Control of Iowa State Institutions of Higher Learning," *Proceedings of the American Association of Collegiate Registrars,* 1935, pp. 231-236.

Sandford, Daniel S. *Inter-institutional Agreements in Higher Education.* Contributions to Education, No. 627. New York: Columbia University Teachers College, 1934.

Smittle, Ray W. "State Coordinating Agencies," *Journal of Higher Education*, x (November, 1939), pp. 437-444.

Starrak, James A. and Hughes, Raymond M. *The New Junior College: The Next Step in Free Public Education*. Ames: Iowa State College Press, 1948.

Stoddard, George D. *The Russell Report: A Memorandum to the Board of Trustees of the University of Illinois*. Urbana: Office of the President of the University, 1951.

Stevens, Edwin B. "Coordinating Boards of Higher Education," *Educational Record*, vii (October, 1926), pp. 280-288.

Warters, J. "Proposal for a State Supported System of Higher Education in Pennsylvania," *Journal of Higher Education*, xix (June, 1948), pp. 313-315.

Webster, William C. *Recent Centralizing Tendencies in State Education Administration*. New York: Columbia University, 1897.

Western Governors' Conference. *Western Regional Cooperation in Higher Education; A Proposed Program*. Chicago: Council of State Governments, 1951.

Whitney, Frederick L. "Educational Research and Statistics: Unitary Board of Control for State Higher Education," *School and Society*, xlii (September 7, 1935), pp. 335-338.

Williams, Robert L. "Single Board of Control for State Supported Higher Education," *School and Society*, lxxi (January 14, 1950), pp. 17-21.

Wisconsin Legislative Council. *Interim Report on Higher Education*, Madison: the Council, 1954.

# Index